James
Mirror for the Soul

James
Mirror for the Soul

Lessons from the Epistle of James

by

Ed Rickard

 **The Moorings Press**

Printed copies of this book can be obtained from Amazon.com. It is also available as a Kindle eBook. Most of the content originally appeared and is still accessible on the author's website, *Bible Studies at the Moorings,* at themoorings.org.

All Scripture quotations, unless otherwise noted, are from the King James Bible (KJV).

ISBN: 978-0-9896510-1-1

revised 1/8/20

✤ DEDICATION ✤

The Law of God

O Lord, when we dare look upon your law,
A brilliance like the sun subdues our eyes.
The glory of your goodness without flaw
So shines that we our own pretense despise.

– Ed Rickard –

✛ ABOUT THE AUTHOR ✛

Ed Rickard (full name: Stanley Edgar Rickard, Jr.) received a B.S. with highest honors from Wheaton College in 1963, then a Ph.D. from Northwestern University in 1967. His undergraduate major was chemistry, and his graduate field was social psychology with emphasis on statistics and research methodology. His dissertation and two subsequent publications dealt with the causal analysis of correlations.

He began his career teaching at the undergraduate and graduate levels in the field of his doctorate. Later he taught Bible courses at a Christian college. His subjects included the Book of Daniel, Christian evidences, and graduate apologetics. More recently, he has served as principal of a Christian academy.

For a leading publisher of Christian school curricula, he wrote a high school physics text that has been widely used. His website, https://www.themoorings.org, has been a source of Bible studies since the early days of the web.

His wife and high school sweetheart, Julie, received an M.A. in French from Northwestern University and for many years taught high school French in video classes available to Christian schools and homeschools. In all her husband's endeavors, she has been an indispensable adviser and helper.

Ed has two sons, seven grandchildren, and one great-grandchild. His older son is a pastor and his younger son is a minister of music. He counts all his family as a great blessing from God.

+ ABBREVIATIONS +

Chron.	Chronicles	Judg.	Judges
Col.	Colossians	Lev.	Leviticus
Cor.	Corinthians	Matt.	Matthew
Dan.	Daniel	Mic.	Micah
Deut.	Deuteronomy	Num.	Numbers
Eccles.	Ecclesiastes	Pet.	Peter
Eph.	Ephesians	Phil.	Philippians
Exod.	Exodus	Prov.	Proverbs
Ezek.	Ezekiel	Ps.	Psalm or Psalms
Gal.	Galatians	Rev.	Revelation
Gen.	Genesis	Rom.	Romans
Heb.	Hebrews	Sam.	Samuel
Isa.	Isaiah	Thess.	Thessalonians
Jas.	James	Tim.	Timothy
Jer.	Jeremiah	v.	verse
Josh.	Joshua	vv.	verses

+ LESSONS FROM THE EPISTLE OF JAMES +

Contents

✛ INTRODUCTION ✛

Lesson 1

The Lord's Brother

Author

The general opinion of Bible students is that the Epistle of James was written by James, the brother of Christ. The eldest of four younger brothers (Matt. 13:55), he was throughout the years of Jesus' ministry, at least in the latter portion, an unbeliever in Jesus' claim to be the Messiah and Son of God (John 7:2–5). How could a man so close to Jesus fail to recognize who He was? Growing up in the shadow of an older brother who was perfect in every way had no doubt been a sore trial to a boy with ordinary imperfections. It was impossible for Mary and Joseph not to treat Jesus with a special respect that tempted His younger siblings to feel jealous. Perhaps some lingering jealousy in James's heart was the barrier to faith.

Yet James's unbelief melted away when Jesus rose from the dead and personally appeared to him (1 Cor. 15:7). He then became a devout follower of Christ. After Jesus ascended to heaven, James was among the 120 who waited in the Upper Room until they received the baptism of the Spirit on the day of Pentecost (Acts 1:14). In the following years he quickly rose to eminence in the church. At the church council recorded in Acts 15, he gave the final speech, pronouncing a verdict that the council adopted as its official position (Acts 15:13–30). In later years he was the acknowledged leader of the church in Jerusalem (Acts 21:18). Among the Jews generally, especially the poor, he was greatly admired for his pious and self-denying manner of life. He spent so much time in prayer that his knees bore calluses. It was said that they resembled the knees of a camel.[1]

Yet he was not popular with the Jewish leaders. The Jewish historian Josephus records that under circumstances we can place in about AD 61, he met a martyr's death similar to Stephen's. A Sanhedrin persuaded that he was a law-breaker dragged him out of the city and stoned him.[2]

Purpose

Our study of James's epistle must proceed from an understanding of what it is not. It is not a treatise on doctrine. It contains little doctrine beyond the opening statement that Jesus is also Lord and Christ. It is not a book of history or prophecy. And it is not a letter of advice from a spiritual leader seeking to help a particular person or group. Rather, it is a sermon addressing a question of far-reaching significance for all followers of Christ. The question is, what is true godliness. Clearly proclaiming the right answer from pulpits and media is an urgent need in our day, when many even in conservative churches are drowning in self-satisfied pseudoreligion.

The author illuminates the right answer from various standpoints. As we will see, the brightest light appears when he provides the term "godliness" with a formal definition. "Pure religion and undefiled before God and the Father is this, To visit the fatherless and widows in their affliction, and to keep himself unspotted from the world" (Jas. 1:27). Obviously, he does not mean to limit charitable works to the one he chooses as an example. Rather, he means that any religion that does not produce a life devoted to helping other people is empty and worthless. But, lest anyone think that charitable works alone are genuine religion, James adds a second requirement: to remain unsoiled by the world. Unless a church excels in meeting both requirements, it cannot glow with godliness, showing that God dwells among them. Personal separation from the world without practical expressions of love for fellow believers as well as for unbelievers is sterile. It chokes off a vibrant testimony for Christ and leads to a dead church. But good works without personal separation are pointless. They produce a church that, although it may seem prosperous, lacks the power of God to gain eternal results. God will not pour favor on a church that fails to draw its spiritual babes away from the power of sin.

James gives central place in his epistle to the question, what is godliness, because it serves as a stepping-stone to his main message. He wants above all to convince us that we should earnestly strive to be godly. To overcome any carnal inertia that may be holding us back, he reminds us that godliness is the natural and inevitable outgrowth of saving faith. He goes so far as to say, "Faith without works is dead" (Jas. 2:20).

Because of its emphasis on works as proof of faith, the Epistle of James has always been a theological battleground. Martin Luther, trailblazer of the Protestant Reformation, considered it a "straw epistle," unworthy to be included in the canon.[3] He charged the author with teaching that salvation requires both faith and works. Later in his career, however, Luther came to recognize the value and authority of James's contribution to the New Testament.[4] In fact, the Epistle of James is not intended to show the reader how to be saved. Nowhere does it present the gospel. Rather, building on the assumption that the reader is already saved, it shows him how to live the Christian life.

Themes

To make godliness concrete, James warns us against the many ways we might fail to practice the cardinal Christian virtues. Altogether, the virtues that he treats either briefly or at length number fourteen.

1. Humility (1:1; 4:6–10).
2. Endurance through trials (1:2–4; 5:10–11).
3. Wisdom (1:5; 3:13–18).
4. Effective prayer (1:6–8; 4:2-3; 5:13–18).
5. Contentment in poverty (1:9).
6. Distrust of riches (1:10–11; 5:1–6).
7. Victory over sin (1:12–18, 21; 4:1–2, 7–10, 17).
8. Discipline in speech (1:19–20, 26; 3:1–12; 4:11–12; 5:9).
9. Agreement between profession and life (1:22–25; 2:14–26).
10. Meeting the needs of others (1:27; 2:12–17; 5:19–20).
11. Separation from the world (1:27; 4:4–5).
12. Treatment of all brothers as equals (2:1–11).
13. Submission to God's sovereign control of the future (4:13–16; 5:7-8).
14. Speech without swearing (5:12).

In discussing these virtues, James does not move through the list one by one. Rather, he designs his epistle to be like a symphony. Each virtue is a theme that runs through the whole work, sometimes becoming prominent on the surface and at other times receding into the background, sometimes appearing alone and sometimes in combination with other themes so that we can see relationships between them. The epistle is also like a tapestry woven of long threads spanning the two ends. In between, each is visible in places and hidden elsewhere. The structure helps us to learn by giving us the main ideas repeatedly. It also brings these ideas into different contexts, so as to enlarge their application.

Sources and parallels

The Epistle of James is one of two New Testament books addressed to Jewish believers. The other is Hebrews. (The meaning of the opening words in 1 Peter is debatable.) The feature marking James's work as Jewish is its preoccupation with living according to the law. Jews did not lose their zeal for the law when they became believers in Christ. Certainly James did not. He was a strong voice in the church arguing that the law should remain the proper rule of life for any Jew (Acts 21:18–24). But in his epistle, James is less concerned with the letter of the law than with its spirit. He says nothing about the sacrifices and ceremonies of the outmoded Mosaic system. He refrains from dwelling on particular commandments in the Old Testament. Although he often refers to the law, it is the law viewed in its essence, as a prescription for making love practical. He endorses Jesus' teaching that the law governing relations between man and man may be summarized as an obligation to love our neighbor as ourselves (Jas. 2:8; compare with Matt. 22:37–40), and he makes this obligation supreme by giving it such titles as the law of liberty (Jas. 1:25; 2:12) and the royal law (Jas. 2:8). Therefore, since the Epistle of James perfectly reflects Jesus' own view of the law, it is good reading not just for Jews, but for all believers. And by teaching us that love should be the standard for our behavior, it succeeds in its purpose, which is to encourage true godliness.

In its topics and phraseology, the epistle is similar to the so-called Wisdom Literature of the Old Testament—the portion incorporating the books of Job, Proverbs, and Ecclesiastes. Compare, for example, James 1:19 with Proverbs 10:19, 16:32, 17:27, and Ecclesiastes 7:9. Other examples of convergence include James 4:6 with Proverbs 3:34; James 4:13–16 with Proverbs 27:1; and James 5:2 with Job 13:28.

Yet the epistle overlaps even more the Sermon on the Mount, at times almost reproducing Jesus' words. The agreement is most striking in James 4:9 (cf. Matt. 5:4), James 4:11 (cf. Matt. 7:1–5), James 4:17 (cf. Matt. 7:12), James 5:2 (cf. Matt. 6:20), and James 5:12 (cf. Matt. 5:34–37). It would not be far wrong to characterize the epistle as a commentary on the Sermon on the Mount.

The parallels between the two works illustrate how profoundly James's thinking was molded by his older brother. Yet James had not been one of the disciples who walked with Jesus day by day during His ministry. Perhaps the mind of Jesus shines out so clearly from the writings of James because he listened to his brother all through his formative years. Many of the ideas that Jesus presented in His public ministry must have taken shape during His youth. If so, it would not be at all surprising if He shared them to some extent with His own family.

Self-Test

1. Is my relationship to brothers and sisters still clouded by sibling rivalry?

No doubt you remember that in your childhood, you and your siblings did not always live in perfect harmony. When our family went on trips, my wife and I sitting in the front of the car, my two sons in the back, we sometimes heard the older cry out that his brother was jabbing him, or otherwise "picking on him." We then dutifully lectured the younger on how to behave while we were all riding together, and the commotion stopped, at least for a while. It was not until years later that we discovered the true story of life in the back seat. The cause of strife was usually the older brother, who, in very subtle and quiet ways, teased the younger until, exasperated, he fought back.

That sort of friction between siblings is not confined to a car. It is part of everyday life and can lead to deep-seated rivalry. The older view the younger as a nuisance. The younger see the older as having a superior attitude. But all this is childishness we should outgrow.

Make sure that today you truly value and love your siblings. They may not be perfect, but God put them in your life as an opportunity for lifelong ministry. Keep in touch with them. Express your regard for them. Help them when they need it. Remember that except for some minor reshuffling of genes, they are exactly like you, so if you deserve the best in terms of God's mercy and grace, so do they.

2. Do I understand and apply the principle that the road to true success is not self-promotion but self-denial?

The church raised James to the place of leadership not simply because he was Jesus' brother. He was a man whose life centered on helping others. He exemplified Jesus' teaching, "And whosoever of you will be the chiefest, shall be servant of all" (Mark 10:44). How do you measure your own stature? How do others measure it? Do you—do they—give first consideration to how unsparingly and lovingly you reach out to meet the needs of people both inside and outside the church. Serving others at the cost of self-sacrifice is the only criterion of greatness that counts in heaven.

3. In my own life, do I seek both good works and separation, and do I keep them in balance?

It is easy to emphasize one at the expense of the other, but you need to cultivate both. Just as a church cannot prosper if it ignores either duty or gets them out of balance, so the same mistakes can keep you personally from being a fruitful servant of God.

It is spiritually meaningless to stay in such isolation from the world that you become wholly preoccupied with yourself. What are you really accomplishing if you never look at the TV or internet, never attend any shows or dances, never dress in anything doubtful, and never let anything unhealthy pass through your lips, but if at the same time you never share the griefs or cares of others, never speak a word of witness to the lost, and never give a cent to a good cause?

But it is also spiritually meaningless if, to help publicans and sinners, you adopt their way of life. You accomplish nothing worthwhile if, besides eating with them as Jesus did (Matt. 9:11), you echo their suggestive humor, copy their clothing, and follow them to all their places of sin.

The Christian life requires <u>both</u> separation and good deeds.

4. Do I have a proper view of moral law—that it is God's prescription for making love practical?

We are prone to dislike anything labeled as law. We see it as a burden better done away with. To be "legalistic" is something bad.

But do you understand that the law of God, even though it convicts us as sinners, is a glorious testimony to God's spotless character? It exalts Him by defining His perfect holiness. Yet we tend to see holiness in the wrong way. We do not look into it deeply enough to find its core, which is love. To be remote from all manner of evil is what love demands, because evil, large or small, is an attack on God's beloved creatures. It is a threat to their welfare. The Ten Commandments, the grand summary of all good laws, is simply a manual on how not to hurt anybody, whether ourselves by estrangement from God or others by taking what is theirs. Thus, as Jesus said, all law deriving from the Word of God merely expresses two basic obligations: "Love the Lord thy God with all thy heart, and with all thy soul, and with all thy mind," and "Love thy neighbor as thyself" (Matt. 22:37, 39).

5. In my own life, do I cherish the Wisdom Literature and the Sermon on the Mount as daily guides to my priorities and decisions?

These resources for building wisdom cannot help you much unless you study them—to be more precise, unless you memorize them. Other Scriptures are equally deserving of your time, but these are especially helpful for teaching you good judgment as you travel the road of difficult moral choices. Add to these, of course, the Epistle of James, another treasure trove for anyone desirous of becoming more like Christ in his everyday conduct.

Review Questions

1. What was the relationship between James and Jesus?
2. How did James become a disciple?
3. What position did he attain in the church?
4. What was his manner of life and how did he die?
5. What is the purpose of the Epistle of James?
6. How does the epistle define true godliness?
7. Why did Luther regard it as a straw epistle?
8. To whom is the epistle addressed, and what does James emphasize for the sake of his intended audience?
9. Whose view of the law do we find reflected in this epistle?
10. What other portions of Scripture does it resemble?

✛ James 1:1–4 ✛

> **1** James, a servant of God and of the Lord Jesus Christ, to the twelve tribes which are scattered abroad, greeting.
>
> **2** My brethren, count it all joy when ye fall into divers temptations;
>
> **3** Knowing *this*, that the trying of your faith worketh patience.
>
> **4** But let patience have *her* perfect work, that ye may be perfect and entire, wanting nothing.

Lesson 2

The Writer's Opening Thoughts

Greeting. James addresses his epistle to the "twelve tribes which are scattered abroad" (v. 1). He is referring, of course, to the twelve tribes of Israel. After Solomon's day, ten tribes seceded from the Davidic kingdom and established a new kingdom in the north, leaving a kingdom of two tribes in the south. The northern ten are known as the lost tribes because it is commonly believed that they forgot their identity after Assyria conquered them in the eighth century BC and resettled many of their people in far-flung places. But this old idea is somewhat of a myth. At the time of division, many from the north moved south so that they could continue to worship God at Jerusalem. From then on, the southern kingdom was a composite of all twelve tribes (2 Chron. 11:13–17). Also, when the Assyrians took many northern Israelites into captivity, they left many behind. The southern kings later extended their domain to include this remnant, in effect integrating them with the whole nation (2 Chron. 34:3–6, 9). As a result, when Babylon conquered the southern kingdom in the sixth century BC and led away many to Mesopotamia, the captives included members of the ten tribes. Likewise, when Persia released the Jews from exile, members of the ten tribes were among those who returned to Palestine, although for many, their exact tribal lineage was by now a vanishing memory.[5] Then in the next several centuries, both the repatriated Jews and the Jews still in Persia became a highly mobile group, establishing settlements throughout the ancient world in pursuit of economic gain, so that all the tribes became scattered far and wide. In New Testament times, they were known as the Jewish *diaspora* (dispersion).

Humility. The author begins by weaving into his greeting a striking illustration of one of the virtues he will emphasize throughout his book: the virtue of humility. He does this in two ways. First, he puts aside all the childish rivalry that he once felt toward his older brother and lifts Him to a plane far above his own, calling Him Lord (v. 1). Second, he lowers himself to the same plane as every other believer, calling himself the servant of God and of Jesus (v. 1). He might have boasted in his connection with the Lord. Yet he does not even tell us that he is Jesus' brother.

Trials. The author exhorts us to "count it all joy" when we fall into various temptations (v. 2). How can we view them all as occasions for joy? The exhortation strikes us at first as a little extreme. The rendering "temptations" misses the point, however. The corresponding Greek word does not speak of temptations to sin, but of testings or trials, commonly in the form of suffering.[6]

What is the joy in suffering? The joy consists in anticipating the spiritual result. There is no joy in suffering itself. To seek suffering as if the experience of pain will be, or should be, enjoyable is a false spirituality.

The asceticism practiced by monks and Eastern mystics rests on a false concept of virtue. There is no spiritual merit in depriving yourself of a truly harmless pleasure, such as a good meal that you can acquire without robbing another person of something good. And there is no spiritual merit in hurting yourself by foregoing sleep or lashing your back or crawling along hard pavement.

No, suffering is a form of evil that can exist only in a fallen world. Yet in the midst of suffering, while under no delusion that it is good, we can have joy in our hearts because we know that God will use it to teach us patience (v. 3).

"But let patience have her perfect work" (v. 4). In other words, when you are suffering, do not resist the work that God wishes to do in your life. Do not complain. Do not choose bitterness rather than joy. Do not try to wriggle out of suffering at the price of compromising moral principle or shirking spiritual duty. For example, the right way to handle an unhappy marriage is not to forsake it, but to pursue the solutions made possible by the power of faith and love.

The result of submitting to suffering is that we will become "perfect and entire, wanting nothing" (v. 4). Here we have three synonymous expressions. James's admonition could be translated, "that ye may be complete, complete, and complete." Only by accepting God's work in our lives can we avoid gaping holes in our character.

Patience. The primary mark of completeness is patience. Although patience is a prime virtue, it is not easy to define. In ordinary use the term means to restrain wrath or annoyance or other negative reactions when we suffer provocation. How should an adult respond to a child who innocently makes the same mistake repeatedly? Patience smiles and waits for improvement. An explosion of bad temper makes the child feel that he is hopelessly stupid. Patience in a spiritual sense has much the same meaning. It is holding back our tendency to grumble during suffering, to indulge feelings of self-pity, to toy with the idea that God is not being fair, to confront God with our complaints, alleging that we could do a better job of running our lives. So, in essence, patience is restraining our negative reactions to trouble.

Parallels. Some commentators in the past have argued that the writings of Paul and James conflict with each other. But what we really find in their writings is perfect harmony. Compare, for example, James 1:3 and Romans 5:3. The two authors speak with one voice. The purpose of tribulation and trial is to teach us patience.

Brokenness. Why is patience so important? Why does it rank as one of the traits that God wishes most to instill in us? The reason is simple. Patience is submitting to whatever God puts into our lives. It is therefore the same as yielding to His will. It is a form of obedience.

Yielding to God fully, raising no question about His motive or His wisdom in allowing us to suffer, can happen only if our will has been broken; that is, only if our will has lost the desire to be contrary and rebellious. Brokenness is the prerequisite of patience.

We understand God better if we view Him as the perfect Father. A wise earthly father knows that his object in training a small child is to break his will but not his spirit. That is exactly what God seeks to do with us. He wants to teach us that our will leads only to disaster. So instead of trusting ourselves, we should deny ourselves and take up a cross and follow Christ (Matt. 16:24). The meaning is that we should decide to emulate His obedience to the Father's will, for Christ was "obedient unto death, even the death of the cross" (Phil. 2:8). He was our example of perfect obedience. For us to attain it requires total surrender, which presumes a broken will.

Yet God does not want us to suffer oppression by sadness, or to fall under a sense of failure, or to spend our days in bitter sighing for deliverance from the trials of life—all these being signs of an unhealthy spirit. He wants us to be filled with hope, generating a positive outlook and a serene attitude. His prescription for a healthy spirit is to view every circumstance as an opportunity for joy. Joy keeps brokenness in the will from spreading to the whole person.

How can we gain joy? We can gain it only if we choose it. By God's grace, we must reach out and take it, as with every other benefit that God offers. The immediate provider of joy is the Holy Spirit. Joy is a fruit of His filling (Gal. 5:22).

Self-Test

**1. How do I introduce myself? Do I seek some borrowed lus-
ter by name-dropping?**

Although you cannot boast that you are Jesus' brother, you can
certainly find other ways to make yourself look good. One way is by
name-dropping. To tell about the important people you know scores
easy points in your favor.

Paul said that he had been a student of Gamaliel (Acts 22:3), but
he was not boasting. He was giving hostile Jews useful information
about himself so they might fairly judge his credibility as a witness to
new divine revelation. It is altogether different to mention bigwig acquaintances for the sole purpose of making yourself look a little bigger. And if your connection with them is casual at best, or even
rather distant, you are simply being dishonest.

**2. When I meet someone, do I seek to glorify myself or to
show love?**

You can try to impress people by casually mentioning your own
achievements and education. But how much more helpful to show
interest in the person you are meeting! Make him or her the topic of
conversation.

**3. Am I willing to represent myself as simply a servant of
God?**

Whenever the situation allows, you should describe yourself as
someone whose only real attainment is to love and serve Christ. Of
course, if they are too many or too sanctimonious, humble words can
come across as phony piety. You must always use discretion in advertising anything about yourself, even your humility.

**4. When there are circumstances in my life that I wish God
to remove, how do I pray for their removal?**

Do you go to God with a demanding attitude? Or do you please
God by stating your willingness to remain under the heel of trouble if
He wants you to endure it? Just imagine how a child might react if
he sees his brothers and sisters receiving a larger portion of dessert.
He might raise a loud protest, demanding his fair share in no uncertain terms. Be careful not to behave like a foolish child when you
approach God.

5. When I go through a trial, do I threaten God by letting Him know that if the trial continues, I will stop doing His will?

For example, if a problem in your church lingers, do you entertain thoughts of leaving or cutting back your involvement? If you fail to escape from financial woes, do you float the idea of withholding your tithe? If you continue to suffer a physical affliction, do you inform God that you might as well stop praying since He refuses to listen anyway? Just to describe such reactions is enough to show how childish they are.

6. Generally speaking, how do I react to difficulties and frustrations in life?

Do you become restless and discontent? Do you constantly push against adversity in an effort to force your way out of it? Do you try to change things through the power of the flesh? Or do you leave the problem to God and rest in confidence that He will work it out in His own way and time? He may require you to take initiative, but you must exercise it only under His direction and only with a right spirit—a spirit of submission to His will whatever it might be.

You must look upon your trial as an opportunity to pursue patience and true joy.

7. In every trial, do I keep myself from murmuring against God?

The people of Israel murmured against Him in the wilderness, complaining that He was failing to provide decent food. All He gave them was the same boring manna. Finally on one occasion He responded to their griping by filling the camp with quail (Num. 11:31–34). Even as the people were feasting on the birds, God sent a deadly plague that took many lives. The ones who died were apparently the ones who gathered the quail most greedily.

In other words, be careful. God may give you what you want and you may live to regret it.

8. Do I cultivate an outward radiance and an inner peace when trials are hardest?

These virtues almost come easier then, because God gives special grace. He is freer with His grace when someone you love dies, for example, than when your roof leaks or pipes freeze.

9. Do I make it my priority to show others an example of victory in suffering?

Do you stand up and give a testimony as readily when trials crowd you as when the path is free and smooth?

10. Do I daily seek the filling of the Holy Spirit, the source of joy?

He is the source of every virtue (Gal. 5:22). The importance of joy is made evident by its position in Paul's list. It stands second after love, the supreme virtue telling how anything good differs from anything evil.

Review Questions

1. To whom is the Epistle of James addressed?
2. How does James at the very outset of his book demonstrate humility?
3. How must we be careful even in striking a humble attitude?
4. What is the meaning of temptations?
5. What is the good that trials accomplish in our lives?
6. What is patience?
7. On what key point do James and Paul agree?
8. Why is patience so important?
9. What kind of brokenness does God want us to shun?
10. How can we have joy instead?

✢ James 1:5 ✢

> **5 If any of you lack wisdom, let him ask of God, that giveth to all *men* liberally, and upbraideth not; and it shall be given him.**

Lesson 3
Wisdom

Our generous God. Two words here are a bit old-fashioned. God gives "liberally," which means "generously," and declines to "upbraid" anyone who seeks His favor. "Upbraid" just means "scold."

Why would anyone think that God might scold a man seeking wisdom? Because a human father is capable of being driven to impatience by constant demands from his children. He might even come to feel that they are pestering him. So James reminds us that God's patience cannot be exhausted by our requests. If we ask Him for wisdom, He will not scold us for bothering Him.

Breadth of wisdom. As a Jew steeped in the writings of the Old Testament, James viewed wisdom as broader in meaning than we do. We think of wisdom as good judgment in dealing with the difficult practical issues that might complicate anyone's life in a real world. But the Old Testament expands the concept to every kind of understanding. It says that Bezaleel knew how to craft the tabernacle and its furnishings because God had given him wisdom (Exod. 31:1–6). It says that the wisdom of Solomon was evident in his ability to name and describe all living things and to compose a large body of sayings and songs (1 Kings 4:29–34). His wisdom also took the form of being able to recognize the liar in a difficult court case (I Kings 2:16–28). The creation of the universe, an engineering feat producing a smoothly operating machine of breathtaking size and complexity, is called a work of wisdom (Ps. 136:5). In the Wisdom Literature—Job, Proverbs, and Ecclesiastes—the focus is on moral wisdom, beginning with the fear of God (Prov. 9:10) and flowering in a life of righteousness (Prov. 2:6–9). Yet even in these books wisdom has a larger reach, taking in the advice of a military strategist (Eccles. 9:14–16) and the skill of a craftsman (Prov. 24:3). The proverb just cited doubtless has a secondary reference to building a family and an enduring family line, these also being works that require wisdom.

It is important to allow wisdom a wide sense so that we do not limit the promise in this verse of James. When it says that God will give us wisdom, it means that He will give us any kind of wisdom that we need, even the wisdom to do a job, or to escape from a moment of danger, or to comprehend the world around us.

Requirement for wisdom. To obtain wisdom, all we must do is ask God for it. But notice that to ask for it means that we already have it in some measure. Why? Because the fool does not realize that he needs wisdom (Prov. 1:7). Ignorance carries no mirror. A fool is content with what he already knows, for he supposes that he already knows everything, whereas a man who truly owns some knowledge can see its limits, and he longs to discover what lies beyond. So, both the first requirement and the first discovery in the quest for wisdom are the same—to realize that we need it.

To ask God for wisdom is wise in itself also because we are going to the ultimate source. There is a wisdom of this world, but in God's eyes it is no better than foolishness (1 Cor. 1:20). Those who seek wisdom from a secular education that ignores God may obtain some specialized knowledge, but they will graduate as narrow technicians deprived of any guidance on how to use their knowledge for God's glory. Moreover, much of what their education presents as knowledge is nothing but an elaborate system of excuses for sin and unbelief.

To obtain wisdom from God is impossible without a right view of the giver. We must fear Him (Prov. 9:10). In other words, we must perceive the consequences of scorning His will. At the core of our being we must have some sense of the bad things we will suffer and the good things we will miss should we displease Him.

The worst tragedy will befall those who displease God even to the extent of refusing salvation in Christ. How awful, how shattering, how devastating will be the eternal outcome! Our Maker sets such high importance on every created thing performing its function that He will discard anything that altogether fails. Should we be surprised at that? What do we do with a pen that no longer writes, or a broken chair, or a worn-out pair of shoes? Do we pack them away in an attic and preserve them in a sort of heaven for useless things? No, we throw them away.

A wholesome fear of God puts us on the path of pleasing Him through our obedience and love. It is the path of wisdom for two reasons: (1) by requiring a traveler to negotiate many difficulties, it teaches great spiritual understanding, and (2) it leads to places that a wise traveler wants to find—places of great spiritual blessing.

Equality of saints. One of the principal themes of James is introduced in this verse. The Jews had great respect for their rabbis, who were highly trained in the Scriptures, and they viewed them as on a higher plane of wisdom than ordinary men. Yet James challenges this sort of elitism. Wisdom, he says, is available to "any of you." In their capacity to obtain the wisdom they need, all believers are absolutely equal, although some may be able to advance farther in wisdom less needful. Even the humblest member of the church can become a wise man and enjoy a deserved reputation for being wise. The wisdom that can be attained by every believer who lets his mind be molded by the Spirit of God is so great that Paul was willing for the "least esteemed in the church" to judge matters that otherwise would go to a court of law (1 Cor. 6:1–4).

Measure whether you are appropriating all the wisdom God wishes to give you.

Self-Test

1. Do I humbly recognize my need for wisdom, or am I a know-it-all? Do I voice a loud opinion on every question, or do I readily admit my ignorance whenever a question exceeds my competence?

New teachers are tempted to pretend they know everything. When a student catches them in a mistake, they are embarrassed, and may even try to defend their mistake as truly correct. But to pose as perfect does not enhance anyone's credibility. Older teachers have learned by experience that it is far better to admit being wrong. In years past, I have offered students extra credit if they could spot an error in anything I wrote on the board.

2. Am I a good listener?

From time to time I attempt conversation with someone who wants to do all the talking. He tells me about all his troubles past, present, and future, or, if he feels upbeat, about all his accomplishments past, present, and future. As he rambles on, he lets me speak hardly a word. Never does he inquire about my experience in life or my opinions. I always walk away scratching my head, wondering how that person ever managed to learn anything. He seemed to have no interest whatever in acquiring new information.

Some people try to dominate conversation because they are insecure and talking is a way of seeking others' approval. But more often, refusal to keep silent long enough to listen is simply an outgrowth of a vanity void of wisdom. True wisdom sets a high priority on drawing out the wisdom of others.

3. Where do I get my opinions?

Do you get them from your family background, from the prejudices of your class and culture, from what you learned in school, from the latest talk show, from your own free-wheeling guesses—or, do you get them from the Word of God? If they are truly based on the

Word of God, they are not really opinions. They are reliable wisdom (Ps. 1:1–2).

Today there is much confusion about a man's role and a woman's role, about how to conduct a marriage, about how to rear children. You are wise if you discount everything you hear from contemporary media and rely instead on guidance from the Bible.

4. When I meet a problem in life, how do I react?

Do you conceive a plan of attack in your own mind and then go forward, relying on human might and cleverness? Do you employ the arm of flesh? Do you try to make things happen by pushing people and tinkering with circumstances? Or do you first go to God and seek His guidance? When Joshua failed to consult God before making a treaty with the Gibeonites, he gave away valuable land that God had wanted the Israelites to possess (Josh. 9).

In one of our moving adventures, I drove our van into a rest area and parked it on what seemed like level pavement. When I returned, I found that the van had rolled down a hill into a fence. If I had been talking to the Lord all along, He would have advised me to set the parking brake.

5. Do I seek divine wisdom for every problem, small or great, spiritual or practical?

Do you appreciate what a wonderful resource you have at your disposal? Divine wisdom is available for every problem that arises, whether a broken pipe or a stain in the carpet, whether an unruly child or a disagreeable neighbor, whether a sickness or a shortage of money, whether a family crisis or a crisis in the church. From God we can obtain wisdom equal to every challenge.

6. Do past failures make me shy of asking God for wisdom in the present?

Are you afraid that your many mistakes have removed you so far from God that He will turn a deaf ear to your plea? Remember, He "upbraideth not." He will not shun you or scold you if you go to Him with a humble heart. Indeed, if your heart is right, He will rejoice to meet your need for wisdom or for anything else.

7. Do I fear God? When I look down the road of some wrong choice, does it make me tremble, or do I feel safe from any consequences?

Whether sin frightens you is a pretty good test of whether you really know the God of the Bible.

When you happen to see a provocative woman, or when you

notice an easy way to cheat on your income tax, or when you feel like wagging your tongue about someone in the church, or when you think the time has maybe come to complain about some trial that God has allowed in your life, do you tremble at the consequences of yielding to temptation?

8. Do I regard Bible study as the special province of pastors and Christian workers, or do I accept responsibility to study the Bible myself, so that I might have a wisdom in no way inferior to theirs?

Every layman should read the Bible both in personal and family devotions, and he should take time for additional Bible study. Moreover, he should read good books about the Bible. In my father's day, many laymen in the church had a shelf of commentaries and Bible study resources at home, and many had experience in preparing both lessons and sermons.

Toward the end of my father's life, his habit in the evening was to take out a volume of *The International Standard Bible Enclyclopaedia* (better known as ISBE) with the intent of reading it until bedtime. But generally after a while he fell asleep. Then when some internal alarm told him that bedtime had arrived, he suddenly woke up and said, "That was sure interesting." I tell this story because it shows the heart of many men in my father's generation. They loved to study the Bible.

Review Questions

1. What does God promise if we seek wisdom?
2. What does the concept of wisdom include?
3. What is the sole requirement to obtain wisdom?
4. Yet what must we have before we desire wisdom?
5. What is not real wisdom?
6. What is the beginning of wisdom?
7. What is the danger in continuing in foolishness?
8. To whom is wisdom available?
9. What standard does Paul set for wisdom?

> **6 But let him ask in faith, nothing wavering. For he that wavereth is like a wave of the sea driven with the wind and tossed.**
> **7 For let not that man think that he shall receive any thing of the Lord.**
> **8 A double minded man** *is* **unstable in all his ways.**

Lesson 4

Effective Prayer

The unstable man. After exhorting us to seek wisdom, James moves to another of his principal themes—prayer that gains results. He says that a man who petitions God for wisdom must ask in faith. But as James expands upon the necessity of faith, he clearly does not mean to limit his advice to one kind of prayer, the prayer for wisdom. He expects us to understand that faith is the condition for any successful prayer, whatever it may seek. Faith is the key to unlock the storehouse containing all of God's benefits.

The Epistle of James is rich in uncommon words and unusual figures of speech. We find several examples here in the opening discussion of faith. He contrasts faith with "wavering" (v. 6). The word refers to a struggle within the mind, arising when a man's thoughts take both sides in an internal debate. A debate over what? There are two possibilities. Since James does not tell us which kind of wavering he means, he likely means either one. It is wavering if a man is not sure whether God will in fact hear and answer his prayer. Likewise, it is wavering if, despite God's promises to be our guide in all things including prayer, he is not sure what to pray for. Either kind of wavering compromises faith and reduces to doubting. Therefore, good alternative translations for "wavering" and "wavereth" are "doubting" and "doubteth."

In a striking simile, James compares the doubting man to "a wave of the sea driven with the wind and tossed" (v. 6). The Greek expression does not picture a single wave, but a whole seascape of waves sweeping first one way and then another as constantly shifting winds play upon the water.[7]

James declares that such a man will not receive anything from the Lord (v. 7). His petitions will hit the ceiling and come right back. The throne room of heaven will shut out his voice. Such a man suffers from a grievous flaw in his character. In seeking to describe this flaw, James found himself at a loss to convey the idea with any familiar word, so he coined a new one, or at least he used a word that occurs nowhere else in ancient literature.[8] He says that a doubting man is "double minded"—literally, "with two souls" (v. 8).[9] Perhaps he was fashioning a Greek equivalent for an expression employed twice in the Old Testament (1 Chron. 12:33; Ps. 12:2): "double heart" in English and "a heart and a heart" in Hebrew.[10] The Hebrew expression, suggesting a divided heart, speaks of a man who is insincere, whose statements cannot be depended on either because he has divided loyalty or because he is downright dishonest. In his use of the comparable Greek term, James gives it a different sense, referring to a man who prays with a heart divided between faith and doubt.

The tragic outcome is that he is "unstable in all his ways" (v. 8). The word "unstable" suggests something that is not planted firmly on the ground—something that is unsteady and likely to topple over. James means that wherever a double minded man walks, he will have a hard time staying on his feet. He will stagger along rather like someone who is intoxicated, and as a result He will always be slipping and falling. In other words, he will be constantly getting into trouble.

Faith as a prerequisite. In his emphasis on faith, James again shows the mind of his older brother, Jesus. One of Jesus' core teachings was that with faith, nothing is impossible. Although the first three Gospels, called the Synoptics, differ sharply in their coverage and style from the Gospel of John, they all agree with John that Jesus viewed prayer as an instrument with unlimited power (Matt. 7:7–11; John 16:23). Jesus taught clearly throughout His ministry that the condition for successful prayer is faith (Mark 9:23). The immediate inspiration for James's remarks on faith, setting it in contrast to doubt, seems to be the following saying of Jesus: "Jesus answered and said unto them, Verily I say unto you, If ye have faith, and doubt not, ye shall not only do this *which is done* to the fig tree, but also if ye shall say unto this mountain, Be thou removed, and be thou cast into the sea; it shall be done. And all things, whatsoever ye shall ask in prayer, believing, ye shall receive" (Matt. 21:21–22).

The promise that all things are possible through the prayer of faith is stunning in its magnitude. It is absolute. There are no hedges on "all things." Can we begin to conceive what "all things" might include? To urge us to greater imagination of the possibilities, Jesus affirms that by faith we could move mountains. How much faith do we need to accomplish great things? Not much. An amount comparable in dimensions to a tiny mustard seed will do (Matt. 17:20). Even with so little faith, nothing is impossible. But although Jesus promised that by faith we could move mountains, we feel mighty pleased with ourselves if by faith we manage to move a few spadefuls.

We find a comparable promise elsewhere in the teachings of Jesus: "And the Lord said, If ye had faith as a grain of mustard seed, ye might say unto this sycamine tree, Be thou plucked up by the root, and be thou planted in the sea; and it should obey you" (Luke 17:6). Why do we not see Christians moving trees and mountains? So far as I know, there is no recorded instance of a believer casting a mountain into the sea or uprooting a tree and transplanting it elsewhere just by the power of prayer. Why not?

Sometime ago I planted trees on my property. As I was doing the work, I naturally could not help but notice the many eye-catching specimens of flowering trees and shade trees in the yards of other people around town. Why did I never command one of their trees to move to my property, and if I had done so, why would God never have granted my desire, though I prayed with perfect faith? Because I would have been stealing somebody else's tree.

On my own property, I have many trees and shrubs growing wild out in the draw behind my house. Many are strong, attractive, and flourishing. Many would be more useful if they were relocated to barren ground. What if I commanded one of these to pluck itself up and replant itself in my front yard? I own the tree. Making it move would not be stealing, and it would serve me better in its new place. So, if I prayed for God to move it, I would be seeking a good thing.

Or would I? Basically, I would be seeking to escape from work. God never performs a miracle just to suit our laziness. In His view, answering my prayer for relocation of the tree would not yield a good result, but an evil result. Look down a few verses. "God cannot be tempted with evil" (Jas. 1:13). God cannot be persuaded to do evil even by the prayers of His children. That is why many prayers are never answered. They are seeking evil, not good.

Now we understand why Christians do not go around removing mountains and trees. It is hard to imagine any circumstance when casting a mountain into the sea or transplanting a tree would be necessary to accomplish any good thing. Can you think of any? I cannot.

Then why does Jesus use the moving of mountains and trees to illustrate what we can accomplish by faith? Because these are clearly impossible things. You cannot move a tree, much less a mountain, just by speaking a word. Jesus is teaching us that by faith we can do the impossible. His illustrations are especially helpful because they show that there is nothing beyond the reach of spiritual power. The power of prayer can affect not only hearts and minds, but also the world of nature.

Why is faith the fuel for great spiritual power? Because faith, like doubt, can be either of two kinds, and both please God. Just as doubt can be uncertainty about what to pray for, so faith can be certainty that God is guiding our words. Just as doubt can be unbelief that God will answer, so faith can be belief that He will. Either kind of faith shows God that we are becoming exactly what He wants us to be.

The first kind of faith shows that we are growing in spiritual judgment. Through long fellowship with the Father and meditation on His Word, we have come to understand what things we should seek. We have acquired the mind of God as we survey possibilities in the future. God is certain to reward a prayer for good things, for as we seek and acquire them, we not only bring His grace and goodness to the world, but we turn away from seeking things that are spiritually ruinous.

The second kind of faith shows that we think God is good. Any doubt that He will answer a prayer for good things insults Him. It makes Him out to be morally neutral, or stingy, or impotent. Faith is really a way of praising God for His goodness, His generosity, and His power. We credit Him with having all three attributes beyond measure when we pray in faith. No wonder God is then open to our request. It puts us in the place of fulfilling the purpose for which we were created—to bring glory to God.

Self-Test

1. If I really believe that prayer is no less powerful than God Himself, surely I will be constant in prayer. But am I?

How much time do you actually spend praying? How many requests do you actually bother to raise before God?

Suppose I gave my wife an amazing new invention—a supersmart, multifunctional robot capable of doing every manner of housework. Would she use it or store it away in the basement? You can be sure that she would never scorn a labor-saving device. Yet we have a tool more capable than any robot—prayer.

You cannot see answered prayer if you never pray. And if you fail to let God show Himself real through answered prayer, your faith will grow weaker. It will atrophy, like a muscle never used. Faith is always growing stronger or weaker, and the difference usually depends on whether we pray.

2. If Jesus said we could move mountains, am I praying for benefits as large as He promised? Or instead of "all things" (Matt. 21:22), am I praying for small things?

It is childish to pray only for recovery from colds and for good weather at the church picnic. You should pray in faith for souls, for a great work of God in your community and in your nation, for worldwide revival. You should go beyond requests that might be fulfilled in the natural course of events.   You should pray for obvious miracles.

Looking back over our lives, I can see that God has often moved mountains for us.   He has granted healing or relief of many serious afflictions.   In every difficult move to a new home, he has smoothed the road.   He has faithfully provided for the spiritual welfare of our children, grandchildren, and beloved sisters and brothers in Christ. He has always taken care of us financially, even giving us far more than we actually need.

Unanswered prayers have fallen in two categories.

a. He has not granted our prayers for the salvation of certain people.   Why?   Because God is not always willing to override a person's stubborn contempt for the truth.   Sometimes He may (2 Tim. 2:25-26), but sometimes He may not.   When Samuel persevered in praying for Saul, the Lord turned a deaf ear to the request, advising Samuel that Saul's rejection would not be reversed (1 Sam. 16:1).

b. God has not always granted healing for the aged.   He did not, for example, deliver my mother from her last illness.   Well into her nineties, she had outlived her usefulness in Christian work.   To prolong her life would have condemned her to more suffering and mental decline.   God gave her something far better than healing.   He gave her heaven.

3. If faith is necessary for successful prayer, do I actually pray in faith?

You are not demonstrating much real faith if you pray with a sleepy or distracted mind.   Then you are just mouthing words.   It is essential to engage your mind in what you are saying so that you can be clear and decisive.   James addresses this issue again later (Jas. 5:16), exhorting us when we pray to wake up, get involved, and put both heart and passion into our petitions.   We especially need to affirm our confidence that we are seeking something good and our confidence that God will give it.   But is that how you pray, or do you grope and mumble and apologize?   Of course, we know that God will refuse a request that is not good, yet that possibility should not keep us from praying with confidence.

4. To be sure that I am asking for good things, do I first exercise myself to find out the mind of God?

Do you pray only after you have contemplated His Word and consulted the Holy Spirit?   Or do you run ahead with requests that may only be spasms of selfishness?

How can you tell the difference?   James will deal with that question later.   Here, we can say that one test is whether other godly people are willing to join in the same request.   That is why the agreement of two or three is grounds for assurance that a prayer will be answered (Matt. 18:19).

Review Questions

1. What is the prerequisite to achieve answers in prayer?
2. What kind of man does God decline to hear, and to what is he compared?
3. What does double minded mean?
4. What kind of life can such a man expect?
5. What promise of Jesus does James recall?
6. How much faith is required to be effective?
7. Why do we not see believers moving trees or mountains by faith?
8. What then does the promise mean?
9. What is the first kind of faith, and why does it please God?
10. What is the second kind of faith, and why does it please God?

> 9 Let the brother of low degree rejoice in that he is exalted:
> 10 But the rich, in that he is made low: because as the flower of the grass he shall pass away.
> 11 For the sun is no sooner risen with a burning heat, but it withereth the grass, and the flower thereof falleth, and the grace of the fashion of it perisheth: so also shall the rich man fade away in his ways.

Lesson 5

Rich and Poor

Flowers of a field. James has advice for two special classes of believers: for the poor, such as many in the church at Jerusalem (Rom. 15:26), and for the rich. He exhorts both classes to rejoice, the first because God has raised them to a high estate, the second because they will soon perish like flowers in a field (vv. 9–10).

The phrase "of low degree" (v. 9) might refer to anyone with low status in society, but because James contrasts the brother of low degree with the rich man, it is clear that he is speaking specifically of the lowly who are poor.

Whether the rich man in these verses is a Christian has been the center of quite a debate. Is James instructing a wealthy believer on what attitude he should assume, or is he pronouncing judgment on the wealthy unbeliever? The better reading sees "brother" in verse 9 as applying to both the poor and the rich. The other reading puts James in the position of advising a lost man to rejoice in his damnation. Such words would not only be devoid of ordinary compassion, but absurd. If God takes no pleasure in the death of the wicked (Ezek. 33:11), surely the wicked themselves cannot be expected to take pleasure in the terrible destiny awaiting them unless they repent.

James says that the rich man will fade away like "the flower of the grass" (v. 10). "Grass" here takes in all the green vegetation that covers a field after winter passes and life is renewed.[11] In Palestine, the fields of springtime erupted in colorful blossom. An eye scanning the landscape saw carpets of flowers. But these did not last long, because the weather soon evolved into a hot, dry season that extinguished them. The rising sun of the summer morning brought from the Arabian desert a searing east wind called the sirocco. Under the heat of the sun and the heat of the wind, the flowers withered, shedding their petals to litter the ground (v. 11).[12]

James uses language suggesting that the passing of a little flower is a sad event. "The grace of the fashion of it" (v. 11) can be translated, "the beauty of the face of it."[13] "Beauty" is another of his unusual words, found nowhere else in the New Testament.[14] He means that the face of each little flower is a thing of beauty. No doubt he learned his appreciation for the inconspicuous delights of God's creation from Jesus Himself, who said that the flowers are more beautiful than Solomon in all his splendor (Matt. 6:28–30).

James concludes by saying that just as the flowers perish, so "the rich man will fade away in his ways" (v. 11). "Ways" means "goings," a term picturing his moving about in pursuit of worldly gain.[15] But although one day he is a man to be reckoned with, the next day he is gone.

The joy of a poor man. A poor man who knows Christ ceases to be a man of low degree. In worldly possessions he is poor, but in the possessions of real value because they last for eternity, he is wealthy beyond his present comprehension (Eph. 1:18), for he is joint heir with Christ of all the riches that Christ will receive from the Father (Rom. 8:17). Thus, in the protocols of God's kingdom, he ranks as a son of God (Phil. 2:15). What higher position could a man want, or even imagine? Yet, supreme exaltation is available to the humblest, poorest, most deprived human being on earth. Anyone can become a prince of heaven just by believing in Christ. Here is the joy of a poor man, who must throughout his days on earth suffer being despised by the privileged.

The joy of a rich man. The joy of the rich man is that God has brought him low. His debasement takes the form of being denied the privilege of holding on to his earthly wealth forever. He will soon die and lose the things of this world. Why should he rejoice in his inevitable loss? For many reasons.

1. That future loss will really be a rescue. Earthly wealth is a snare that easily traps the unwary in foolish schemes to gain more wealth and to multiply pleasure (1 Tim. 6:6–10). The safest way to handle wealth is to give it away (1 Tim. 6:17–19).

2. The fact that he will soon lose his wealth helps a rich man keep his priorities straight. It reminds him day after day that he needs to be compiling a good record for eternity rather than building an empire here.

3. The same fact helps him view his poor brothers with proper love and respect. It protects him from feeling superior. After all, his present position in society is only temporary. Although now he can treat a poor brother with condescension and exact his obedience, the time will come when they will stand before God as equals, and the rich man will give account for his treatment of the poor man. Then God will right any injustice.

Rich or poor? Which of these men are you? Few among us

would admit to being rich. Because we know people who have bigger houses and cars than we have, most of us feel that we are just average folk. But comparing ourselves with wealthier acquaintances is like the Empire State Building in New York comparing itself with the Willis Tower in Chicago. From street level, they both look gigantic. Likewise, in comparison with past generations and with people in third-world countries today, the middle class in Western nations is fabulously wealthy. Think of it. What are you lacking that you could reasonably want? There is a restaurant nearby to satisfy any craving your belly might conceive. You have more clothing in your closet than many of your ancestors possessed in a whole lifetime. Your houses and gardens would, in past generations, have set you just below the highest nobility. Kings of old would have gone to war to acquire your cell phone, your air conditioner, your car, your television. If we recognize that we are rich, we can learn from James's advice. His advice is that we should rejoice in how transitory our wealth is.

Self-Test

1. Do I think that I have acquired my wealth through my own devices, or do I credit the true source, God, who has, for reasons of His own, seen fit to give it to me?

Before Israel entered the Promised Land, Moses warned the nation, "And it shall be, when the LORD thy God shall have brought thee into the land which he sware unto thy fathers, to Abraham, to Isaac, and to Jacob, to give thee great and goodly cities, which thou buildedst not, and houses full of all good *things*, which thou filledst not, and wells digged, which thou diggedst not, vineyards and olive trees, which thou plantedst not; when thou shalt have eaten and be full; then beware lest thou forget the LORD, which brought thee forth out of the land of Egypt, from the house of bondage" (Deut. 6:10–12). God intended to heap material blessings upon Israel, but the danger was that someday they would forget the source and imagine that they had become prosperous through their own cleverness and hard work. Self-satisfied, they would see their wealth as a reason to boast of themselves rather than as an opportunity to thank the Lord.

We who live in the midst of modern plenty face the same danger. We dare not slip into the mentality of the successful entrepreneur who imagines that he is a self-made man. As with life itself, so also with our possessions, "The LORD gave, and the LORD hath taken away; blessed be the name of the LORD" (Job 1:21).

2. Seeing how soon my wealth will pass away, do I keep a loose hold on it, not caring greatly whether I have it or lose it?

One test is how much you worry about the state of the economy. You are too fixated on financial security if you are keeping a close eye on unemployment and inflation rates, the stock market index, and other measures of national prosperity. As responsible citizens, we should encourage wise economic policies, but we should view them mainly as a tool to help others, not ourselves. For ourselves, we should rest in God's provision as we faithfully fulfill our responsibilities in the home, the church, and the workplace. Trends that might make us a bit richer or a bit poorer should not be our preoccupation.

Nor should we vote primarily on the basis of our economic interests. Gaining a larger piece of the pie is not a godly objective. How a candidate stands on questions related to budgets and taxation is indeed important, but not nearly as important as whether he will resist the tides of corruption sweeping over the world today. He deserves our support if he opposes the chief threats to moral decency:

- the murder of unborn babies,
- the sentencing of many children to be reared not in normal families but by homosexual couples,
- the legalization of recreational drugs that damage the rational thinking and wholesome motivation of young people, and that endanger the lives of everyone on roads traveled by drug users,
- the removal of all censorship protecting the young and vulnerable from life-shattering sexual addictions, and
- the proliferating power of the media and other social engines committed to destroying traditional values.

3. Do I thank God for what He has given me?

Thanksgiving should be the theme of your life, as you look around at all the blessings that God has piled upon you (1 Tim. 4:4–5).

4. Do I accept my obligation to give my wealth back to God?

That is, do you make it available for uses He will show you—uses that will bring glory to Him, not to yourself?

5. Do I use my wealth in the light of eternity?

Do you readily share your wealth with the needy? Do you come forward without hesitation to help finance Christian work and Christian workers? How much do you give above your tithe in order to support missions?

6. Do I face the dangers in wealth and protect myself from

them? Do I guard myself from becoming a covetous person, always seeking more?

One temptation we all face is to collect things, but in this we can easily go overboard. I am speaking to myself as well as to you, because I have a distinct weakness for collecting books. When possessed by a collection mania, we soon find ourselves spending good money to acquire what is really junk, or what is hardly different from what we have already, or what will sit around never to be used and rarely to be looked at. How much better to use the same money to promote the work of God. How much better to be a cheerful giver than an incorrigible pack rat.

7. Do I discipline my use of money, so that I am not living primarily to satisfy carnal appetites?

Overeating is now a serious problem in our society. Portion sizes have increased markedly in the last generation, as has daily per capita food consumption.[16]   The result is that obesity has become epidemic.[17]

Review Questions

1. What is James's advice to the rich and the poor?
2. Is the rich man he is addressing a believer or an unbeliever?
3. Why was the comparison to flowers especially vivid to his readers?
4. How does James regard the beauty of a flower, and whose example is he following?
5. What will happen to the rich man?
6. Why can a poor believer rejoice?
7. For what three reasons can a rich believer rejoice in the prospect of being brought low?
8. Are we in America rich or poor?

---

12 **Blessed** *is* **the man that endureth temptation: for when he is tried, he shall receive the crown of life, which the Lord hath promised to them that love him.**

Lesson 6

Enduring Trials

Blessedness. "Blessed is the man." James echoes the language of Jesus in the Sermon on the Mount, where He pronounces nine blessings on those who seek God and a life of godliness (Matt. 5:3–11). As used by Jesus and His younger brother, the term "blessed" is not equivalent to our word "happy," which has become almost meaningless through overuse. We say we are happy whenever some little thing makes us feel good. But to be blessed is a far greater benefit. It is to receive favor from God, and His favor is not confined to a single kindness. Rather, His favor introduces us to a life where every experience, large or small, is guided by a loving hand, and where every moment fits into a larger plan to enrich us with good things. So, whereas happiness is to feel good in the present moment, blessedness is to experience nothing but good forever.

The classic picture of the blessed man is, of course, in Psalm 1. He is blessed because, in forming his own opinions, values, and goals, he has turned away from the world's influence and taken guidance from the Word of God (Ps. 1:1–2). God's thoughts are so important to him that he meditates upon them day and night. They are his foundation for life.

Job's example. Turning back to the Epistle of James, we find that a special blessing comes to "the man that endureth temptation." Here again the temptation James intends is not the kind that offers opportunity to sin, but the kind that subjects a man to hardship and loss. To endure means not just to get through the trial. A man can survive yet fail to endure. "Endure" means to stand firm in faith and testimony. The prime example was Job. His trial was perhaps the most severe any man has suffered. He lost his possessions and family and finally his good health. The devil took everything but his wife, and he left his wife so she could tempt Job. Her faith collapsed under the weight of her anger against God. She urged Job to curse God and die (Job 2:9).

We should not deny her our pity, however. We remember Job's sufferings, but we may not remember that his wife suffered nearly as

much. Yet although her faith faltered, it was later restored. How do
we know that? Because God blessed her by making her the mother
of another family.

Earlier, when she turned against God, Job did not follow her example. In fact, he declared, "Though he slay me, yet will I trust in
him" (Job 13:15). The steadfastness of his faith brought him the
blessing that James says will come to any man who endures temptation. At the end of Job's sufferings, God repaid him double for everything taken away (Job 42:12–13).

As we go through a trial, the promise of blessing helps us endure,
for whatever we lose, we know that God will, in His own good time,
whether in this world or the next, give us compensation. Not only
will we receive blessings, but blessings with greater value than anything we lost.

The crown of life. Some distort the Epistle of James by claiming that he teaches works salvation. One text they offer to prove their
interpretation is this: "For when he is tried, he shall receive the
crown of life." The idea they find here is that a man must earn eternal life by enduring temptation. But we can say emphatically that
James is teaching no such thing. The word "tried" suggests the
testing of a precious metal to see whether it is genuine.[18] Thus, the
purpose of trials is not to make someone a Christian, but to show
that someone is a real Christian already. Before the visible world of
men and the unseen world of angels and demons, they put his faith
on display and bring glory to God, for a steadfast faith in the heart of
a mortal, sinful man must be a divine work.

The reward for enduring is a crown of life. "Crown" here is the
usual word *stephanos,* which can refer to a victor's crown or a king's
crown.[19] James evidently views it as a token of victory. He could be
referring to an actual crown, but more likely the meaning is figurative. That is, he is merely saying that after we have completed our
passage through this vale of tears, God will bestow upon us eternal
life, a reward priceless and beautiful like a crown. Eternal life is
what God has promised to those who love Him.

Love as our motive. The crown of life is promised to them that
love God. James brings in the concept of love at the right moment to
show the importance of love in God's program. Love is the reason we
are willing to endure trials. Except for our love of God, we would
never accept the suffering that He permits in our lives. Instead, we
would be consumed by resentment and hate. What enables a child
to accept a spanking from his parents? Love for the parents. What
enables a parent to put up with his child's foolishness? Love for the
child. Likewise, love of God is what motivates us to obey God and to
keep a sweet confidence in His goodness despite all the troubles of
life. Indeed, these troubles make us love God even more, for each
time we choose to praise Him instead of complain, our love grows
stronger.

So now I will state a principle that is one of the most important I could ever teach you. If you grasp it, it will give you a spiritual perspective that will enable you, when you meet the hardest moments in coming years, to understand their purpose instead of sinking into doubt and despair. It is this. The whole scheme of earthly human life is designed to produce creatures who will give God a measure of love that He finds satisfying. The basic reason He puts us through trials and suffering is therefore to build our love for Him.

God created us because He wanted to receive love in return for His love. His love was so great that God in the flesh, Jesus Christ, died a horrible death to save us from sin. Our love for God is naturally weak by comparison and needs strengthening. Even the hardest trial is a strengthening tool if we choose by faith to believe that God has intended it for our good.

Self-Test

1. Am I looking for fleeting happiness rather than true blessedness?

The happiness afforded by the things of this world can never satisfy for more than a few measly moments. Watching a football game on TV or browsing at the mall may not be wrong in themselves, but they will never make you blessed. Only the blessedness attained by pleasing God will give satisfaction forever. So, examine how you spend your resources and energy. Do a time study of your life. Find what percent is transient in its impact and what percent is eternal. The things of lasting value include good works, attending church and supporting its ministries, Christian service, reading the Bible, prayer, and wholesome family life.

2. In pursuit of happiness, how much time do I spend indulging and entertaining the flesh?

Giving mastery to the flesh will not only waste your life on what is transient, but also entangle you in sin. Several years ago my son went through great soul-searching as he pondered whether his family should be watching videos. The problem is that after you buy the best and least objectionable, you eventually get tired of them. So you must replace them with others, which are usually less desirable. As you acquire more and more videos, your standards tend to slip, and you begin looking at entertainment that you would not have tolerated in the beginning. My son decided that his family would cut back video-watching and develop other activities in its place, and these have proved to be both profitable and enjoyable.

3. Do I serve God first and let Him add to my life such comforts and pleasures as He deems good for me?

The navy's slogan, "Join the navy and see the world," resembles Jesus' promise to the warriors for His kingdom. "But seek ye first the kingdom of God, and his righteousness; and all these things shall be added unto you" (Matt. 6:33). Do you enjoy sight-seeing? Join God's service and He will give you a traveling ministry. Do you enjoy exotic food? He will send you to the mission field. Do you enjoy sports and games? He will put you in youth work. Do you like people? He will give you as many opportunities to minister to people as you can handle. Do you like to talk? He will make you a preacher or teacher.

4. To know what will please God and gain His blessing, do I, like the man in Psalm 1, meditate upon His Word day and night (Ps. 1:2)? Or do I relegate the Bible to the coffee table and leave it there to gather dust?

Sometimes when I teach a Bible class, I feel that many sitting in front of me have not been digging into the Word. Perhaps they have been reading short texts for devotions, but they have not been taking time to master the content and doctrine of the Bible. Let the Bible be your meditation day and night. Believe me, it will surgically remove the cancerous growths in your heart, dig out the weeds in your mind, and jump-start your conscience.

5. Do I respond to trials as Job did, with a refusal to complain against God? Do I trust Him even as He is taking away what is dear to me?

Whenever you undergo a painful loss—death of a loved one, being fired from your job, a serious illness—you should view it as a test of your faith. Remember the last great loss in your life and consider whether you handled it correctly. When my sister's husband died, I was angry at God for what He did to her. He left her a widow with four children, the youngest little more than a year old. It was a hard blow, especially for a woman who had lost her own mother when she was a girl. The dark night my sister had to endure was one of my excuses for turning my back on God for several years. She, on the other hand, submitted to God's will and nourished her faith. As a result, her life evolved into a beautiful thing, harmonious in all its parts, whereas my life unraveled. I did not find a worthwhile direction again until I decided to let God be God.

6. Do I think of my faith as being on display?

If you do, and if you love God, you will strive to maintain a strong faith even when you are passing through tribulation. Especially then, you will want to protect God's honor and bring credit to His name. When you find fault with God, you unwittingly lend support to the devil's age-old contention that man does not deserve God's love and grace (Job 4:15–21).

7. Do I keep my eyes on the reward for endurance—eternal life with my beloved Savior? Am I heavenly minded? Or do my thoughts dwell solely on life in this world?

Again, examine your thoughts. How much time do you give to thinking about your future life with God? As a result of becoming enthralled with the prospects of love, marriage, children, and career, some young people in the church actually hope that Christ will not return soon. They do not understand how glorious our life with Him will be. It will be a life so satisfying that we will never for a moment regret anything we missed in this world. If given the chance to come back and pursue unfulfilled dreams, we would never take it. We would say, in the equivalent language of heaven, are you crazy?

8. Do I understand how important my love is to God?

You should look upon obedience to His will as an opportunity to show your love. You should look upon endurance through trial in the same way.

9. Do I tell God that I love Him?

Do you say, "I love you," to your spouse, children, parents? You should. But say it every day to the Lord also when you meet with Him.

Review Questions

1. What is the difference between the terms "blessed" and "happy"?
2. Where do we find the classic picture of a blessed man?
3. To whom does James promise blessing?
4. What is meant by "temptation," by "endureth"?
5. Does James mean that enduring is required for salvation?
6. What is the reward for enduring?
7. What should be our motive for enduring trials?
8. What is the secret to gaining a stronger love for God?

9. What is God's purpose for putting us through life in a difficult
    world?

✛ James 1:13–15 ✛

> 13 Let no man say when he is tempted, I am tempted of God: for God cannot be tempted with evil, neither tempteth he any man:
> 14 But every man is tempted, when he is drawn away of his own lust, and enticed.
> 15 Then when lust hath conceived, it bringeth forth sin: and sin, when it is finished, bringeth forth death.

Lesson 7

Resisting Temptation

Blame-shifting. James, using the appropriate Greek words, shifts his discussion from temptations in the sense of trials to temptations in the sense of enticements to sin.[20] He warns the reader against blaming God for them. Holding Him responsible is wrong for two reasons (v. 13). First, God Himself cannot be tempted. Second, He tempts no man.

This is the only time that Scripture states the obvious fact that God is immune to evil suggestions and enticements. There is no chink in His armor, no soft spot in His underbelly, no Achilles heel where wicked ideas can penetrate and poison the Almighty's thoughts.

His absolute righteousness is the first guarantee that He is no man's tempter, for to solicit evil is in itself evil. But lest we fail to draw out this implication, James states explicitly that God tempts no man. Yes, He allows His children to suffer temptation. They must struggle against the world, the flesh, and the devil. But all these sources of temptation are enemies of God's righteous order. God permits them to exist because His children grow stronger in divine character as they struggle against corruption. They emerge from life in this world with a practical righteousness that is battle-hardened.

There must have been people in James's time who reasoned that since God is sovereign, He is the true source of all that happens, both good and evil; further, that the evil He ordains includes the many temptations lining the path of a man's life. So, in a lame effort to excuse their sin they said, "I am tempted of God." Their premise, which they assumed all hearers shared, was that anything coming from Almighty God must be well-nigh irresistible. Ergo, God was to blame not only for the temptation, but also for the sin it produced.

In our day, we seldom hear this excuse in exactly the same words. We are more accustomed to people saying, "I sin because I just can't help myself—that's the way I am—I was born with this problem—it's part of my nature—etc." Or, "I sin because I am the victim of my circumstances—I had a terrible home life and a rotten education—I was raised in poverty—and besides all this, I am saddled with physical and emotional handicaps." Or even, "The devil made me do it." But all these excuses are equivalent to blaming God.

How can that be? Because God is sovereign. He did not create evil. But as a result of creating moral beings with a capacity for choice, He allowed evil to enter the universe, and He suffers it to continue for a season. Furthermore, He is the direct author of everything good. Therefore, your character, your personality, your environment—all the parameters and dimensions of your life—exist by either His permission or His design. It follows that ultimately you are blaming God if you blame your sin on anything but your own wicked heart.

Blame-shifting is as old as the world itself. When the Lord questioned Adam and Eve after they had taken of the forbidden fruit, Adam blamed both the woman and God, and the woman blamed the serpent (Gen. 3:12–13).

The true culprit in sin. James provides the final rebuttal of all man's ingenious attempts to escape responsibility. A man sins for one reason only, because he chooses to sin.

Resorting to figurative language, he describes sin as the child of an unholy alliance between lust and man's free will. In other words, sin occurs when lust tugs on a man's heart until he yields and commits sin. Then, as James says, when sin is full-grown and capable of having its own children, it brings forth death (vv. 14–15). Paul agrees: "For the wages of sin is death" (Rom. 6:23).

Notice that James carefully distinguishes between lust and sin. It is not sin to have lust. The word "lust" can translated simply as "desire," and here it clearly connotes a desire for something unlawful, but as James uses the term, lust refers to a desire arising in a man's heart as an evil suggestion that he can refuse. Lust is a step toward sin, but a step where it is still possible to turn around.

Three kinds of lust. The Bible teaches that we must cope with three kinds of lust—"the lust of the flesh, and the lust of the eyes, and the pride of life" (1 John 2:16). There are three kinds because man is a composite being, with a soul and a spirit besides a body. All three parts of man carry the inherited stigma of the Fall. All three are depraved. The body generates wrong desires rooted in biological drives such as gluttony and sexual lust ("lust of the flesh"). The soul generates wrong desires to possess things perceived through the eyes or the other senses ("lust of the eyes"). You obey this kind of lust when you look at what your neighbor has and want it for yourself. And lastly, the spirit generates wrong desires to put self in the place of God ("pride of life"). This kind of lust becomes your master when

God says to follow a certain road and you defiantly choose a different road.

It must be understood that every lust is the perversion of a desire for something good. For example, the desire for the nourishment necessary to sustain life is hardly sinful, but in excess the same desire swells to gluttony, a form of lust. Likewise, the desire for sexual fulfillment in marriage is wholesome in itself, but is easily twisted into the desire for immoral sex, another form of lust.

Paul said, "For I know that in me (that is, in my flesh) dwelleth no good thing" (Rom. 7:18). What Paul means by the flesh is the whole motivation of man in his mortal state, whether arising from body, soul, or spirit. The flesh is the sum total of all of our natural desires. The "no good thing" that dwells in the flesh is the tendency of every natural desire in a fallen world to go to extremes and seek outcomes that would hurt self or others. This lustful tendency of the human heart is one component of the sin nature that we have all inherited from Adam. It is the component that creates the potential for sin.

Yet if I sin, I cannot absolve myself by blaming my flesh, just as I cannot absolve myself by blaming God. The choice to sin resides in one place alone, in my will, a faculty of my conscious mind. The guilty party if I sin is not my flesh, but me, exercising my own power of choice. Any sin I commit is my own fault, period.

The secret to victory. In a fallen world, the will of man is weak in resisting the flesh. This weakness is the component of the sin nature that turns potential into fact. If a man resists the flesh, he is free of sin. As James says, sin is not born unless a man gives in to the lusts that tempt and entice him. Sin is always the result of yielding.

Yet before we are saved, our efforts to resist the flesh have limited success. In one way or another, sin gains the mastery over us. But at the moment of salvation, we become a new creature in Christ (Rom. 6:6; Eph. 4:22–24; 2 Cor. 5:17). Although we do not lose our sin nature, we escape from slavery to sin (Rom. 6:13–14).

Victory over sin may also be divided into potential and fact. The potential rests on the work of Christ, who defeated sin and Satan. It rests also on the indwelling presence of the all-powerful Holy Spirit, who offers us strength to resist temptation. The fact rests again upon man's will. We must decide to fulfill our potential for victory over sin. To make the right choice requires God's grace, and to implement it requires conscious dependence on the Holy Spirit. If with divine help we set our faces against sinning, we will be able to overcome any temptation to sin. Sin will have no power over us (Rom. 6:13–14).

Jesus set us an example of victory by meeting and refusing every possible temptation. He had all the desires we have, yet He prevailed over every desire to do wrong (Heb. 4:15).

Self-Test

Here are some questions to evaluate whether you are guilty of blame-shifting.

1. Do I ever justify myself by claiming to be a victim? Do I say, "I know I'm mad, but who could stay cool after being so mistreated?"

Anger and wrath are frequently rooted in a sense that we have been wronged. Once we see ourselves as victims of mistreatment or abuse, we tend to think that we have a moral right to feel mad, or even to retaliate. We react just like a rat backed into a corner.

Many years ago when I was in the field of psychology, rats were often used as subjects in research on learning and memory. (As you might expect, that research shed little light on the workings of the human brain, which is not simply a larger version of a rat's brain.) Many times while I myself was performing an experiment with rats, I had to retrieve one of these little beasts from a maze that it was unable to master. A rat is fairly slow on a straightaway, but when backed into a corner, it can attack with the speed of lightning. I always wore heavy gloves, but more than once, a cornered rat, who had spent its idle hours sharpening its teeth on the wire mesh of its cage, bit me so hard that its teeth went all the way through both the glove and my finger. Sad to say, we human beings have defensive instincts similar to a rat's. When cornered, we lash out. Then we tell ourselves that our reaction was not our fault, but the fault of whoever victimized us. We shift blame off ourselves.

But the Bible is not sympathetic to such excuses. "If it be possible, as much as lieth in you, live peaceably with all men. Dearly beloved, avenge not yourselves, but *rather* give place unto wrath: for it is written, Vengeance *is* mine; I will repay, saith the Lord. Therefore if thine enemy hunger, feed him; if he thirst, give him drink: for in so doing thou shalt heap coals of fire on his head. Be not overcome of evil, but overcome evil with good" (Rom. 12:18–21).

2. Do I pretend that the flesh is too strong to control?

Although everyone above early childhood is capable of sexual sin, the most vulnerable are teenagers, since they have the weakest internal controls. It is therefore wise to structure their lives so that before marriage, they will stay away from relationships involving affectionate touching. Some parents oppose strict standards on the grounds that God made the young incapable of wholly restraining their strong desires. I have often seen parents later regret such thinking. When their teenager became involved in impure romance, he or she lost an interest in spiritual things, and in many cases the backsliding led to personal tragedy.

When my sons were still fairly young, I learned that many of the young people I had grown up with in my church were no longer following Christ. What happened in my church was typical. The spiritual casualty rate for children of Christian homes seems to have risen sharply after World War II. In the '50s and '60s, when I was in my formative years, the church as a whole failed to retain maybe half of its young people. (Today, the casualty rate is even higher). What were the reasons for the declining success of Christian upbringing in those days? Doubtless one major reason was the growing moral looseness of teenage society. Dating standards had fallen to a new low after the advent of car dating in the '30s and '40s.

I was determined to protect my own sons from the dating trap, so in the early '80s, when they were entering their teens, I wrote a book called *With All Purity,* which was published by Regular Baptist Press. Its thesis was that to uphold purity, the wise course for the young is to postpone dating until they are old enough to marry. For most, an appropriate time to begin going on dates is during college.

Over the years I have had many parents quarrel with my position. Their objection is usually some variation on the theme, "God did not expect young boys and girls to behave like monks and nuns." I understand that in modern society we have a unique problem. Young people are biologically ready for marriage long before marriage is prudent. As a result, Christian young people today must deny themselves any sexual fulfillment for many years. Is that unreasonable to expect? Are we adults being unfair if we insist on so much self-restraint? No, Christ was capable of all the passions we have, yet He never married and He never sinned. By the power of the Spirit, every teenager can live like Christ. It certainly makes the road smoother, however, if the young avoid premature dating and romance.

Yet many parents do not agree with my standards. Many years ago, I talked to a father about his daughter after I learned that she was involved in a questionable relationship. When I shared this information with him, he did not want to hear it. He said that I was much too strict and that my sons would someday turn against me; also, that we should trust our children, and he trusted his daughter to do right. Sometime later, she was found to be pregnant out of wedlock. How did the father react? He ejected her from the home and disowned her, on the grounds that she had betrayed him. How often have I seen parents blame their children for misconduct the parents had failed to prevent. Here is another kind of blame-shifting. Children are but children. They are weak, naïve, untaught by experience. Parents must accept responsibility for standing in the gap. God has given them the job of protecting their children from life-ruining mistakes.

3. If I have sinned because I could not cope with the troubles of life, have I held God responsible?

Finding yourself in financial trouble, perhaps you have stolen or cheated to gain money. Or overcome with loneliness, perhaps you have sought relief through sexual sin. Or after suffering an injustice, perhaps you have sought revenge. And you have justified yourself by saying that God left you no alternative. But James rebukes such thinking when he says, "God tempts no man."

4. How do I handle criticism? Do I automatically rear back and defend myself?

How you should react depends on what kind of criticism it is.

1. Perhaps it is false and malicious. It can be a shock to discover what others think about you. Some people are quick to pigeonhole you according to prejudice or evil gossip or selfish interest, and then they can always find another unjust person to agree with them. In response to criticism of this kind, you are entitled to explain yourself in a reasonable and kind manner. But what if your critic refuses to hear you? You should turn the other cheek (Matt. 5:39) and leave justice to God. He, the righteous Judge, will come quickly and settle the matter (Jas. 5:8–9). The only time when you need not turn the other cheek is when the attacker is under your authority. Then for the attacker's sake you have a duty to undertake proper corrective measures.

2. Another kind of criticism is false but well-intentioned. The wise response is to hear it graciously and then explain yourself as kindly as you can.

3. But if someone addresses you with just criticism, your duty is to listen and learn (Ps. 141:5). You must be careful to accept responsibility for your faults, rather than denying they exist or putting the blame elsewhere. Do you know someone who is deaf to criticism? One sign of our fallen human nature is that such a person is often quick to criticize others—like the man who said to his wife, "Sometimes I think the whole world is wrong but me and you, and sometimes I have doubts about you." Why is the person impervious to criticism often so critical? It is a form of blame-shifting. You can maintain the illusion that you are always right only by convincing yourself that in conflicts or disagreements with other people, they are always wrong.

5. How do I react when people I love come under criticism?

Many parents are tragically blind to the faults of their children. But unless they stop living in denial about what their children are really like, they can do little to help them. Any effective strategy for correcting their faults must start with admission that they exist.

Every school teacher must deal with parents who use blame-shifting to excuse the misbehavior of their children. Little Johnny is bad because he is going through a phase, or is handicapped by a medical or psychological disorder, or is just seeking attention, or is being picked on by the other kids, etc.

These are the leading excuses. From a teacher's perspective, they constitute the familiar four. Also very familiar are the common excuses for not doing homework. The classic is, "The dog ate it." I have known teachers who actually received homework papers covered with paw prints. The most brazen excuse I ever heard came from a father who insisted that his son's homework papers were missing because the teacher lost them.

6. Can I say, "I'm sorry?"

To live with someone who cannot let down his defensive wall and say he is sorry must be a sore trial. Stubbornness of this kind frequently arises from a habit of blaming others.

A teenager's "I'm sorry" may not be sincere. It may mean I'm sorry because I don't want you to probe deeper and find something worse. Or, I'm sorry because I want you to stop bothering me so I can get on with my life. Or, I'm sorry because I don't want you to punish me. An adult dealing with the issue must persist in questioning and exhorting the teenager until he obtains a real "I'm sorry."

Review Questions

1. Now what kind of temptation does James address?
2. For what two reasons is it wrong to blame God?
3. Why does God allow temptation in this sense?
4. What are the common excuses for sin?
5. Why are they equivalent to blaming God?
6. What is the only reason a man sins?
7. What is the difference between lust and sin?
8. What are the three kinds of lust?
9. What is the flesh in which dwells no good thing?
10. In sinning, where lies the potential and what produces the fact?
11. In victory over sin, where lies the potential and what produces the fact?

> 16 **Do not err, my beloved brethren.**
> 17 **Every good gift and every perfect gift is from above, and cometh down from the Father of lights, with whom is no variableness, neither shadow of turning.**
> 18 **Of his own will begat he us with the word of truth, that we should be a kind of firstfruits of his creatures.**

Lesson 8

The Goodness of God

Seeing God correctly. In the last verses we considered, James confronted sinners who try to blame God for their sin. He bluntly denied that God is a source of temptation. To entice any man into sin would itself be an act of wickedness, and wickedness cannot touch God, for just as He tempts no man, so He "cannot be tempted with evil." James concludes His defense of God's righteousness with a fervent appeal, "Do not err, my beloved brethren" (v. 16). In other words, do not err by harboring in your minds any slight suspicion that God is less than holy and pure to a degree which is absolute.

Far from being the source of anything evil, God is the source of everything good. Verse 17 can be translated, "Every act of giving [something] good and every perfect gift is from above, coming down from the Father of lights."[21] The meaning is that the Father above is the source of every good thing we receive, as well as every circumstance that brings a good thing into our lives. Our God is a dependable giver of wonderful benefits because His very nature is light (1 John 1:5), which in the physical realm provides the energy necessary for life and for every achievement and enjoyment that life makes possible, and which in the spiritual realm furnishes all truth necessary for a relationship with God Himself (John 1:1–14). To demonstrate that He is light, God created the luminous bodies of the sky. James calls Him "the Father of lights," or, literally, "the Father of the lights," referring generally to the celestial bodies, but especially to the sun and moon.[22]

Yet the Creator is greater than His creation, for whereas the sun and moon vary in color and intensity according to their position in the sky and according to conditions of cloud and atmosphere, the Father is perfectly unchanging. His goodness shines with a constant radiance. Also, whereas the moon is sometimes obscured by the earth's shadow and the sun is rarely but occasionally obscured by the moon's shadow, with God there is no "shadow of turning." The idea is that His light is never interrupted or overcome by darkness. His goodness is secure from any setback or defeat.

Notice that James understood basic science. He knew that the shifting darkness that may appear on the moon's surface or sun's surface is basically the same as an ordinary shadow on the earth. Furthermore, James recognized that shadows on the moon and sun come about as a result of "turning"—in other words, as a result of the heavenly bodies moving through their orbits.

Proof of God's goodness. James next proceeds to prove the goodness of God. The primary evidence is that He has offered salvation to man (v. 18). Motivated by love, He has given each of us a chance to live forever, even though we belong to a race of rebels and have gone astray into sin that divine justice must condemn. The destiny we deserve is a second death in an eternal hell (Rev. 20:12–15). Yet God has taken sinners like us and turned us into new creatures through a process of spiritual rebirth. In our new existence we stand united with Christ and partake of His moral perfection. We are without sin at least in our position though not in our practice, and when we shed sinful flesh we will be sinless altogether. Therefore, God will be glad to receive us into His ever-enduring fellowship.

How has God made us fit for heaven? He has accomplished our new birth through the "word of truth." James means simply the gospel. The preaching of the gospel has awakened in us a consciousness of our sin as well as a desire to be saved, and it has also shown us the Savior, who is Jesus Christ. James emphasizes that the winning of souls requires preaching, the same principle we find eloquently set forth by Paul (Rom. 10:13–15).

The consequence of our new birth is that we have become "a kind of firstfruits of his creatures." Firstfruits were the beginning of a harvest. The third in the yearly cycle of feasts that God prescribed for Israel was the Feast of Firstfruits, so called because the first grain taken in the barley harvest was brought to the Temple and offered to the Lord. In his characteristic precision, the Holy Spirit speaking through James says we are "a kind of firstfruits." He avoids saying that we are "firstfruits," because the term better applies to Christ as the firstfruits from the dead (1 Cor. 15:23). Yet we are similar to firstfruits in that we are the first of many creatures that God will yet bring into existence.

It is uncertain what James means. The word translated "creatures" literally means "things made,"[23] so the reference might be either to some creatures, whether living or nonliving, or to the entire system of created things.[24] If he is speaking chiefly to Christian readers of his own time, perhaps he means that they were the first of a great harvest of souls that would continue into succeeding ages. Or if he is addressing Christians throughout the whole Church Age, perhaps he means that they were the first of a new creation that will eventually supplant the present cosmos, which is tainted by sin, infested with death, and subject to decay. We find the latter sense of firstfruits in Paul's epistle to the Romans (Rom. 8:21–23). Both writers view God's work of regenerating believers as the opening phase of His program to make a perfect world that He will be willing to sustain forever.

Self-Test

Pose some questions to yourself to see whether you understand just how good God is, as He is described in verse 17.

1. Do I ever make the mistake of retouching a true picture of God so that He looks more like me?

Perhaps the first idolatry was to worship a man and woman posing as gods. Mankind has always tried to squeeze God into a human box. When they look at Him, instead of seeing God they see a reflection of themselves.

A few years ago, the famous atheist Antony Flew realized he was wrong and admitted that God exists after all. But what kind of being did Flew first imagine God to be? Not like the God of the Bible. Instead of espousing true theism, Flew resurrected the eighteenth-century philosophy known as deism, which believed that after God created the universe, He took no further interest in it. Later, however, Flew said that he had become open to the Christian idea of God.[25] One problem in deism is that it portrays God as rather like the philosophers who have clung to it in place of Christianity—as a calculating intellectual indifferent to moral values and deficient in love.

Do you make the same mistake? When you picture God in your mind's eye, do you see your own mirror image, or the image of a being essentially manlike? Do you think of Him as a kindly grandfather with a white beard, or in some other way do you give Him a human appearance? But our heavenly Father does not look like a man. He has no distinct parts. He is a unified Being clothed in light (1 Tim. 6:16). Moreover, just as He has no human appearance, so He has no human failings. Don't think He is imperfect like you. He is never impatient, mean, selfish, manipulative, or unreasonable. As James says, He is not tempted by evil. Likewise, He is not limited by any of your weaknesses. He never lacks the right answer or the necessary power. He never fails to hate sin or uphold truth. You have the wrong conception of God if you imagine that He approves or tolerates your sin.

I saw a man wearing a T-shirt that bore words to the effect, "Beer was created by God and proves that God wants us to be happy." Like all excuses for sin, this was a specimen of juvenile thinking. Many things exist contrary to the will of God, and many other things harmless in themselves are used contrary to His will.

Here is not the place to address the evils in drinking. I will be content to say that God could not possibly endorse any practice that draws millions into the net of alcoholism, with all of its terrible consequences, destroying mind, body, and soul. Have you known an alcoholic? Have you seen anyone going through delirium tremens? If my example and practice of abstinence can help anyone avoid addiction to drink, then by choosing abstinence I am simply living the Christian life, which is a life of compassion for my weaker brother.

2. Do I give God credit for every good thing in my life?

You probably recognize His hand when He does a miraculous work to help you, perhaps by healing a disease or delivering you from danger. But are you as ready to thank Him for all the simple pleasures of life (1 Tim. 6:17)? Every refreshing moment is a gift of God.

I love a child's laughter, a sunset, a blooming rose, a cheerful song, a thrilling symphony, the touch of my wife's hand, a piece of chocolate. You can make your own list, I am sure. But let us remember that even these small blessings, in addition to every larger blessing we know or imagine, originates in the Father of lights (1 Tim. 4:4–5).

3. Do I see His goodness even in the troubles of life?

Whatever the trouble may be, it is another gift of God. God allows it for many reasons—so that you will grow stronger by wrestling with adversity; so that you will learn to depend on Him for victory; so that you will come to praise Him for His superior wisdom in giving you troubles that you would never choose, yet that prove essential for some good purpose (Rom. 8:28).

When my sons were little, we often went on excursions into the wilderness. Once before our youngest was born and our oldest was still a toddler, we visited Dinosaur National Monument in Colorado. At the trailhead next to the parking lot, we saw a sign that the trail we wanted was fairly short. Normally my little boy would have ridden on my back in a child carrier. But since this promised to be an easy hike, I decided that instead of carrying him, I would let him walk beside me and hold my hand. From the trailhead we could not tell what was coming because the course we would follow was obscured by rocks. After a few minutes of trudging upward, however, we found ourselves on a high ridge not far from a steep drop-off. Then suddenly the trail led us onto an overlook with sheer cliffs on the right and left as well as in front of us. The sides plummeted to a river far below. Surrounding the point was very crude protection. As soon as I saw where we were, I was not afraid for myself but for my little boy, and my grip on his arm tightened like a vice, and he began to whine. If he had been slightly older, he would have said, "Daddy, you're hurting me." For years afterward, I had nightmares about that moment. What might have happened if, in his childish displeasure with my grip, he had succeeded in pulling away from me? Or what if he had pulled away before I saw the danger?

You see what I am driving at. Sometimes we say to God, "Daddy, you're hurting me." But why is He hurting us? Because He can see the cliff. Just as my tiny son had no idea of his peril, so we may not foresee the tragic steps we would take except for God's protection, and often His protection is a troubling or painful experience which, by strengthening our character and molding our will, leaves us capable of choosing a safer path through life.

4. Have I gone through a spiritual rebirth?

You have not begun to experience the goodness of God unless you have received His greatest gift, salvation. Reaching out to accept it by faith makes you eligible for every other divine gift.

But perhaps you say, "Why should you preach salvation to me, the diligent reader of this Bible study?" Or perhaps you say, "Am I not a good church member?" Because the sad truth is that many professing Christians are unsaved. Some are deliberate hypocrites pursuing a personal agenda. Some do not know their true condition.

In one of our churches there was an old man in his nineties, a widower who had belonged to the church for fifty years. He loved to talk about what a wonderful person his wife had been. Indeed, she had a reputation as a godly woman. But after she died, her husband as he grew older became more hardened in his indifference to anything spiritual. None of us ever heard him give a testimony of salvation. If you pressed him about it, he would recall how he and his wife had often invited the pastor for Sunday dinner. Once when I visited him in the hospital, I asked, "Wouldn't it be wonderful to be reunited with your wife in heaven?" His face stiffened and he said nothing. His own daughter, a member of our church, did not think that he was saved. He was very hard to get along with. She doubted that he had ever shown any real fruit of the Spirit. Yet he had belonged to the church for fifty years. Obviously, when he was younger, he had done a better job of playing the hypocrite, But age tends to accentuate and display our real character.

I have seen many similar cases. It is not unusual for a family to join the church together even though the husband or wife is not saved. Then after the passage of years, the Lord generally takes the life of the saved spouse first, giving the other as much time as possible to repent. The Lord's desire is that in his or her loneliness, the one bereaved will pursue the only course that will achieve reunion with the one departed. He or she must submit to the message of salvation through Christ.

I have discovered that some of the unsaved spouses in our churches do not really understand the gospel. They hear it every week perhaps, but its true meaning never registers in their hearts. So let me ask you, "If you died today, do you know for sure that you would go to heaven?" If your answer is just, "I hope so," or "I think so," you are probably not saved, and you need to talk to someone about your soul's destiny. Do not be too proud or too embarrassed to do what is necessary to stay out of hell and enjoy heaven.

If you say that you are sure of going to heaven, the next question is, "How do you know?" Because your parents were Christians? Because you are married to a wonderful Christian? Because you have always attended church? Because you have been a church member for fifty years? Because you've had the pastor over for dinner? If you give any of these answers, your salvation is in doubt. The only right answer is, "Because Jesus died for my sins and I have trusted in Him as my Savior." It is not these exact words that save you, of course. You are not saved by reciting a formula. What saves you is faith. These words are grounds for assurance only if they express what you truly believe.

5. Do I meditate on my future state in a perfect world?

The Bible gives you abundant information about what that state will be like, information that God intended to encourage and cheer you as you deal with this present imperfect world. To gain these benefits, read the closing chapters of the Book of Revelation and see the wonderful future that lies in store for all of God's children.

Review Questions

1. What kind of wrong thinking must we avoid?
2. What kinds of gifts proceed from God?
3. Why is God a dependable source of good things?
4. What proves that God is light?
5. What is one respect in which God is greater than the celestial lights He created?
6. How does James demonstrate understanding of basic science?
7. What is the greatest gift that God provides?
8. By what tool has He brought us to spiritual birth?
9. What do we become as a result of our new birth?
10. What is the likely meaning, especially in light of Romans 8?

✦ James 1:19–21 ✦

> 19 Wherefore, my beloved brethren, let every man be swift to hear, slow to speak, slow to wrath:
>
> 20 For the wrath of man worketh not the righteousness of God.
>
> 21 Wherefore lay apart all filthiness and superfluity of naughtiness, and receive with meekness the engrafted word, which is able to save your souls.

Lesson 9

Being Teachable

When to be swift and when to be slow. In verse 17, James shows us God in His character as the author of every good gift. Then in verse 18 James describes God's greatest gift of all. That gift is our salvation, which has so transformed us that we have lost our former identities and become wholly new creatures, the firstfruits of a perfect creation enduring forever. The instrument God used to produce the miraculous change was "the word of truth."

Now in verse 19 James brings out the crucial application. If the Word of Truth is so powerful in accomplishing good, we had better give it central place in our lives. He issues a strong appeal to heed the Word. He says, "Wherefore." In a nutshell he is saying, "The appeal I am now going to make rests upon what I have just shown you." Then he addresses his readers exactly as he did three verses earlier, calling them "my beloved brethren." He wants them to know that the motive constraining his appeal is love and only love. Counsel proceeding from real love can be trusted to seek above all the welfare of the beloved. He is implying that because his words come from a loving heart, his readers should listen closely. He is going to state what he truly believes is the great need of their souls.

That need is to "be swift to hear, slow to speak, slow to wrath." "Swift" and "slow" in this context do not refer to speed. By "swift" he means "eager." He wants us to be ready and eager to hear. By "slow" he means that we should exercise restraint. He wants us to speak only after carefully weighing our words and to show anger only after determining that it is right and necessary for a good purpose.

There are many other warnings in Scripture against speaking rashly (Prov. 10:19; 13:3; 17:27; Eccles. 5:1–2) and many other warnings against anger (Prov. 14:29; 16:32; 17:27 again; 29:11; Eccles. 7:9). But the general principle that we must keep our speech and temper under control is not all that James is teaching here. He is teaching also how we should react to the Word of Truth. It will not be profitable to us unless we are swift to hear, slow to speak, and slow to wrath. We must hear it with minds poised to believe. Rather than permit quarrelsome outbursts that will negate its wholesome influence, we must bind our tongues to thoughtful questions and applications. And finally, we must not allow the Word to become an excuse for wrath and fighting.

The wrath he means is evidently the kind that arises when two brothers disagree over a point of doctrine or practice within the church. Confirmation that he is thinking of this kind of wrath appears in his next comment; "For the wrath of man worketh not the righteousness of God" (v. 20). Human wrath of a fleshly kind never attains a result that a righteous God can approve. Yet when do men most easily fall into the trap of thinking that their wrath serves God's interests? When they have embarked on a passionate crusade against what they define as sin or heresy. It is then that they easily get riled up with anger which they pretend is righteous anger. They fool themselves that unless they take a strong stand and defend their ground with fussing, fuming, and fighting, darkness will tighten its hold on the world. They fail to see that when they let themselves be possessed with carnal rage, darkness wins, for this kind of wrath is a vehicle of hatred, not love. It divides rather than unites. It hurts rather than helps. It destroys rather than builds.

There is a place for defending the Word of God. Later we will discuss when and how it is appropriate to defend it.

Sin as dirt. James next puts his finger on the root cause of all our wrong responses to the Word of Truth. Why are we not swift to hear but slow, not slow to speak but swift, and not slow to wrath but swift? Because of sin. Sin is the great wall that keeps truth from penetrating deep into our hearts (Acts 28:26–27). Therefore, James admonishes us to "lay apart all filthiness and superfluity of naughtiness" (v. 21). Another translation is this: "Put off all dirt and all abundance of wickedness."[26] He is comparing sin to the filth that readily accumulates on our bodies and clothing as we interact with the world around us. There is dirt everywhere, and we pick it up without trying. So also it takes no special effort to multiply our sins. By nature we are sinners and we are always sinning. Just as we must regularly cleanse ourselves of dirt, so we must regularly remove the sin clinging to us. Otherwise, we are unprepared to profit from the Word of Truth.

If we deal with sin by confessing and forsaking it, then we will be able to "receive the engrafted word, which is able to save your souls" (v. 21). "Engrafted" is literally "implanted."[27] James is thinking of the Word as seed sown in the soil of our hearts. Here is one example of his close dependence on the teaching of Jesus. The imagery he employs recalls Jesus' Parable of the Sower, telling of the farmer who goes forth and scatters seed in his field (Matt. 13:3–9, 18–23). The seed is the Word of God, and the sower is anyone who shares the Word with others. In some soil the seed cannot take root. In other soil it germinates but soon withers. In yet other soil it grows up among weeds and never produces fruit. But in the remaining soil it yields a great harvest. Thus, when James pleads with his readers to receive the implanted Word, he means that they should let it grow and be fruitful.

Exactly what must they do? As they hear the Word, they must respond with faith. By believing the gospel, they gain salvation if they have not been saved already. As James says, the Word "is able to save your souls." Yet salvation is only the first work that the Word performs in our hearts. It not only puts us in the position of sons who are legally entitled to inherit heaven, but it also does a continuous work of transformation that makes us fit for heaven. This ongoing work is the subject of the next verses.

The virtue of meekness. The virtue that makes our hearts tender to the Word is meekness. The opposite of meekness is, of course, pride. The main reason men resist the Word is that they feel no need for it. In their pride, they are satisfied with what they know already, or with what they think they know. As they hear the Word preached or taught, many professing Christians reject anything they do not agree with. They may claim that the Bible is their ultimate authority, but in reality they accept the Bible only to the extent that it fits into the framework of their own thinking. They are not really open to new ideas, especially if these challenge sinful attitudes and practices. They are not teachable, and at the core of their resistance is pride. Thus, Jesus says, "Blessed are the meek, for they shall inherit the earth" (Matt. 5:5).

Self-Test

First, consider whether you are swift to hear.

1. Do I take every opportunity to hear good preaching and teaching?

The best test is your attendance record. If your church is properly organized, it surely notices when you stay away, but you need to understand that God keeps attendance too. He is not going to teach you much unless you meet the requirement He states in Jeremiah 29:13: "And ye shall seek me, and find me, when ye shall search for me with all your heart." You can hardly claim that you are keen on finding God if you do not even go to the place He has appointed for meeting with Him, the church.

If you are content to wallow in spiritual ignorance, very likely you do not think that Bible teaching and preaching have much to offer. Maybe the reason is that you do not really believe the Bible, and you are a hypocrite.

Years ago I knew a well-educated man who attended church but showed little appetite for spiritual things. I discovered the reason when he confessed to me in private that he had put his own spin on Christianity. As he shared his thinking, I realized that he had come to views which he called Christian, but which were outrageously unchristian. His favorite book was, *Zen and the Art of Motorcycle Maintenance,* one of the most influential books in the early New Age Movement. He blithely informed me that he was a god.

Few of the marginal people in our churches who give little place to the Bible and Bible teaching have fallen into such weird beliefs as this man embraced. Yet they are just as guilty of making themselves into gods if they do not put God's Word above their own ideas and God's will above their own desires. The proof that you give priority to His Word and His will is that you take every opportunity to hear good preaching and teaching of the Bible. Not only do you attend church faithfully, but also you attend with a glad spirit, rather than with a grudging spirit as if you were performing an unpleasant duty.

2. As I listen, do I keep an attentive mind?

You must stay awake and alert, unlike poor Eutychus who fell out of a window while Paul was preaching,. You know the story (Acts 20:7–12). It should be obvious why God included it in the Bible. He was warning all you sleepyheads what might happen to you if you drowse off during the sermon. You might drop dead.

3. Do I shun a critical spirit, causing me to focus on minor faults in the teacher's ideas and delivery, and instead do I dwell on the good things he is saying?

You should harvest all the helpful truth you can find rather than sift through the main substance for small reasons to quibble and complain. In other words, as my father often advised, don't make a mountain out of a molehill. Your strategy as a student should always be to overlook the bad and discover the good.

I am speaking on my own behalf as a teacher. If I say something in this commentary that is not exactly right or that is poorly expressed, pay no attention. Concentrate on the better things I say, and if you look for them, perhaps you will find them.

4. Am I careful not to reject the Word of Truth just because it contradicts my own ideas? Am I swift to learn something new?

One reason that many Bible-believing churches are not growing is that although they can attract new people, they have trouble holding on to them. When people come into our churches and learn what the Bible says, many are offended because it sharply contradicts the humanistic worldview they have learned in the schools and the media. Indeed, these shapers of public opinion have brainwashed them to think that people who instead hold a Christian worldview are crackpots of the first magnitude. Where do we fall so wide of the mark? We reject the three cornerstones of modern thinking: evolutionism, pragmatism, and relativism. But as we show in Appendix 1, all three are absurd.

I trust that none of you will reject what I am teaching here just because it does not agree with the philosophy imposed on you by today's unbelieving world. Be swift to hear. If you are a new Christian, come to Bible teaching and preaching with a heart of faith and let the Holy Spirit instruct you in a whole new way of thinking that will give you a true picture of the world you dwell in, that will show you the true purpose of life, and that will lead you down the path to true happiness.

The secret to being teachable is to receive the Word with meekness. When you hear something new or contrary to your beliefs, you should consult the Holy Spirit and seek His mind. The meekness required of you is to admit that you might be wrong.

Next, consider whether you are slow to speak.

5. When I ask questions of a teacher, are they of a profitable kind?

Do you belabor the teacher with questions that proceed not from a real desire to know, but from a desire for attention, or from a desire to show yourself clever, or from a desire to make the teacher look foolish? Do you ask questions that you could easily resolve yourself if you sought instruction from the Holy Spirit? Do you ask questions that the teacher just answered but you were asleep?

There is no evil in questions, but you should confine yourself to good questions. Every teacher occasionally has a student who, when he raises his hand, everybody groans. Don't be that kind of student.

6. More important, do I argue with the Word of Truth?

How often have I known people who cast aside good Bible teaching because it made no sense to their carnal minds, darkened by unbelief! You may encounter people like this when you go out witnessing. I sometimes receive letters to my website from people with a scornful and argumentative spirit. For example, I had one man write to me at great length to register furious objection to my stand against polygamy. Another took issue with my insistence that all men are sinners. He assured me that he is not. I responded by asking whether his wife agrees.

Also, consider whether you are slow to wrath.

7. Do I become embroiled in debates over the Bible and Christian living?

As you should not argue with the Word itself, so you should not argue with others because they disagree with your interpretations. Church history is a sad tale of bitter and divisive fights over doctrine, often leading to broken fellowship or even to violent conflict. We must defend the fundamentals of the faith, yet we must defend them charitably and gently (2 Tim. 2:24–26).

There are exceptions to this rule. When opposing a false teacher, someone with spiritual authority may resort to severe or harsh language if thereby he can save any of the flock from being devoured. We find many illustrations in Paul's conduct (Gal. 1:8–9).

Nevertheless, when we honestly disagree with real brothers in Christ, we must altogether avoid rancor. When debate shifts from the ground of peaceful and pleasant dialogue to the ground of hot contention filled with suspicion, accusation, and denunciation, it becomes a fleshly work as bad as any other gross sin (Gal. 5:19–21). It becomes "hatred, variance [contention], emulations [jealousy], wrath, strife, seditions [dissensions], heresies [factions]." Paul says, "They which do such things shall not inherit the kingdom of God" (Gal. 5:21).

8. Do I come to the Word with a clean heart, able to learn?

The first step in your daily devotions should be confession of sin, so that nothing will hinder the Holy Spirit as He seeks to instruct you through the Word and through His still small voice. It is the custom in our churches to close each preaching service with an invitation, but it would also make good sense to put an invitation at the beginning of a service, giving people a chance to clear away sin before hearing the Word. Because they recognize the need for self-examination before approaching God or God's Word, most churches provide a quiet moment before the service and perhaps others during the service.

Review Questions

1. How does James assure us that we can trust his counsel?

2. What in his judgment is the great need of our souls?
3. What does each of the three admonitions mean?
4. How does each describe a right reaction to the Word of Truth?
5. What is the great barrier that keeps the Word from being fruitful in our lives?
6. What comparison shows how we should deal with our sin?
7. What is involved in giving ourselves a good cleaning?
8. What picture of the Word shows its place in our lives?
9. What is the first benefit of hearing the Word, a prerequisite for all others?
10. What is at the core of all resistance to the Word, and therefore what virtue enables us to profit by it?

> **22** But be ye doers of the word, and not hearers only, deceiving your own selves.
> **23** For if any be a hearer of the word, and not a doer, he is like unto a man beholding his natural face in a glass:
> **24** For he beholdeth himself, and goeth his way, and straightway forgetteth what manner of man he was.
> **25** But whoso looketh into the perfect law of liberty, and continueth *therein*, he being not a forgetful hearer, but a doer of the work, this man shall be blessed in his deed.

Lesson 10

Being Sincere

Self-deception of hypocrites. James has been giving counsel on how to obtain the good gifts that are available in abundance from the Father of lights, as he calls our heavenly Father in verse 17. He has taught that by asking in faith, we can obtain wisdom. By enduring trials, we can gain the crown of life. And by receiving the Word of Truth, we can appropriate a power capable of saving our souls. Yet in the verses we will now consider, he shows that he conceives of this Word as an instrument not only for saving us, but also for transforming our hearts and minds and deeds.

So that the Word will work in us with full effect, without hindrance, we must, however, do more than obey James's instruction in verse 19. There he exhorts us to be swift in hearing the Word, slow in raising questions about it, and slow in making it a center of controversy. We must also do more than obey James's instruction in verse 21. There he tell us to receive the Word with meekness. Besides these good responses, another is crucially important. We must let the Word shape our conduct (v. 22). Giving assent to it is not enough. The Word lays out complex and complete instructions on how we should live. In response, we should be "doers of the word, and not hearers only." We should put into practice all the moral precepts we find in the Word. In the opening verses of James, we have learned some of those precepts, such as the necessity to pray in faith and the requirement to resist lust, and we will learn others as we go through the book.

Hearing the Word without applying it is, as James says, a form of self-deception. We imagine that God will be pleased just because we

give His Word our attention and our assent, even though we neglect
to give it our obedience. Lip service without a corresponding lifestyle
is just hypocrisy. James is right in warning us that a typical hypocrite is self-deceived; that is, he has no insight on his true condition.
He genuinely feels right with God, even though sin clutters his life
and suppresses his conscience.

The Pharisees. The classic example of hypocrisy is the Pharisees. The Jewish people held them in high esteem, allowing them
seats of honor in the synagogues and at banquets, calling out re-
spectful greetings to them as they walked by in the marketplace, and
addressing them as Rabbi, a title full of prestige (Matt. 23:5–7). The
Pharisees had no less esteem for themselves. Jesus tells us how one
Pharisee prayed in the Temple. "God, I thank thee, that I am not as
other men are, extortioners, unjust, adulterers, or even as this publi-
can. I fast twice in the week, I give tithes of all that I possess" (Luke
18:11–12). The irony in this boasting is that Jesus held the Pharisees guilty of the very sins they saw in others.

He specifically mentions "extortion" (Matt. 23:25, the Greek word
referring to stolen goods[28]), accusing them of devouring widows'
houses (Matt. 23:14; Mark 12:40; Luke 20:47). We are not sure exactly what evildoing He was describing.[29] It is possible that in deciding inheritance, Jewish courts gave preference to male relatives, so
that if a man died without sons, his house and other possessions
might pass to a brother or nephew rather than to his widow. The
widow, as a result, might be evicted from her home. Pharisees were
responsible for her loss whether they claimed the inheritance or sat
on the court deciding against her.

Jesus also accused the Pharisees of failure to be just (Matt.
23:23). And in the Sermon on the Mount, He taught that the law
against adultery forbids divorce, a common practice of the Pharisees
(Matt. 5:31–32). One school of rabbis believed that a man could divorce his wife for any reason, even if she served him a bad supper, or
even if he found a prettier woman to take her place.[30]

Hypocrisy has never ceased to plague the work of God. In one of
His Kingdom parables, Jesus warned that tares—that is, hypocrites—
would exist in the church alongside the wheat—true believers—until
the end of the age (Matt. 13:24–30, 37–43). We see here that the ultimate fate of hypocrites will be no less horrific than the fate of outright sinners. They will be cast into a furnace of fire, where there is
wailing and gnashing of teeth. God's wrath against the self-satisfied
Pharisees was so great that Jesus threatened them not only with hell
(Matt. 23:33), but also with greater damnation (Matt. 23:14). The
worst judgment awaits the man who poses as a minister of the gospel
but who abuses his trust by harming God's people and living in self-
indulgence. He will be cut to pieces before being cast into hell (Matt.
24:48–51).

Doers contrasted with hearers. To make more vivid the difference between doing the Word and not doing it, James compares two men who look at their reflections in a mirror (vv. 23–25). "Glass" is a mistranslation, since the mirrors used in the ancient world were not glass, but handheld plates of polished metal, generally bronze.[31] What is the mirror these men use? It is the "perfect law of liberty"— literally, "the perfect law, that of freedom."[32] But although they both view the same picture of self, they react differently. One looks with no more than a glance. After beholding his face and noticing some flaw needing a corrective touch, he goes away and forgets what he saw. He saw the flaw, but did not think it very serious, or else he would have remembered it and done something later to remove it. The second man looks at his face more carefully. The words "looketh into" suggest that he stoops over and gives it close inspection.[33] Then he "continueth," meaning that he does not stop examining himself. His purpose is to let the law of liberty expose all his faults and sins.

What is the perfect law of liberty—that is, the perfect law that brings freedom? The answer appears a few verses later, where James employs "law of liberty" as a name for the requirement to love our neighbor (Jas. 2:8–12). This requirement is indeed a perfect law, in the sense that it gives precisely the right guidance for every moral decision affecting the people around us. Jesus said that it is the summation of the law governing relations between man and man (Matt. 22:37–40). The same requirement is also the law of liberty. It is liberating in two ways: first, because it simplifies our moral duty by eliminating the need to consider any narrower regulations. We need not work our way through a long rule book to find a rule tailored to our specific problem. We only need consider what is the loving thing to do. Second, it is liberating because to act always in love is a life of freedom not only from sin, but also from any sense that God is oppressing us with His demands. Obedience is no longer a grim necessity, but a joyful opportunity. It is a wonderful privilege to feel and show love. To live in such a way that we never fail to love our neighbor is a happy life.

Gazing intently into the mirror of God's Word shows how God sees us. Then we have a choice. We can go away and forget what we saw, resuming our normal habits as if we were already good enough in God's eyes. But if we take that direction, we will continue in our sins and act the part of a hypocrite. Or we can respond by remolding our life according to God's will. If we become doers of the Word we have heard, we will gain a great reward. We will be, as James says, blessed. In a previous lesson (p. 29), we discussed what blessedness means. It means to experience nothing but good forever. Now the blessed get up every morning and go through the day as children of the King. Someday they will inherit the Kingdom itself, where they will stand in line for any treasure in God's storehouse that they might fancy.

Self-Test

The main question that this lesson presents for your consideration is obvious. Are you a doer of the Word? Yet to help you come to
a good answer, we will be more specific.

**1. When I read the Word or hear it preached, does it simply
blow through my mind as familiar words, or do I allow it to gen-
erate thought?**

You must consciously consider whether it demands changes in
your life. You dare not leave out the application stage as you process
the Word of God.

2. Do I meditate on the Word?

The application stage takes time. Thus, it is not sufficient just to
read or hear the Word. You must spend time thinking about it.

In your morning devotions, it is not enough to read a psalm and
recite your usual list of maybe ten requests; then, when you are
done, to say, "OK Lord, that's it for today. See you tomorrow." No,
you should include other portions of Scripture as well, and as you
bathe your mind in the Word, you should ponder how it applies to
your life. Then afterward sit quiet for several minutes and meditate
on what you have read. Think of all the demands and challenges of
the coming day, and ask God for wisdom and strength to meet them.
Seek specific guidance from the Word and from the Spirit for the decisions you will be making. Let your devotions be your means of
transport into heaven's throne room to gain practical direction for
your life.

Also examine yourself during the invitation after a sermon. What
did the preacher say that God wanted you to hear? Which of the
preacher's words were really God speaking to you personally? Both
then and after you go home, meditate on the Bible-based truth you
have heard from the pulpit.

**3. When I make choices during the day, do I filter them
through the wisdom in God's Word? Or am I content with my
own wisdom?**

Paul cautions us against being wise in our own eyes (Rom.
12:16). You must always use the Word as a sounding board for your
decisions. One benefit of doing this for a number of years is growth
in discernment. Like any other skill, good discernment takes practice.

For the spiritually mature, the right choices are usually pretty obvious.

4. Am I self-deceived?

Here is a question that cannot be avoided. It is my duty to recommend it as a question you should ask yourself. Indeed, as I exhort you further, I cannot avoid being even more blunt. Are you one of those Pharisees who thinks he stands in the center of God's favor when really he teeters on the verge of God's wrath? In other words, are you a real Christian or a fake? There are basically two tests.

The first is the pride test. The distinguishing mark of every Pharisee is a wall of pride shielding him from honest self-evaluation. Can you accept the kind of criticism that comes through reading or hearing God's Word? Or do you always justify yourself? There are many easy ways to whitewash your heart. You can redefine sin so that you feel outside its boundaries, or you can minimize sin by comparing yourself with worse sinners, or you can find someone or something to blame for your sin, or you can tell yourself that your sin is outweighed by your good works.

The second is the sin test. If you have a chronic sin that gives a bad odor to your pretense of being religious, you are self-deceived. Others may detect the odor even if you do not.

The last question is even more unpleasant to consider, but again I have no choice but to include it.

5. Am I in fact a deliberate hypocrite?

Are you consciously playing a game when you claim to be a believer? Do you come to church solely in pursuit of some selfish advantage or some other purpose irrelevant to faith? What can I say to you except to warn you that every man will be judged according to his knowledge (John 15:22; Acts 17:29–31; Rom. 2:12)? The more truth you heard about God's will for your life, the more severely God will punish you if you failed to respond with obedience and faith. Notice in Revelation 21:8 that Jesus puts the fearful and unbelieving first. The implication is that these who heard the truth will suffer worse damnation. The fearful are those who heard it but turned away because they were afraid to be identified with Christ. The unbelieving are those who heard it but responded with unbelief.

Review Questions

1. What else does the Word accomplish besides saving us?

2. What response to the Word is essential to enjoy its good influence?
3. How does James describe hearing the Word without applying it?
4. Who were the classic example of hypocrisy?
5. How did the Pharisees break every law which they prided themselves for keeping?
6. What will be the fate of hypocrites, and which hypocrites face the worst consequences?
7. What imagery does James use to contrast the doer and the hypocrite?
8. What is the perfect law of liberty?
9. In what two ways does the perfect law have a liberating effect?
10. What is the reward for obeying the law of liberty?

---

26 If any man among you seem to be religious, and bridleth not his tongue, but deceiveth his own heart,
this man's religion *is* vain.

Lesson 11

Speech to Avoid

An unbridled tongue. The verse preceding this one is a strong
plea to live in obedience to the Word of God. James has said that a
man who not only hears the Word, but who also performs what he
has heard, will enjoy divine blessing. Now he goes on to give three
tests of whether the Word is truly a man's rule of life. The first test,
found in verse 26, is negative, for it identifies a common sin that he
will cast aside. The last two, which will be the subject of the next
lessons, are positive, for they identify two key virtues that he will
cultivate.

The sin that will be missing in a godly life is the loose speech of
an unbridled tongue. James says, "If any man among you seem to be
religious, and bridleth not his tongue," he "deceiveth his own heart."
The underlying Greek for "seem" does not actually speak of a man
who looks religious to others. Rather, it refers to how a man thinks
about himself.[34] The opening phrase could be translated, "If any
man thinks he is religious." How could a man imagine himself religious if he is not? Because he might be satisfied with practicing only
the external side of religion, including all pious observances that are
on public display. What James is saying, therefore, is that a man
with a loose tongue is deceiving himself if he thinks that going
through the motions of religion will make him right with God. Even
though he endures all the trouble in showing up at church every
Sunday and posing as a good church member, he has not gained a
clean heart. His heart is still black with sin. Why? Because his
tongue is out of control.

Since speech can be as broad in content as thought itself, there
are no limits on the sins the tongue might commit. To catalog them
is impossible within a short space. Yet it will be profitable to consider some of the more common sins.

Using the tongue to manipulate. The chief method of manipulation is flattery, which the Bible roundly condemns (Ps. 12:1–4;
Prov. 26:28). Flattery is insincere praise in an effort to gain some advantage, as when a salesman flatters a customer to secure a sale, or
a man flatters a woman to seduce her, or people pay you compliments

to keep you from noticing that they are stabbing you in the back. It is, of course, never wrong to give people praise if your motive is to encourage them or build them up. Whether your nice words are right depends solely on your motive. As an expression of love, you may even tell people that they look good when they do not, according to general opinion. If, for example, a little old man totters into church with his clothes rumpled and unwashed, his face poorly shaven, his skin mottled with age, and his hair unkempt, it is an act of pure kindness to say, "Hi, Mr. Jones! Happy to see you! You're looking good today!" Is that flattery? No. Is that a lie? No. It is looking at Mr. Jones from God's perspective, not from a warped human perspective. Because the man has done his best to dress up and go to church, he looks good in God's eyes.

Using the tongue to deceive. Lying is an abomination to God (Prov. 12:22; 6:16–19). The Lord commands that we as brothers and sisters in Christ should altogether renounce lying in our dealings with each other (Col. 3:9). One reason God hates lying is that it is the invention of His chief enemy, Satan (John 8:44). Lying, a favorite instrument of selfishness, is always employed to avoid some loss or penalty that comes with truth. But as the saying goes, "The truth will out." In other words, any supposed benefit in lying is never more than temporary. Sooner or later the lie will be exposed for what it is, and the liar will face judgment either by man or God. But a liar is generally blind to the certain consequences of his sin. In the absence of repentance, the ultimate consequence is, of course, damnation (Rev. 21:8, 27; 22:15).

Lying comes natural to children, as they try out the many ways of getting their own way, and adults must take firm measures to teach them not to lie. A grown-up liar is someone who was deprived of good training when he was a child. He is mired in an especially juvenile form of sin.

Using the tongue to attack. In a previous lesson (p. 53), to display the many sins proceeding from wrath, we examined Galatians 5:19–21. A large portion of the list, "variance" as well as "strife," "seditions," and "heresies," may be considered sins of the tongue. Wrathful speech is a terrible sin because it arises from hatred and, if unrestrained, leads finally to wrathful deeds, even murder. Jesus held hatred in any form to be a violation of the commandment, "Thou shalt not kill" (Matt. 5:21–22). The weapon that wrath most often uses is the tongue. Although the tongue cannot tear flesh, it can shred another's reputation, wound deeply his self-respect, brutalize discussion, and decimate bonds of love. There is never any excuse or extenuating circumstance or measurable benefit to justify hateful speech (Eph. 4:31–32).

Yet sometimes the motive for attack is not exactly hatred, but only a desire to look superior, a manifestation of pride. Then the tongue resorts to ridicule or sarcasm or put-downs of one kind or another. Although much of this may masquerade as good fun, God sees it as unacceptable because it destroys the atmosphere of sweetness and love that He desires to fill the church (Eph. 5:4).

Using the tongue to gossip. Gossip has always been one of the most prevalent sins in churches. Yet God hates gossip (Prov. 11:13; 18:8; 26:20). A few of the many reasons that gossip is wrong are discussed in Appendix 2.

To relay the good news that someone is getting married or the bad news that someone has died is not gossip, because no one is unjustly hurt by it. Real gossip has two characteristics. It tells something the subject would not wish to be said, and it violates Jesus' guidelines for handling any complaint against a brother (Matt. 18:15–17).

Jesus' guidelines. If you feel that a brother has transgressed against you, the right first step is to talk with him privately in an effort to resolve the issue. If you fail to make progress, then you can bring one or two more parties into the discussion. If the matter still cannot be settled, you can ask the church to get involved, presumably the leaders first, then the whole church if the leaders do not succeed in restoring harmony. Finally, if the offender will not listen to the church, he must be removed from fellowship.

What faults in a brother call for this procedure? Its scope is not limited to personal frictions and grievances. Even if you do not feel that your brother has wronged you personally, you have an obligation to confront him if you see a sin in his life that is hampering his spiritual walk or endangering the testimony of the church. Any sin a brother commits hurts the whole body and is therefore an offense against you. In such cases, Jesus' guidelines demand that you approach him and discuss your concerns face to face rather than make his sin a subject of gossip.

There are some exclusions from these guidelines.

1. One is whenever you have truly good reason to believe that someone has committed a criminal offense. Such matters lie outside the jurisdiction of the church and fall within the jurisdiction of the state.

2. Another exclusion is whenever the source of the complaint is a minor under parental authority. His parents have the right to stand in his place in any discussions seeking to resolve the matter.

3. There is also a third important exclusion. If you have a complaint against Mr. Smith, you need not talk to him before you talk to your wife. Your one-flesh relationship with her supersedes any obligation you may have to Mr. Smith. Indeed, talking with her first is probably a good idea. She might tell you that Mr. Smith is right, and that you will make a fool of yourself if you confront him. Generally speaking, Jesus' guidelines for resolving complaints within the church were not intended to restrict communication within families.

But there is no other exclusion from these guidelines. There is none, for example, based on rank or role in the church. The guidelines apply equally to pastors, deacons, and laymen, to men and women, and to children and adults. Even a pastor has no right either to hear or to spread a negative report about a member or former member of his congregation if he is stepping outside proper procedure. It does not matter whether the pastor is talking to other pastors, or to leaders in his own church, or to others who also have complaints against the accused. He has no right to wag his tongue in disregard of Jesus' guidelines. In general, no one—leader or layman—has a right to engage in any behind-the-scenes discussions or maneuvers that set these guidelines aside.

It should now be obvious that much of the talk that passes between people is really gossip, in violation of Matthew 18. Why do we all find it so hard to handle complaints the proper way, according to Jesus' guidelines? Because when we feel offended by someone, they require us to confront the offender. Yet confrontation is often unpleasant and often does not come to a satisfactory resolution of the problem. So we are afraid to embark on it. To put it bluntly, we do not have the courage to do right. But we dare not allow our cowardice to hinder the work of God. Let us be men of courage and women of courage.

Christian forbearance. I do not wish to leave the impression that we should always be confronting people. In Matthew 18, Jesus is merely giving us a procedure to follow if we wish to deal with another person's sins. But if we are the sole victim and the sins are not of a grievous or criminal nature, we always have the option to overlook them and get on with life. Indeed, the course of wisdom is generally to overlook the minor faults of others, and also to accept their petty slights without resentment or comment. This is known as Christian forbearance (Eph. 4:2; Col. 3:13). Nevertheless, if you elect not to deal with a problem directly, through confrontation, make sure that you are truly forbearing. Do not dig at the offender behind his back. Do not give him the cold shoulder. Do not cast innuendos in his direction. Either confront him, or grin and bear it. If the matter is serious, however, you have a duty to sit down with the offender and talk. If you choose to remain silent, you will be denying him valuable help, and the complaint will probably rankle in your heart and poison your relationship with him.

Proper confrontation. What is the right way to confront someone? Profitable confrontation, including all forms of Christian counseling, requires attention to six rules.

1. As we have already said, you must engage the other person privately, one-on-one.

2. You must approach him with a desire to be just. You must assume he is innocent until proven guilty, you must patiently hear his defense, and while hearing it you must do your best to factor personal bias and self-interest out of your judgment.

3. Do not be a Pharisee. Do not feel proud of your own righteousness compared with his black deeds. What did Jesus say to the accusers of the woman taken in adultery? "He that is without sin among you, let him first cast a stone at her" (John 8:7). View your conversation as between two sinners saved by grace.

4. If you are rebuking him for a sin that also troubles you, deal with your problem first before trying to help him (Matt. 7:1–5).

5. Be careful that the sinner does not recruit you to his sin (Gal. 6:1). Do not accept any of his excuses, lest they lead you astray.

6. Be nice. The Bible commands gentleness (2 Tim. 2:24–25; Titus 3:2).

Self-Test

The questions we must ask follow directly from our discussion.

1. Do I use my tongue to manipulate?

Do you use flattery to get ahead in your job or to boost your success in selling a product or service? Do you use it to gain the attention of important people? Do you use it to escape the consequences when you have done wrong? For example, if your boss sees you coming in late, it is tempting to shower him with compliments to avoid his wrath. But again, it is never wrong to say nice things if they are motivated by a desire to be a blessing, as when you praise someone on the margins of the church, or if they are sincere, as when a husband tells his wife how wonderful she is.

2. Do I use my tongue to deceive?

The temptation to lie is always greatest when you are caught in a sin. Scripture furnishes us the example of Saul. The Lord through Samuel had instructed Saul that when he defeated the Amalekites, he should destroy their flocks and herds. Perhaps they carried diseases that the Lord wanted to keep away from the livestock of Israel, but Saul paid no heed. Upon his return, to hide his decision to spare the beasts of Amalek, he lied to Samuel, saying he had fully obeyed the Lord's commands (1 Sam. 15:12–14). Since Samuel was God's spokesman, Saul was in essence lying to God. Also, whenever you refuse to admit sin, you are lying to God. But it is folly to compound sin with cover-up. Then, sin lodges more firmly in your heart and exerts greater control over your desires and decisions. It drives you away from God and makes the punishment much worse when He finally deals with you.

3. Do I use my tongue to attack?

Every ounce of negativism in your speech is, when stripped clean of all pious pretexts, a form of attack. It may be aimed at something impersonal like a policy or duty, but the true target is the person who made the policy or prescribed the duty. It may be aimed at a simple circumstance of life like the weather, but the true target is God, who made the weather. Complaining is so common because it quickly becomes a habit. It even becomes a frame of mind that we continually express first to our family, then to our friends, then to others around us. How much of your speech is complaining? How much negativism is there in what you say? You may use your tongue for accomplishing worthwhile tasks, dealing with problems, expressing inner virtues (Gal. 5:22–23), edifying others (Eph. 4:29), and praising God (Eph. 5:19). But any use that strays into sour criticism is wrong and comes under the heading of attack.

4. Do I use my tongue to gossip?

You know perfectly well whether you gossip. Just reexamine your recent conversations with other people. Did you ever place an absent person in an unfavorable light? Did you pass on juicy tidbits that you had no right to share? Did you consciously seek to run somebody down to advance your own prospects or interests?

5. Have the social media, such as Facebook, drawn me into improper speech?

All four kinds—flattery, lying, complaining, gossip—are rife in today's digital world.

Review Questions

1. If a man is a doer of the Word, what common sin will he put out of his life?
2. What manipulative speech does Scripture especially condemn?
3. What misuse of the tongue is an abomination because it derives from God's enemy?
4. What speech violates the commandment against murder?
5. How may gossip be defined?
6. How did Jesus direct us to handle complaints?
7. What are the three exclusions from His guidelines?
8. What often keeps us from following His guidelines?
9. What is sometimes a legitimate alternative to confrontation?
10. What six rules govern confrontation?

> **27 Pure religion and undefiled before God and the Father is this, To visit the fatherless and widows in their affliction . . . .**

Lesson 12

Helping the Needy

A positive test of true religion. In the last verse, James confronts a professing Christian who cannot control his tongue and brands his religion as vain. Now, after exposing hypocrisy, he goes on in verse 27 to give the two marks of genuine religion.

As we remarked in our introductory lesson, verse 27 provides the term "godliness" with a formal definition. "Pure religion and undefiled before God and the Father is this, To visit the fatherless and widows in their affliction, and to keep himself unspotted from the world." In other words, the positive side of pure religion has two components. It combines personal devotion to good works with personal separation from every evil work.

As we said before, James obviously does not mean to limit good works to the one he chooses as an example. Rather, he means that one mark of an authentic Christian is commitment to helping the needy, whether a widow, an orphan, or someone else. But lest we think that good works alone are genuine religion, James adds the requirement to remain unsoiled by the world. Generous charity without separation from worldly sin is pointless, for nothing in a sinful life can win the approval of a righteous God or advance His program. If a church is dominated by unseparated lifestyles, any of its attempts to help the needy will be wasted effort, gaining no eternal results. God will not pour power and blessing on a church that fails to draw its spiritual babes out of sin's bondage.

Yet, although personal separation is the second mark of true religion, the first mark is to practice good works. A religion bearing the second mark but not the first is sterile, because good works are a natural outgrowth and visible expression of love for those who receive the benefit. A distinguishing feature of Spirit-filled believers is a rich godly love both for the brethren and for unbelievers (John 13:34–35). A church that neglects good works on behalf of either shows that it lacks this unique love. It is, or will soon become, a dead church, for a loveless religion is not the religion of Christ.

Widows and orphans. As chief examples of the needy, James mentions widows and orphans. In Bible times, a widow reduced to poverty by her husband's death was helpless to support herself. She could not take a job. Unless she was a trained craftsman she could not make anything to sell. As a result, she was completely dependent on relatives. Since relatives can be stingy, it was common for widows to be extremely poor. Likewise, orphans had no means of support apart from relatives, who might give them very little or neglect them completely. James's own concern for these bereaved members of society won him the admiration of the poorer class in Jerusalem. Touched by that concern, James says that our duty as believers to widows and orphans is to "visit" them. No doubt the word "visit" is referring mainly to visits for the purpose of taking them material assistance. Yet also within the compass of this phrase are visits for the purpose of showing sympathy and relieving loneliness.

The poor brother. Yet if we are animated by the kind of compassion that pleases God, we will not restrict our charity to widows and orphans. We will help anyone who is going through difficulties. One common case is a brother trapped in poverty. Throughout the Bible we are commanded to supply his needs (Jas. 2:15–16; 1 John 3:17; Acts 20:35; Rom. 12:13; Gal. 6:10; Eph. 4:28; 1 Tim. 6:17–19; Heb. 13:16; Matt. 5:42; Lev. 25:35). From these texts we learn three principles:

1. Charity of this kind is the most basic and indispensable obligation of brotherly love.

2. Charity is a special obligation of the rich.

3. Brothers in Christ have first claim upon charity. In other words, they should always be the first to receive it.

Giving to the poor does not exhaust our duty to help others. The Bible urges us also to visit the sick and those in prison (Matt. 25:34–36), to bear one another's burdens (Gal. 6:2), and to share the sorrow of any who are grieving (Rom. 12:15). Such forms of charity may involve material assistance, but the greater need is usually emotional support. Of course, the greatest need wherever trouble strikes is for prayer, but true Christian love always combines prayer with down-to-earth ways of giving help.

Self-Test

The following questions will search out whether you are meeting your obligation to show compassion for the needy.

1. As I think about the widows and orphans that I know, can I

say that I have inquired about their needs, and if I have discovered any needs, have I offered help?

In our society, where life expectancy far exceeds what it was in Bible times, there are hardly any orphanages, and few orphans are left without care. But since women tend to outlive men, there are many widows. Perhaps you say, "In our society they need no money from me. They have social security and Medicare." But their social security and medical coverage may nevertheless be inadequate. And many who start off retirement with enough financial resources find themselves unable to keep up with inflation, which is a great evil upon the backs of the elderly. The small increases in social security designed to offset inflation may keep pace with some rising costs, such as food, but they may lag woefully behind many others: for one, medical care; for another, property taxes. If an elderly person has the misfortune of owning property in a desirable location, he will soon be taxed out of house and home.

As they cope with financial pressures, the elderly may rapidly deplete their resources and end up on Medicaid and other welfare programs. These hardly provide a decent way of life. Yet some of the elderly are too proud or too debilitated even to apply, and they languish in deepening poverty.

Who should carry the burden of helping the elderly, especially widows? Paul provides a clear answer. They should be cared for by their own families, and he defines the responsible family as younger relatives, especially children and grandchildren (1 Tim. 5:4, 8, 16; the world translated "nephews" in v. 4 means "descendants"[35]). He does not wish to make life even harder for elderly sisters and brothers. If someone in his declining years has no family to meet his needs, then it is the obligation of the church to fill the gap (1 Tim. 5:3, 5–7, 9–10, 16).

2. What am I doing to help the elderly whose lives have been reduced to the confines of a nursing home?

Within the body of Christ, they are perhaps the poorest of all. Their lives have been reduced to a bed, a chair, and a bathroom. They may be attended by people who view them as mere objects, with no real value. They may be granted little privacy and modesty. Their calls for help may be ignored. In some of the cheapest establishments they may even be subjected to abuse. The least we can do is to let them know they are not forgotten and to give them a sense of our love.

When in her seventies, my mother started a nursing home ministry that continued over ten years. Toward the end, she was older than most of the people she visited. She was appreciated not only by the nursing home residents, but also by the caregivers and administrators, who gave her special recognition in the form of awards and plaques and publicity. In every respect her outreach to the elderly was an effective testimony for Christ.

3. Am I helping others who are poor?

But you say, "In America there are no poor people apart from those who have allowed laziness or some other vice to overmaster them and drag them down into degradation." Yes, sin may be the reason for poverty in some cases, and certainly we would not question that the poor are sinners. They are sinners because they belong to a race consisting entirely of sinners except for Jesus. But we can rejoice that God offers all humanity His mercy. Are you not a sinner? Has His mercy not come to you? Why, then, should you decline to show mercy to another sinner like yourself? Your helping hand to that single welfare mom living in squalor with her seven kids, or to that derelict on the street corner, or to that druggie and his freakish looking girlfriend is the hand of God's mercy. You may not see any good result, but God will repay you. And occasionally your effort may snatch a soul from the brink of hell.

4. What am I doing to help brethren who are not exactly poor, but who have far less financial power than I have and who, as a result, are deprived of privileges that I take for granted?

One family can afford to give their children a good Christian education. Another cannot. This kind of inequality does not belong in the body of Christ, for one child is as valuable in God's eyes as another.

The more prosperous should always sacrifice <u>luxuries</u> to provide the less prosperous with <u>necessities</u>. What the more prosperous lose through generosity may not be good for them anyway. The luxuries they set aside may have fostered carnality rather than spirituality, leaving them more in love with this world than with the world to come.

Sharing among believers has a strong precedent in the practice of the early church, a church filled with the Holy Spirit and submitted to His leadership to a degree never seen again in church history. As a result, "Neither said any of them that ought of the things which he possessed was his own; but they had all things common" (Acts 4:32).

5. What am I doing to help poor brethren around the world?

Many of God's people live in societies far less prosperous than our own. Paul expected the gentile Christians in Greece and Asia Minor to help their much poorer Jewish brethren in Jerusalem (Rom. 15:25–27; 2 Cor. 8:13–14; 9:1–4, 7, 12). So likewise, we should help our poorer brethren in other nations. How may we do this?

In years past, some mission organizations offered food and other assistance to converts in the churches they were planting, but this kind of help proved to be unwise. It produced too many false converts, who remained on the fringes of the church in good times, then disappeared in times of persecution.

Still, material gifts to foreign believers may serve a good purpose. Especially helpful is money to provide medical services, school facilities and staffing, or church buildings. Relief in a time of famine or natural disaster is always of critical importance. Both as individual believers and as church bodies, we should be alert to such ways of helping our brethren abroad.

6. Am I helping believers with other kinds of needs?

Do you show concern for the sick and seek ways of easing their burden? Do you mourn with the bereaved as much as you rejoice with the blessed? Do you give encouragement to the despondent and guidance to the confused? When a family goes through crisis as a result of strained relationships, do you enter the spiritual fray on their behalf, wielding the weapons of counsel and prayer? Do you notice new people in the church and respond to their needs? Their primary need is to feel welcome, and you meet it by showing hospitality. Do you notice new believers? What they need, of course, is discipling. Do you make time for any one-on-one ministry?

Review Questions

1. What are the two positive marks of genuine religion?
2. Is helping widows and orphans enough of a good work to achieve pure religion?
3. Why are good works pointless if there is no personal separation?
4. Why is personal separation sterile if there are no good works?
5. Why in James's day were widows and orphans especially needy?
6. What does James mean when he tells us to visit them?
7. Who else should receive our help?
8. Giving help is a sign of what basic virtue?
9. Who has a special obligation to help the poor?
10. Who has first claim upon our help?
11. What other forms of charity does Scripture recommend besides material assistance?

+ James 1:27b +

Lesson 13
Unspotted from the World

Legitimate dealings with the ungodly. The second mark of true religion is to keep wholly unspotted from the world (Jas. 1:27). The Bible elsewhere warns us that we should neither love the world (1 John 2:15–16; 2 Tim. 4:10) nor be conformed to it (Rom. 12:1–2). Rather, we should come out from it and be separate (2 Cor. 6:17). What is the world? The world we must shun is not the world of nature, which glorifies God by showing His handiwork (Ps. 19:1–5). Nor is it the world of people. As God loves all men, so must we (John 3:16). Rather, the world threatening us is the world of evil influence—the world of sinners seeking to draw us into sin.

To what extent must we separate from the world? We need not withdraw altogether from ungodly people (1 Cor. 5:9–10). Scripture permits us to mix with them for a variety of purposes.

1. We can live alongside them in their communities. When the apostles started a church, they never required its first members to forsake their homes and build a new community set apart from unbelievers.

2. We can enter the world to conduct business. Paul, sometimes in partnership with Priscilla and Aquila, was a "tentmaker," a common term for someone engaged in leatherworking of all kinds (Acts 18:2–3).[36] Lydia was a seller of purple (Acts 16:14). Paul authorized believers to make purchases at marketplaces patronized by worldly people (1 Cor. 10:25).

3. We can meet socially with unsaved acquaintances, so long as we do not compromise our Christian testimony (1 Cor. 10:27). After all, Jesus ate with publicans and sinners (Mark 2:16).

4. We can, and should, perform charitable deeds on behalf of people outside the church (Gal. 6:10).

5. Jesus counseled us to "render therefore unto Caesar the things which be Caesar's" (Luke 20:25). The question He was addressing was whether God's people should pay their taxes. His answer made it clear that they should be good citizens in every respect. Yes, they should pay their taxes, but also they should not neglect other civic duties. The lesson for today's world is that we should engage ourselves in the political process. By voting and other means,

we should strengthen what is good in society and counter what is bad. It is even appropriate for us to hold public office. In his letter to the Romans, Paul mentions a prominent believer who was also "the chamberlain of the city" (Rom. 16:23).

6. Among those who received the gospel proclaimed by the early church were some in the Roman army (Acts 10:1, 24, 44). Nowhere in the New Testament or in records of the early church do we find any suggestion that soldiers converted to Christ were expected, if possible, to leave military service or, if not possible, to stop cooperating with higher command.

7. The last way we can mingle with the world is not simply a privilege and convenience, but a duty. We must go into the world and mix with worldly people in order to give them the gospel (Acts 1:8).

Where to draw the line. Exactly what forms of interaction with the world are illegitimate? We draw our rule of separation from Psalm 1:1, which is a series of vignettes comparing two men, one who receives the blessing of God and another who forfeits His blessing. The difference between them lies in their response to the world. The one who is blessed turns away from it. The other is pliable to it and, by degrees, comes under its complete control. At first, while conducting his own business, he happens to meet the ungodly on the road. Attracted to their company, he travels beside them and listens to their conversation. Later, he seeks them out in public places and lingers in their presence. Finally, he follows them into their homes, sits down, and joins in their scornful way of thinking and speaking. His downfall is the result of engaging the world under circumstances that allow the world to affect his thinking. We conclude that a believer should shun any practice that would make him receptive to worldly influence.

The first rule of separation. This might be called the influence test. And it may be stated thus. **We stay away from the world if the result will be exposure to influence of a kind that will damage our innocence or our faith.**

Yet we cannot altogether avoid worldly influence. In the course of earning a living, we may encounter ungodly people who pressure us to compromise our integrity. Work associates may assault our purity with obscene language or foul suggestions. A boss may ask us to lie or cheat. Even in the course of serving God, we may run into severe temptations. Anyone who has done Christian work in a slum or ghetto knows that ministry may necessitate going into extremely sordid situations. For example, on one occasion when I was a young man working in a ministry on the south side of Chicago, my team, consisting of myself and two older college girls, entered the apartment of a harlot. We went there with food on the basis of a tip from another apartment dweller that the harlot's children were on the brink of starvation. Upon arrival, we easily gained entrance, probably because the woman herself was hungry, and found several children, all with distended stomachs and severe mental impairment. We reported their plight to the authorities, who quickly removed them to better care.

Nowadays you can run into sordid situations almost anywhere as you reach out to meet people and help them. Therefore, the primary rule of separation requires a secondary rule.

The second rule of separation. It is this. **We can expect God's protection from worldly influence if we encounter it while doing something necessary and legitimate.**

To make this protection effective, we must submit to it. That is, we must cooperate with the help that God is willing to provide. Suppose we are moved by Christian compassion to visit someone in the hospital, but once inside the hospital room we find it impossible to turn off an objectionable program on TV. Then we must ignore the program as much as we can. If we look at it, we lose God's protection. We must handle ourselves in a similar fashion in the other situations we described. If we hear dirty jokes in the workplace, we must react with quiet disapproval. If the boss urges us to do wrong, we must meekly decline.

Whenever we are doing something necessary and legitimate, we must rely on the help of the Holy Spirit. He will not only show us how to conduct ourselves in a godly manner, but also He will shield us from any corrupting effects. When we leave the hospital room, we will forget the program on TV. We will forget the dirty jokes we heard at the office. The boss's pressure to be dishonest will not undermine our integrity.

The third rule of separation. From the second rule of separation, we can derive a third. **We cannot expect God's protection from worldly influence if we accept it as the price we must pay for our own pleasure or success.** This rule teaches us that two forms of interaction with the world are especially dangerous. The first is to become a spectator of worldly entertainment. The second is to pursue a worldly education. Entertainment and education bring a believer under influence of an extremely potent kind. Moreover, the influence is one-way.

When I watch TV, it communicates to me exactly what it wants to communicate. But I can say nothing in reply. I cannot speak to any of the people whose images and voices are electronically reproduced before me, nor can I exert any influence upon them. Yet everything they do and say has been designed by ingenious men to manipulate me. And I subject myself to this influence for no good reason except to please myself. I am deluded if I think the Holy Spirit will intervene to protect me from the consequences.

Likewise in the classroom of a public school or university, the student is helpless to counter any devilish lies coming from the teacher. The teacher is in control, and a teacher committed to attacking

Christian faith may have developed clever strategies for making any student look ridiculous who dares to raise objections. So, by speaking up, Christian students may position themselves as a negative rather than as a positive witness for Christ. Moreover, they may hear such a smooth and sophisticated presentation of the secular worldview that they will be unable to resist it. It will damage or destroy their faith. Perhaps it will reshape their thinking without even being recognized as a challenge to their faith. However devoted to Christ they were when they entered the classroom, they will go away weaker Christians. Why does the Spirit decline to give them more protection in a public school? Because when they go there, they are violating the clear command of Scripture not "to sit in the seat of the scornful" (Ps. 1:1); that is, in the seat the scornful have provided so that the one sitting there can hear all the scorn.

Going to a public school in a modern secularized society is legitimate only for students who have no alternative. Perhaps they are required by law to attend a public school. Or perhaps they must go there for necessary vocational training. Any student who cannot escape from entering a classroom hostile to faith can be sure of the Spirit's help if he or she earnestly seeks it.

Self-Test

Unless you guard yourself from the world, its tentacles will gain hold of both your thinking and your conduct. Let's examine your thinking and conduct separately.

The prevailing system of thought today is known as secular humanism. This is the worldview that denies the existence of God and puts man in God's place, giving man ultimate authority to judge what is true and false and what is right and wrong. Test yourself as to whether secular humanism has infiltrated your own thinking. As we have taught in an earlier lesson, the three cornerstones of this worldview are evolutionism, pragmatism (the denial of moral absolutes, claiming that whatever works is right), and relativism (the denial of absolute truth). Let us revisit these modern delusions.

1. Do I accept any form of evolutionism?

Do you think that the universe is billions of years old? Do you believe that life evolved from non-life and that higher life forms, including man, evolved from lower life forms? Do you think that mankind is progressing to a higher level and that beings more advanced than man already exist in the universe? If your answer is "yes" to any of these questions, you have accepted an evolutionary lie, seeing history as an upward development over protracted time.

In the Bible we find the true story of our world's past and future. We learn that the physical universe originated a few thousand years ago; that the various kinds of living things sprang into existence at the moment God created them; that the last kind He created was man; that the entire work of creation was accomplished within six days; that sin and evil arose shortly afterward; that before sin there was no death; that sin and evil are getting worse; and that God will soon put a stop to them when He destroys the present cosmos and replaces it with a cosmos perfect in righteousness and eternal in duration.

2. Do I subscribe to any form of pragmatism?

In other words, do you believe that man, either individually or collectively by means of public opinion, has the right to determine his own moral standards, even though these disregard God's standards set forth in His Word, the Bible? The acid test is what position you take on the many social issues that are now being hotly debated. You have renounced the world's pragmatism if you side with the Bible rather than with today's opinion leaders. The Bible condemns divorce, premarital sex, adultery, homosexuality, and abortion, and it supports male leadership in the home as well as in the church.

3. Have I swallowed the lie that truth is relative?

When brought into the religious realm, the lie takes the form of claiming that all religions lead to God. But the Bible clearly teaches that the only way to find and know God is through belief in Jesus Christ (John 14:6; 5:22-23; Matt. 11:27). The test of whether you have purged your mind of relativism is whether you understand the peril of those who have never heard the gospel. If you fully comprehend that every responsible adult without Christ faces damnation, you will have a great burden to reach the lost.

Consider also whether the world is shaping your behavior. For the sake of time, we cannot look at all dimensions of its possible influence, so we will focus on three kinds of conduct that are especially prone to worldliness. These are dress, speech, and amusements.

4. Is my dress befitting my identity as a child of God, or does it show my desire to copy the world?

Your dress is worldly if it is immodest in any degree, or freakish, or transsexual, or elegant to the extent of making other Christians feel like social inferiors.

5. Does my speech always minister grace to the hearer, or does it veer into the crudeness, unkindness, and vanity that mark the speech of someone estranged from God?

Speech is crude if it is vulgar or impure or marred by profanity. As children of God, we dare not take His name in vain, using it flippantly as a mere expletive or blasphemously as a swear word or curse word. Speech is unkind if it cuts down other people, if it seeks to hurt rather than to help, if it assumes that to be insulting is funny. And speech is vain if it vaunts self at the expense of others. A person who is truly great does not need to speak of his greatness. Even when cloaked in modesty, excellence shines out clearly for all to see. The luster soon fades, however, if boasting sets the cloak aside.

6. Are my amusements unspotted by the world?

We could present a very extended critique of the modern entertainment industry and its products, but a believer sensitive to the Spirit of God needs to consider only one question when evaluating something he might choose to view, read, or hear. The question is, would Jesus Christ enjoy it? Jesus is here now, although we think of Him as remote, and He is there whenever you are using the media to amuse yourself. At the moment you begin, imagine turning to Christ and asking, "Will this offend you? Knowing that you are here with me, can I enjoy this without shame?" And as you ask the question, remember that you are talking to a holy God, one who cannot condone sin. He cannot overlook immodesty or provocative behavior. He cannot approve of unmarried people kissing and hugging like lovers. He cannot laugh at suggestive or malicious humor. He cannot view as a hero or role model anyone who is dishonest, or who uses manipulation to accomplish his goals, or who reacts to trouble with childish tantrums, or who handles frustration by breaking windows. He cannot accept God's name—that is, His name—being abused or cheapened. He cannot endorse any portrayal of life that denies Him first place.

Review Questions

1. What is not meant by "the world" we must shun?
2. What is meant by this term?
3. What forms of interaction with the world are legitimate?

4. What text especially clarifies the line between legitimate and illegitimate forms?
5. What forms of interaction with the world are illegitimate?
6. What is the first rule of separation?
7. What is the second rule of separation?
8. What must we do to obtain God's protection while doing right?
9. What is the third rule of separation?
10. What two forms of interaction with the world are especially dangerous?

1 My brethren, have not the faith of our Lord Jesus Christ, *the Lord* of glory, with respect of persons.
2 For if there come unto your assembly a man with a gold ring, in goodly apparel, and there come in also a poor man in vile raiment;
3 And ye have respect to him that weareth the gay clothing, and say unto him, Sit thou here in a good place; and say to the poor, Stand thou there, or sit here under my footstool:
4 Are ye not then partial in yourselves, and are become judges of evil thoughts?
5 Hearken, my beloved brethren, Hath not God chosen the poor of this world rich in faith, and heirs of the kingdom which he hath promised to them that love him?
6 But ye have despised the poor. Do not rich men oppress you, and draw you before the judgment seats?
7 Do not they blaspheme that worthy name by the which ye are called?
8 If ye fulfil the royal law according to the scripture, Thou shalt love thy neighbour as thyself, ye do well:
9 But if ye have respect to persons, ye commit sin, and are convinced of the law as transgressors.

Lesson 14
Impartiality

Respect of persons as another sign of hypocrisy. Toward the end of chapter one in his epistle, James mounted an attack on religious hypocrisy. He put a spotlight on the man whose life does not match his profession and labeled him as self-deceived. To help this wayward soul recover his steps from the path to destruction, James held up to his face the mirror in God's Word, the only mirror that gives a true likeness of inner character. Then in the man's image James pointed out some telltale signs of a hypocrite. Plain for all to see was an unruly mouth (v. 25), an indifference to the needy (v. 26), and a fascination with the world (v. 26).

In chapter two, James begins to expand his treatment of each topic introduced in chapter one. He has already identified charity toward the poor as a mark of true religion. Now he discusses one sin that hinders charity, a sin so damaging that he devotes much of this chapter to warning us against it. It is the sin of partiality; that is, the sin of giving preference to people with a higher position in society (v. 1). He refers to partiality as "respect of persons." To shame any reader guilty of this sin, he declares that it is absolutely inconsistent with "the faith of our Lord Jesus Christ, the Lord of glory." Indeed, it is another telltale sign of hypocrisy.

The title that James assigns our Lord is difficult to translate. The clearest rendering in our language is probably, "our Lord Jesus Christ, [the One] of glory."[37] The exact wording here is highly significant both as a testimony of James's own faith and as a strong argument against partiality. Though he was the human brother of Jesus, he does not hesitate to identify Jesus as the man who is more than just a man. To Him also belongs the divine glory, as John likewise declared (John 1:14). In other words, from Him proceeds that dazzling radiance which God alone possesses as a natural property. Thus, by calling Jesus "the One of glory," James underlines the fundamental equality between Him and the Father, creator of all the lights (Jas. 1:17) manifesting His own nature as light (1 John 1:5). James's testimony to the glory of Christ is meant not just as a tribute, but also as a rebuke. How can mere mortals, each pitifully inferior to God in all His glory, presume to make distinctions among themselves, as if any of them were significantly better than any other?

A scene which is cause for shame. James continues by illustrating partiality (vv. 2–3). He describes a scene that probably occurred many times in the churches he was addressing. Two men come into a meeting of the church body. The word is actually "synagogue," the name Jewish Christians gave their churches.[38] The first is a rich man "with a gold ring, in goodly apparel." The second is a poor man in "vile raiment." Our English translation greatly diminishes the contrast James intended. Actually, the first man is "gold-fingered" and wears "shining apparel."[39] The meaning is that his fingers are jammed full of gold rings. It was the custom among the Romans to load the left hand with rings as a token of wealth.[40] The man's apparel is shining probably because it is pure white, without any of the soil that would accumulate through toil or long wear. The poor man's, however, is contemptibly dirty and ragged. How does the congregation react? With great deference they invite the rich man to sit in a good place, but they do not even offer the poor man a seat. He is told, probably with scant courtesy, to stand in the back or sit off in a corner.

James severely condemns such treatment of the rich and poor (v. 4). He says that when the church makes a distinction between them, they set themselves up as unjust judges, swayed by evil thoughts. What is the evil? Based solely on the appearance of the two men, they are judging the rich man to be better. Indeed, by giving him preference in the body of Christ, they are assuming that Christ sees him as better. But how foolish!

God's love for the poor. James protests by pointing out that insofar as God has any preference, He prefers the poor (v. 5a). Jesus in His teaching emphasized that the poor enjoy the special blessing of God (Luke 6:20). If that blessing is not evident in their outward circumstances, where does it appear? It appears in their very poverty. A life of hardship and deprivation makes them more receptive to the gospel. They can see that this world ultimately cannot satisfy the deepest longings of the heart, so they more eagerly embrace the promise of a better world. Their experience of scrimping and scrounging to survive is fertile ground for faith. From such unpromising meagerness of life arises a faith that James calls rich.

As a further reprimand of their partiality, James points out that good church members are treating people as inferiors who will someday be their equals, for God has chosen the poor to be heirs of the Kingdom (v. 5b). Be careful then not to despise a brother because of his poverty. Consider how embarrassed you will be in heaven to find that he now occupies a splendid mansion next door!

James next exposes the folly in admiring rich people just because they are rich. He wants the churches to understand that whereas human beings are impressed by wealth, God is not. Indeed, many of the rich have made choices that will bring the wrath of God upon their heads. Many use their wealth as a weapon to accrue more wealth through robbery and oppression (v. 6). Who but the wealthy can manipulate the legal system to their own advantage? While they carry out schemes for taking property from the poor, they may protect themselves under a cloak of legality. In a masquerade of true justice, they may hire lawyers to manufacture false charges or bribe judges to secure favorable verdicts.

Another sin common among the rich, especially the rich Jews known to the Jewish churches James was addressing, was to blaspheme the name of Jesus (v. 7). Instead of accepting Him as their Messiah, most of the rich people in Jewish communities had sided against the church Jesus founded.

Throughout this passage, James is trying to deflate the natural human tendency to flatter and honor rich men, a tendency rooted in the greedy hope that they will let their friends enjoy some of their wealth. Such a tendency cannot be tolerated in the church, because the church was designed by God to win and nurture souls, and most of the souls God intends to reach are poor, not rich. Its welcome for the poor must therefore be in no way less enthusiastic than its welcome for the rich.

The royal law. The churches will not fail in their duty if they simply heed the royal law, which, as we said before (p. 4), is the requirement to love our neighbor as ourselves (v. 8). The term "neighbor" lacks any tags that would justify giving more love to the prosperous than to the poor. The poor have an equal claim on our love. This law is called royal perhaps because it is the most suitable rule of life for all heirs of the Kingdom. As such, they are royal. They are kings and priests before God (Rev. 1:6). If they heed the royal law, demanding selfless love, they will acquit themselves like royalty, for they will emulate the Prince of Peace Himself, Christ, who is the God of love (1 John 4:16).

If, on the other hand, the churches show partiality, they will be guilty of sin (v. 9). Not only will they transgress the royal law, but also many lesser regulations intended to enforce impartiality. These are no less prominent in the Old Testament (Lev. 19:15; Deut. 1:17; 16:19) than in the New (1 Tim. 5:21; here in Jas. 2 also). Hence, whether from the perspective of law or grace, partiality is wrong. Fundamentally, it is wrong because it is contrary to the very nature of God, who is no respecter of persons (Matt. 5:45; Acts 10:34; Gal. 2:6; Eph. 6:9).

Self-Test

The following questions probe whether you show partiality in your dealings with people in the church.

1. Am I part of a clique?

Special interest groups and cliques form wherever people assemble outside the church. It is sad that cliques may also spring up inside the church. But God intends the church to be a place where all manner of people can mix together and yet no one becomes marginal, much less a misfit or an outcast; where there is neither Jew nor Greek, bond nor free, male nor female (Gal. 3:28); where any random selection of people is as happy in each other's company as any other random selection.

2. At church socials, am I willing to talk to anybody, or do I prefer my friends?

You should be able to sit with any individual or group and enjoy their company. If you are a senior, do not talk just to other seniors. If you are young, do not seek out others of the same age and ignore everybody else.

Teenagers have a special proneness to restrict their attention to peers. They tend to create their own little world, set apart from adults and even younger children. Parents, pastors, and others who supervise teenagers should work at teaching them to mix with adults and make adult conversation. At hand-shaking time, the young should notice people other than their friends. Likewise in every other situation, they should see the world as larger than a few buddies. Staying within their own group is a form of self-centeredness that the young must learn to reject as contrary to Christ and Christian love.

Yet the problem has two sides. Adults also tend to ignore the young. On social occasions both inside and outside the church, they should from time to time approach a young person and show a personal interest in what he thinks and feels. Both teenagers and younger children need to sense that adults view them as important members of the body of Christ.

3. Within the church, do I prefer the company of people with high social status?

Paul cautions us not to hobnob with the wealthy and important, but to give as much attention to little people (Rom. 12:16).

4. Do I give more attention to newcomers who appear to be of a higher social class?

This is the problem that James especially addresses. We must see the infinite potential of everyone who walks through the door. It does not matter what they look like now. Imagine what they would look like as God's child in eternity, when they have all the beauty and breathtaking power and radiant holiness of an immortal being. No man or woman alive has any less potential.

Review Questions

1. What is another mark of a hypocrite?
2. How does James identify Jesus?
3. How does the exalted nature of Jesus show the absurdity in making distinctions among ourselves?
4. What scene does James use to illustrate partiality?
5. Whom does God prefer?
6. How will the poor rank in heaven?
7. What is the folly in admiring rich people because they are rich?
8. What are two characteristic sins of the rich?
9. What is the royal law, and why is it called "royal"?
10. If we show partiality, how will God view it?

> **10** For whosoever shall keep the whole law, and yet offend in one *point*, he is guilty of all.
> **11** For he that said, Do not commit adultery, said also, Do not kill. Now if thou commit no adultery, yet if thou kill, thou art become a transgressor of the law.
> **12** So speak ye, and so do, as they that shall be judged by the law of liberty.
> **13** For he shall have judgment without mercy, that hath shewed no mercy; and mercy rejoiceth against judgment.

Lesson 15

The Judgment of Believers

Working for church growth. In the foregoing verses, James has been trying to bring down one of the great obstacles to growth in the church, an obstacle not only in the Jewish churches he is addressing, but in all churches. That obstacle is the natural human tendency to give the wealthy and privileged a warm welcome, while treating the poor with indifference. Favoritism hinders progress of the gospel in two ways.

1. To make the poor feel unwanted contradicts God's own character. He is no respecter of persons. Therefore, a class-conscious church offends God and loses His blessing.

2. Partiality toward the rich disregards the best strategy for church growth. Christian outreach generally reaps a larger harvest of souls among the poor than among the rich. Thus, God expects that churches will always make a special effort to reach the poor.

Error in excusing any sin as minor. In the verses now under consideration, James continues with another strong argument against favoritism. He has just pointed out that it is a violation of the law, both of certain specific regulations (mentioned in the last lesson) and of the great commandment to love our neighbor. Now he anticipates the likely reaction of his readers. Instead of owning up to their partiality, they will run from his accusing finger and hide behind their reputations as good church people. They will recite all their good deeds and boast of all their victories over other sins, including many they regard as far worse than partiality. But James warns them that to break one law makes them guilty of the whole law (v. 10). If they have practiced partiality, they are in God's eyes as much of a law-breaker as any murderer or adulterer. Why? The answer is that the whole law comes from a single source, God (v. 11). It is He who expresses His mind and speaks His will in every point of the law.

Still, how does the law's origin in a single source put every offender's guilt on the same level and make us all equally bad? How does violation of what we would regard as a minor regulation, such as the rule against partiality, plunge us into the depths beside the blackest of criminals? Because whether we choose to obey any law coming from God shows our heart toward the law-giver. Though we break only one minor regulation, we put ourselves in the position of rebels.

Adam and Eve had only one law to follow. What kind of law was it? Did God tell them, do not kill the mate I have given you; or even, do not get into squabbles with each other; or even, do not be hard to live with? No, He said they should not eat the fruit of a certain tree. The only behavior off-limits was to enjoy a mouthful of luscious-looking fruit. From man's perspective, the law seems of little consequence. We cannot see that they did great harm by breaking it. Yet their failure to keep that small requirement brought upon them the worst conceivable penalty—death in this world and damnation for eternity. The reason for God's severity is that they broke the law deliberately, with full knowledge of what He had said and in willing cooperation with His enemy, the serpent. They became rebels as black in their treason as any doer of an outwardly greater sin.

Likewise when we disobey any divine law, though it be a lesser law such as His prohibition against partiality, we reenter the Garden of Eden, as it were, and stand in the place of our first parents. As they did, we deliberately set our faces against God's will and join in Satan's cosmic insurrection against God. Thus, our guilt is no less than it would be if we broke every law.

There is another reason why breaking one law makes us guilty of all. One transgression is enough to show that under the right circumstances, we would commit any other transgression. If a sinner chooses a somewhat moral life, he is merely serving his own convenience. He is upholding his moral pride by avoiding the bad conscience that would follow greater sin. If any social penalties would also follow, he is avoiding them as well. But if these penalties were altogether removed, conscience would afford little protection. Only one slip into sinful pleasure would leave his conscience weaker, so that a second sin would be easier than the first. Then, against the fading resistance of conscience, the third would be easier than the second, and the fourth easier than the third, until the course of his life became a gradual slide into thoroughgoing hedonism. Somewhere along the downward slope his conscience would cease to function, and the silencing of its voice would leave him capable of every sin. Formerly he limited his transgressions to indulging fleshly appetites. Now he can attack others and leave them devastated. He can even commit murder.

Cruelty always lies at the end of sin's progression to worse forms. Generally when a person first falls into sin, he sees it as a good time, but later, after sin becomes habitual, he realizes that to go on satisfying himself, he must pay the price of hurting somebody else. Sin then has such a strong hold on his will that, sooner or later, he will agree to the terms, especially if he feels secure from social penalties or, blinded by passion, fails to consider them. There will not be enough love or pity or common decency left in his heart to hold him back.

Thus, every sinner is capable of every sin. The proof is that the sins of the human race soon leaped beyond the pleasure-seeking disobedience of Adam and Eve. In the next generation, brother murdered brother.

The prospect of judgment. Having stressed the enormity of sin, James gives his readers the most sobering reason of all to shun it. He reminds them that they will stand in judgment before God (v. 12). So, they must live and act and speak accordingly. It is one of the great consolations of the Christian life that we will not stand before God at the Last Judgment, when He sits upon His great white throne (Rev. 20:11-15). All who stand there will be condemned. Nevertheless, after all dead believers are brought up from the grave and all living believers are raptured, the whole church will appear before the Judgment Seat of Christ. There they will give an accounting for both their good deeds and their bad. For their good deeds they will receive rewards (Matt. 10:42; 25:23; Luke 6:35; 1 Cor. 3:13-15; Eph. 6:8; 1 Cor. 9:25). For their bad deeds that have never been confessed and put away, they will incur penalties (Rom. 14:12; 2 Cor. 5:10-11; 1 Pet. 1:17; Luke 12:48). Notice Paul's exact wording in 2 Corinthians 5:10. He says that every believer "will receive the things done in his body, according to that he hath done, whether it be good or bad." Addition of "or bad" is an obvious threat of unpleasant consequences.

The law of liberty. James counsels his readers that the only safe way to prepare for our dreadful accounting before God is to live according to the law of liberty (v. 12). As we said before, he is referring to the law enjoining us to love our neighbor as ourselves. Indeed, if we go through life consistently practicing love toward all around us, we have nothing to fear when we meet God in judgment. A life of bringing grace and blessing to others will doubtless earn us those wonderful words of commendation that we all long to hear from the lips of Christ: "Well done, thou good and faithful servant: . . . enter thou into the joy of thy lord" (Matt. 25:21).

The blessing in being merciful. Our interpretation of the law of liberty is confirmed by what James says next (v. 13). He teaches that regular obedience to this law so fashions a man's heart and character that he becomes outstanding in mercy. Indeed, the way of mercy is the way of love. God is so pleased with mercy that He is willing to extend His own mercy to the merciful. In putting forward this principle, James is alluding to one of the most famous sayings of his brother. In the Beatitudes, Jesus said, "Blessed are the merciful, for they shall obtain mercy" (Matt. 5:7).

Mercy is one of a trio of related virtues. Just as we must be merciful to obtain mercy, so must we forgive to be forgiven (Matt. 6:12, 15), and so must we refrain from judgment to escape judgment (Matt. 7:1). In Jesus' mind, not judging and forgiving appear to be synonymous with mercy. Our imprecise notions of these virtues easily obscure their real meanings. All three refer to a decision not to punish.

James reminds us that habitual mercy is the only quality of a man's soul that sets the standard for God's treatment of the man himself. In the day of judgment, the unmerciful man will receive no mercy, whereas the merciful man will have reason to rejoice, for God will be merciful to him. God will be lenient when judging his failings. The last statement in verse 13 could be translated, "And glories [or boasts] mercy over judgment." James chooses the word "glory" and sets it first to show how triumphant mercy will be. Our Lord's mercy and love will easily be great enough to set aside the strict requirements of justice. Where we deserve His wrath, we will see His smile.

The application James wishes his readers to make is to their treatment of rich and poor. If they heed his counsel and gladly receive the poor into their churches, they will be showing mercy and building credit for the day of judgment.

Self-Test

1. Do I treat small sins as serious? Or do I take them lightly, with the excuse that I am doing pretty well just to keep away from larger sins?

There is a difference between small sins and large sins. Being upset with a brother is obviously not the same as killing him. In the day of judgment, the Lord will no doubt consider the degree of evil involved in each sin. Yet we must always remember that all sins are equal in the sense that they are all sufficient grounds for condemnation. In that sense, a transgressor of one law is a transgressor of all. Thus, we must never excuse any violation of God's law or God's will as a minor offense, as a mere peccadillo, or, as the Catholics say, as a venial sin as opposed to a deadly sin. Notice Romans 6:23. It does not say that death is the wages of some sins. No, the offense deserving the ultimate penalty is defined as sin; by implication, any sin. Every sin is deadly.

2. Does the prospect of judgment enter my thoughts and affect my decisions?

If at no other time, we should certainly think of coming judgment when we stand in the midst of temptation and coddle the impulse to yield.

3. As I think about the Judgment Seat of Christ, do I view it with sober respect, recognizing all the ramifications of being accountable to a holy God?

When Paul considered his future moment of judgment, he sensed a degree of terror (2 Cor. 5:10–11). If such a fruitful servant of God was nevertheless apprehensive that he might fall short of God's approval, surely we should not be complacent about our summons to the Judgment Seat of Christ.

That future moment may seem far away, but James elsewhere reminds us that the Judge stands at the door (Jas. 5:9). He means the door of heaven, which Christ will open when He returns to gather His people. But we can also think of it as the door to the courtroom. So understood, the warning is that Christ is about to enter and hear our case.

4. Is the law of liberty the controlling principle in my life?

In previous lessons, we have discussed the manifold ways that a believer will make love practical.

5. Is mercy the habit of my life?

Do others see in you the outworkings of a merciful heart? All our dealings with others should be governed by a resolve to minimize and overlook their faults. Our dominant purpose must always be to extend help rather than to exact justice.

A person in authority must enforce obedience to rules and policies, but even when discipline is required, there may be a choice between being harsh and being more moderate. The right option is never to be harsh.

Review Questions

1. In what two ways does partiality hinder the work of the gospel?

2. How does James deal with the excuse offered by those guilty of partiality that overall they are pretty good Christians?
3. Why does one sin make us guilty of all?
4. What was so bad about the sin of Adam and Eve?
5. What is another reason that one sin makes us guilty of all?
6. What always lies at the end of sin's progression to worse forms?
7. How was this demonstrated in the history of the human race?
8. What prospect should deter us from sin?
9. What rule will keep us away from sin?
10. What virtue sets the standard for God's dealings with us?
11. To what other virtues is mercy equivalent?
12. What is one practical opportunity to show mercy?

14 What *doth it* profit, my brethren, though a man say he hath faith, and have not works? can faith save him?

15 If a brother or sister be naked, and destitute of daily food,

16 And one of you say unto them, Depart in peace, be ye warmed and filled; notwithstanding ye give them not those things which are needful to the body; what *doth it* profit?

17 Even so faith, if it hath not works, is dead, being alone.

18 Yea, a man may say, Thou hast faith, and I have works: shew me thy faith without thy works, and I will shew thee my faith by my works.

19 Thou believest that there is one God; thou doest well: the devils also believe, and tremble.

20 But wilt thou know, O vain man, that faith without works is dead?

21 Was not Abraham our father justified by works, when he had offered Isaac his son upon the altar?

22 Seest thou how faith wrought with his works, and by works was faith made perfect?

23 And the scripture was fulfilled which saith, Abraham believed God, and it was imputed unto him for righteousness: and he was called the Friend of God.

24 Ye see then how that by works a man is justified, and not by faith only.

25 Likewise also was not Rahab the harlot justified by works, when she had received the messengers, and had sent *them* out another way?

26 For as the body without the spirit is dead, so faith without works is dead also.

Lesson 16

Faith and Works

The basic issue. In the closing portion of chapter two, James continues with his attack on empty religion. As throughout his epistle, he is firm and uncompromising in his estimate of any nominal believer whose life is devoid of good works. He says bluntly, "But wilt thou know, O vain man, that faith without works is dead?" (v. 20).

To comprehend the full force of this question, let us examine the whole passage verse-by-verse.

Verse 14. James begins with a searching rhetorical question, clearly demanding a "no" answer. Faith without works cannot save a man. Therefore, right at the outset James raises the possibility that a man who claims to have faith may not be saved.

Verse 15. He then shows a kind of faith that is unprofitable. He imagines a scene where two believers meet. One is a brother or sister living in a poverty so severe that he lacks basic necessities. He is "naked," a term that might describe someone wearing only an undergarment, or having only rags to cover an undergarment.[41] The poor brother is also hungry. The phrase "destitute of daily food" means that on the day the rich brother finds him, the poor brother has eaten nothing and has nothing to eat.

Verse 16. The rich brother is full of pompous compassion, effusive in showing concern, but heartless in withholding assistance. In a charade of Christian piety, he intones a blessing on his brother, wishing him peace when he really needs food, and commanding him to depart when he really needs to stay and receive help. And the rich brother covers up his callousness with a sweet voice such as he might use in inviting the poor brother to dinner. Someone nearby who caught his voice but not his meaning would never imagine that he was telling his poor brother to get lost. And to make his phony religion even more disgusting, he says, as if he were raising a prayer to God, that he hopes the poor brother's needs will be met. In other words, he pretends to be a man of faith, confident that God will provide. It is as though he says, "I'm praying for you, brother." But he is merely making excuses. What help comes from good wishes? And what help comes from prayers rising out of a stingy heart? While posing as a good man, the rich brother does nothing at all to lift his poor brother from the trash heap of society. James is not impressed. He says the man's faith is worthless.

Verse 17. Even worse, his faith is dead. The Greek word rendered "dead" means nothing else but dead.[42] If the man has no living faith, then he has no faith at all. Therefore, he is not saved, for faith is the prerequisite for salvation.

Verse 18. Now James considers an objection. Someone says, "Thou hast faith, and I have works." To interpret this correctly, we must understand that in James's mind, the objector is a third party seeking to mediate between James and the person who lacks works although he professes faith (v. 14); also, that James treats the works-deficient person as one of his readers. He is "one of you" (v. 16), so James calls him "thou." "I" is James himself. To clarify the third party's objection, we may therefore expand it as follows: "One of you (the man without works) has faith and the other (James) has works. Don't argue between yourselves. You each have a strength—a form of spiritual excellence—that is good for the church. The church needs both a man of works and a man of faith." James's reply, addressing the man whose life is devoid of works, is to challenge his claim to possess faith. Prove it, James says. The only way is to begin acting like a Christian. James continues by denying that he has works only. Far from it. He also has the only kind of real faith—a living faith manifest in works. By implication, he exhorts us all to acquire and demonstrate his kind of faith.

Verse 19. As he seeks to reach the hearts of hypocrites, James senses how they might dodge the cutting edge of the story about the rich brother who refuses to help a poor brother—the story James has just used to illustrate dead faith. The reader might protest that the rich brother was simply a hypocrite, mouthing words he did not believe. The reader might say, "That's not me. My faith is not dead. I really believe in God and in God's Word." Therefore, James continues by showing that a purely intellectual belief in God has no value. Even the devil and his angels, the demons, do not doubt God's existence. Yet they are not saved. No man is saved just because he knows there is a God in heaven. A man whose belief is limited to intellectual assent may be entirely honest in his belief. But his belief is not saving faith.

Verse 20. Next follows James's classic summation of the true relationship between faith and works. "But wilt thou know, O vain man, that faith without works is dead?" The debate between Luther and the Catholic church at the time of the Reformation centered on whether salvation and justification are by faith or by works. Luther correctly taught that justification is by faith alone (*sola fides*). But he carried this principle so far that he could not comprehend such verses as James 2:20. He even proposed to remove the Epistle of James from the Bible.[43] But in this verse James is not questioning that faith alone is the prerequisite for eternal life. He is merely giving us a definition of saving faith. It is a faith productive of works.

We see a parallel in marriage. Its foundation is love, but the love produces a changed life involving an ever-faithful relationship between the spouses. If a man, just two weeks after gaining one woman's assent to marriage, forgets her and proposes to another, how would we describe his love for the first? It is dead, not the real thing. Just as love without faithfulness is dead, so faith without works is dead.

Verse 21. As an example of saving faith, James points to the faith of Abraham, which enabled him to obey God even at the price of sacrificing his own son. James is not teaching that Abraham was saved by works. Rather, he is saying that Abraham could not be justified without the kind of faith that produced obedience to God.

Verse 22. To clarify what kind of faith he means, James says, "Faith wrought with his works." That is, faith reshapes his works, so that they will serve as sterling evidence of faith. "By works was faith made perfect." That is, works bring faith to perfection, or completion.

What does all this mean? A man is saved at the very instant when genuine faith enters his heart and he accepts Christ, even though observers cannot yet see any outward evidence of faith. The change is first inside him. But his new faith is not complete until he acts upon it. Suppose my friend says that he is coming to visit me. Perhaps he fully intends to do so. But his promise is not made complete and perfect until he actually comes. Likewise, faith is not made complete and perfect until it produces works. If it never produces works, it is dead.

Verse 23. Lest we misunderstand him and twist his words into the false teaching of works salvation, James hastens to affirm that justification is by faith alone. Abraham was justified not because he offered Isaac, but because he believed God. In particular, he believed God's promise of an innumerable seed. From that step of belief came all the benefits of a relationship with God: first, imputed righteousness; then, to be reckoned as God's friend. Without righteousness, no man can dwell with God. The righteousness Abraham received was not his own, but Christ's, imputed to him as a free gift in response to his faith.

Verse 24. James's main point in this passage is so important that he uses the device of repetition to make it as strong as possible. In this verse we find the fifth statement of the same principle (also in vv. 14, 17, 20, and 22). It will appear again in verse 26. Seldom in Scripture elsewhere do we find so many affirmations of the same idea within a short passage. James seems to be warning the church down through the ages not to tamper with his message. He presents it in six ways so there is no chance he will be misunderstood and no chance the awkward truth might be cast aside.

Verse 25. James gives yet another example of profitable faith, of the kind that leads to good works. He recalls Rahab's protection of the two spies. The motive leading her to shelter them at great risk to herself was faith. She had decided to place her faith in the God of Israel. But her faith did not remain a hidden loyalty, without peril. Rather, at first opportunity, she expressed her faith by allying herself with the people of God. Thus, as James says, she was justified by works, in the sense that without her works she could not be regarded as having real faith.

Verse 26. As his final observation on the crucial issue of how we gain salvation, James says again that faith must be properly defined. He reminds us that faith is not a true, living faith unless it is accompanied by works.

We must now insert a caution. The orthodox teaching that faith involves works is easily twisted into the heretical teaching that salvation depends partly on man's own efforts. The corrective is Paul's assertion in Ephesians 2:8-10. Four questions are answered in these verses.

1. What does not save us? What is powerless to save is works.

2. What does save us? The answer is etched plain. "We are saved by grace through faith."

3. What accompanies faith? Paul agrees with James that true faith gives rise to works.

4. Where do these works come from? The works issuing from salvation come from God. They are different from the self-generated works that many trust in for their salvation. In fact, a man cannot begin to perform truly good works until he is saved.

Self-Test

1. What am I trusting in for salvation? Is it any form of works?

If you think you are on the road to heaven because you go to church, or because you were immersed, sprinkled, or in some other way doused or sloshed with water inside a church, or because you live near a church, or because you own a burial plot in the church-yard, or because your parents professed to be Christians, or because your mother prayed for you, or because there was one occasion when you actually gave money to a church or religious cause, or because you sometimes check yourself before you use God's name in vain, or because you watch a televangelist, or because God answered you once when you prayed for something, or because you have never committed murder, although you have thought about it, or because you have not committed adultery as often as you wanted to, or because you like the pope, or because you dislike Democrats, or because you have a Bible in your home, or because you send your kids to church, or because your brother-in-law is a preacher—we could go on and on—if you are relying on anything except simple faith in Christ, you are deluded. In selecting reasons that people give for their hope of heaven, we have chosen many that are obviously absurd. We have done so precisely to show that all reasons, even those that many people take seriously, are absurd if they neglect Christ.

None of the reasons we have listed are as plausible and pious as the reasons that many will offer on the Day of Judgment (Matt. 7:21-23). Many will claim very impressive works. Jesus gives this fore-glimpse of future reckoning as a warning that no amount of good in us can outweigh the bad. If our sins are not covered by the blood of Christ, our good works are invisible to God. However good they might be in our estimation, God still sees us as workers of iniquity.

2. Have I received salvation by faith in Christ?

Have you acknowledged that you are a sinner undeserving of

eternal life with God, but deserving only of eternal separation from God? Have you beheld Jesus as very God in the flesh who died on a cross to pay the full penalty of your sin? Have you acknowledged and joyfully received Christ as your Savior so that His payment for your sin might be credited to your account? Have you repented of your sin by desiring in your heart to turn from it by the power and direction of Christ your Lord?

In 1905 and 1906, the prominent American evangelist R. A. Torrey conducted meetings throughout Britain. It is instructive to consider his closing appeal at a gathering of about 11,000 men at Royal Albert Hall in London. He said this:

> Now without a song, without any further persuasion, I want to ask every person in the building, old or young, who will here and now yield to the love of God, who will accept Jesus Christ as your personal Savior, surrender to Him as your Lord and Master, begin to confess Him as such publicly before the world, and live from this time on to please Him in everything day by day— every one who will thus accept Jesus Christ tonight, stand up, all over the building.[44]

Torrey's preaching was never highly emotional, although he spoke with considerable force. Otherwise, in the days before microphones, he could not have been heard by thousands. His strategy was to urge the only decision that was right and reasonable, and as a result of his manly words and bearing, an unusually high percentage of those who responded were men. Three features of his invitation on this occasion stand out as especially interesting.

1. He did not ask anyone to pray to receive Christ. He recognized that salvation is a decision. Today, by emphasizing the prayer, we have ritualized the process. The truth is that the moment of salvation generally precedes an actual prayer to be saved.

2. He incorporated the principles of James 2 in his gospel presentation, telling his hearers up front that receiving Christ is a decision to live for Him. Today we have many false converts because although they recite what we consider to be the right prayer, they do not make the right decision.

3. He required public confession at the start. There was no sneaking forward when everyone's eyes were closed. No harm is done by a private decision for Christ if it is later followed by baptism, which serves as a public confession of faith. Still, a policy of asking for public decisions would probably prevent many false conversions.

3. Is my faith dead or alive?

Has faith in Christ made a difference in your life? Can others see the Holy Spirit in you? Is His presence manifest in the fruit of the

Spirit (Gal. 5:22-23)? Is your religion vital and genuine by the two chief tests that James provides: that is, is it productive of good works, and is it marked by separation from the world (Jas. 1:27)?

4. When people approach me for help, do I put on a pious face as I reject their plea?

Do you ever use words of blessing as a cover-up for the coldness of your heart? If we are honest with ourselves, we will admit that sometimes when we promise to pray for another's need, we are speaking the wrong words. What God wants us to say is not, "I will pray," but, "I will help."

Review Questions

1. What is the message of this whole passage?
2. How does James illustrate an unprofitable faith?
3. How else does he describe a faith without works?
4. How does James reply to the man who thinks that faith and works are just different forms of spiritual excellence?
5. How does James reply to the man without works who nevertheless protests that he really believes?
6. What is wrong in supposing that James is teaching works salvation?
7. Who is James's first illustration of true faith, and how was it proven?
8. How many times does James warn us that faith without works is dead, and why does he repeat the warning so often?
9. Who is James's second illustration of true faith, and how was it proven?
10. What four principles in Ephesians 2:8-10 reinforce James's teaching?

> 1 My brethren, be not many masters, knowing that we shall receive the greater condemnation.
> 2 For in many things we offend all. If any man offend not in word, the same *is* a perfect man, *and* able also to bridle the whole body.
> 3 Behold, we put bits in the horses' mouths, that they may obey us; and we turn about their whole body.
> 4 Behold also the ships, which though *they be* so great, and *are* driven of fierce winds, yet are they turned about with a very small helm, whithersoever the governor listeth.
> 5 Even so the tongue is a little member, and boasteth great things. Behold, how great a matter a little fire kindleth!
> 6 And the tongue *is* a fire, a world of iniquity: so is the tongue among our members, that it defileth the whole body, and setteth on fire the course of nature; and it is set on fire of hell.

Lesson 17

The Iniquity of the Tongue

The call to be a teacher. In chapter three, James turns to a subject that he has already touched on briefly, but now he devotes a long passage to it. In chapter one, he warned a professing Christian with an unruly tongue that his religion is vain. Now he develops a long series of graphic comparisons to illustrate just how dangerous an unruly tongue can be.

He starts by addressing his readers as "my brethren." This expression and the expression "my beloved brethren" recur throughout the epistle. He uses them when he wishes to stress that his counsel comes from love. Here he is entering a subject that will require words of rebuke and censure, so he builds a foundation of love before proceeding. His approach is a good example for us when we practice discipline. Discipline should always take place in a loving context.

James's first admonition is not against an evil use of the tongue, but against a legitimate use without good results. He says that not many should seek to be "masters" (v. 1). The actual Greek word should undoubtedly be translated "teachers."[45] He is advising the churches that the role of teaching others should not be shared by all. By implication, he agrees with Paul that teaching is a special gift that

God imparts to a few (Rom. 12:6–7; 1 Cor. 12:7–10, 28–30). James continues with the warning that whoever stands up and teaches will face a stricter "judgment," the meaning of the word translated "condemnation."[46] In other words, with responsibility goes accountability. The more you undertake in God's service, the more you will answer for when you stand before the divine Judge.

A teacher's words will then be thoroughly sifted. Good words will gain a reward. Words that are careless through lack of study, or false through lack of belief, or unkind through lack of love, or self-serving through lack of humility, or merely tedious and empty through lack of understanding will cause a loss of reward. God expects anyone who fills the vital office of teacher to do well. He must know his Bible. He must be well-educated by the Spirit of God. He must be pure in his motives, without a self-seeking agenda. He must be humble and moderate in his conclusions, restrained in his words, faithful in making applications to real life, fearless in taking unpopular but Biblical positions, and full of love for his hearers. Obviously, then, teaching is not for everyone.

We must remember, however, that James is thinking mainly about teaching as a regular ministry to adults. The counterbalancing truth is that we all should be teachers in a broader sense (Heb. 5:11–14). We all should instruct those under our authority. A man instructs his family. A woman instructs her children. Older men instruct younger men, and older women instruct younger women (Titus 2:3–5). We all can help in one-on-one discipling of new believers, or in the many ministries to youth that a church conducts. Finally, we all should be taking opportunities to reach the lost with the gospel. When sharing the gospel, we are teaching truth. Yet even teachers in this broader sense will be accountable for their words. Thus, before we open our mouths to speak, we must first cleanse our hearts of wrong motives and prepare our minds with understanding.

The power of the tongue. Next, James anticipates a problem universal among teachers. The problem is this: teachers have a tendency to be self-satisfied. Some enjoy getting up in front and talking even when they are doing a poor job. To counter this common failure to practice self-criticism, James reminds us that we all fall short of what we should be (v. 2). We all give offense in many things. Recognizing that the tongue is especially prone to give offense, a teacher must continually monitor his own performance, being careful to stay close to the mind of the Spirit in everything he says. To say only what is true and profitable is a nearly impossible feat for fallen man, but by the help of the Spirit it is possible. The ability to control speech is a mark of a "perfect" man—that is, of a man who is spiritually mature.

A man with enough spiritual strength and discernment to control the small organ in his mouth called the tongue can easily control the whole body with its multitude of surging impulses. To underscore this principle, James uses a series of striking metaphors (vv. 3, 4). The bit in a horse's mouth is small enough to hold in your hand. But if you pull on the reins attached to the bit, you can make the horse turn however you like. Likewise, the rudder of a ship is a small thing compared with the whole vessel. (An ancient ship actually had two rudders, one on either side of the stern.[47]) But the man at the helm can, by operating a fitting of insignificant size, control the whole vessel's direction, even when the ship is buffeted by raging winds and towering waves.

What exactly does James mean when he speaks of the tongue? The correct interpretation must explain how controlling the tongue is the secret to controlling the entire man. James is, I believe, building on a basic fact of psychology. At some point in the unfolding of every reaction to life, the mind must speak, and what it says shapes conduct afterward. If we feel abused, we normally respond by expressing anger with our mouths, and as a result our anger builds, perhaps to the point of fueling violent behavior. But, you say, it is entirely possible just to seethe inside, with no venting of anger through audible words. Yes, but then we speak inflammatory words to ourselves. When James refers to the tongue, he is thinking generally of the role that words play in our conduct and character. If we can control our words, whether silent or spoken, we can control the whole body.

When angry feelings surface, we must think and speak words of forgiveness. What helps us forgive? To remember that God has forgiven us, who by nature are sinners as bad as any in God's eyes. When lustful feelings invade the mind, we must think and speak words of duty to God and of compassion for anyone our lust could victimize. We must persuade ourselves against any wrongdoing, just as Joseph did when he was tempted by Potiphar's wife (Gen. 39:8, 9). When fearful feelings paralyze us, we must think and speak words of courage and of trust in God.

Just as we can put down every sin by well-chosen words, so we can use words, whether silent or spoken, to stir up every good deed. Words of compassion for the needy will produce charity. Words of love for our brothers will provoke us to encourage them, comfort them, and show hospitality. Words of indignation for injustice will motivate us to exercise our Constitutional powers as a free people to stop abuses in society, such as abortion. Words of concern for the lost will arouse us to support evangelism.

The evil in boasting. Yet the power of the tongue is too often employed for the wrong purposes. It is indeed a small member, but because it has the ability to speak, it can serve as a powerful tool of sin. What sin in particular does it make easier and more damaging? The tongue is no less than the chief instrument of pride (v. 5). There is no ambition or pretense or conceit that the tongue cannot express through boasting. Much of what people say is to lift up self, and often the means chosen to accomplish this goal is to put others down, perhaps in ways that do them incalculable harm. The Nazis bolstered their claim of racial superiority by denouncing the Jews and others as worthy of destruction. Although the boasting we encounter in our daily lives may not be so vicious, it still has the usual effect of hurting or demeaning other people. Then what do they do? They often fight back. Thus, James compares the tongue to a little fire, or even a spark, cast into a dry stack of lumber or into a dry forest ("matter" can refer to either[48]). The matter ignites and the fire spreads until it becomes a great conflagration, reducing the whole to ashes and ruin.

The tongue as a fire. Having shown that the tongue is like a fire in this sense, James is ready to bring his indictment of the tongue to a climax with two stinging charges (v. 6a). First, he makes his point explicit. He says that the tongue is indeed a fire. Then he draws another comparison. The tongue is also a world of iniquity. In other words, although the tongue is a small member, there is nothing in the vast realm of evil that it cannot reproduce in some measure.

The effect of evil words is to defile the whole body (v. 6b), just as Jesus also taught (Matt. 15:16–20). The meaning is that a man who sins with his mouth is, in God's eyes, a sinner through and through, for what a man says shows the character of his heart. No word appears on the tongue that the heart has not conceived. A man's words are generally a clear window to his inner being, even the very depths of his soul.

Yet the damage a tongue can do is not limited to its own body. Returning to the image of fire, James says that the tongue can inflame the very course of nature (v. 6c). Literally in the Greek, the phrase is, "the wheel of nature."[49] By "nature" he means the whole complex of events that make up the history of the world. In his choice of the word "wheel" we see that he is thinking of history as a machine that is moving ever onward. He is conveying the idea that one little tongue can kindle a blaze so destructive that it causes history to take an evil turn. How many horrendous wars have issued from the cruel commands of a single demonic tyrant?

James now furnishes another reason why he equates the tongue to fire. The reason already evident is that both are destructive. But the reason he gives now is that when the tongue speaks wickedly, it is doing the bidding of hell, here used as a figure of speech to represent Satan and all his hosts (v. 6d). The tongue is fire because the source of its wickedness is hell fire, or, as James says, "It is set on fire of hell"; that is, "by" hell.[50] He is trying to instill in his readers a realization that whenever they let their tongues go out of control, they are joining Satan's rebellion against God and allowing him to accomplish his purposes through their mouths. Indeed, they might even be speaking under the direct influence of Satan or one of his cohorts. Remember what Jesus said to Peter when Peter rebuked Jesus' announcement that He would be killed in Jerusalem (Matt. 16:23)? If

Peter could become a puppet of Satan, we are also at risk of serving as Satan's mouthpiece if we speak hastily from a proud heart.

"Hell" in the original is Gehenna,[51] which refers to the Valley of Hinnom outside Jerusalem, whither all the refuse of the city was carted and burned.[52] When people within the city walls looked in the direction of this garbage dump, they saw perpetual flames ascending on the horizon. The fires were never quenched. No doubt for this reason Gehenna was the name Jesus often used for the eternal lake of fire (Matt. 5:22, 29, 30; 10:28; 18:9; 23:15, 33; Mark 9:43, 45, 47; Luke 12:5).

Self-Test

1. Have I tried to fill a teaching role that God has not gifted and called me to fill?

I must quickly add that I do not wish to discourage anyone from teaching simply because they lack self-confidence. I merely wish to urge a sober examination of God's true calling in your life. How can you know if He wants you to teach? You must first consider whether you have or can acquire the necessary Bible knowledge, spiritual maturity, and speaking skill. You must consider also what your spiritual leaders think and what the people who hear you think. Another test is whether God blesses your efforts with spiritual fruit. Last but hardly least, you must have an inner assurance of what God wants. It is perfectly natural to have doubts about your ability. If all the other signs of God's will point to a teaching role, pay no attention to doubts. They merely show a desirable humility that will increase your dependence on God's help. Humility is never a disqualification from a role in serving God.

2. Am I doing the kinds of teaching that do not require a special gifting or call?

You are conducting a vital teaching ministry if you are instructing children under your authority, giving counsel to younger people in the church, or witnessing to the lost.

3. Am I teachable?

If you are under someone's authority, do you heed his or her instruction? If you are younger, do you prize and seek the wisdom of older saints? In our society, respect for the wisdom of older people has all but vanished. But do not play the fool by supposing that there is no advantage in experience (Lev. 19:32).

4. Do I understand that control of my tongue is the secret to moral victory in my life?

Do you check your thoughts if they are going in a bad direction? Do you consciously cultivate a thought life centered on praising God and designing good deeds for others? Do you monitor your words before you speak and squelch those you would be ashamed to hear on the Day of Judgment? Do you make an effort to say things that are constructive and encouraging?

5. Do I ever fall into the trap of abusive speech?

Remember that abusive speech can destroy a home by ripping apart the fabric of family love. It can even destroy a life if it causes the targeted person to plunge into suicidal despair. One great evil in abusive speech is that you cannot take it back. If you tell someone that he is worthless, how can you truly apologize? You can say that you did not mean it, but your attempts at erasing your previous outburst will not be very convincing. What you said first will be remembered as the true expression of your heart and mind.

6. Have I ever, like Peter, served as Satan's mouthpiece?

Perhaps you have heard someone in a rage or in a fit of abusive speech make statements that would never have occurred to him in his right mind, or even make statements exceeding his own knowledge. Where did that extra dimension of malice or knowledge come from? Doubtless from demonic influence. Paul warns that losing your temper puts you at risk of becoming a tool of Satan (Eph. 4:26–27).

Review Questions

1. What is always the right context for discipline?
2. Why should someone be careful before entering a teacher's role?
3. What responsibilities do we all have as teachers?
4. What problem is universal among teachers?
5. In what two ways does James illustrate the power of the tongue?
6. What does James likely mean when he talks about the tongue as an unruly member?

7. What sin in particular does the tongue make easier and more damaging?
8. To what especially does James compare the tongue when used wickedly?
9. To what else does he compare a wicked tongue?
10. What evil effect does someone suffer who misuses his tongue?
11. The tongue can do damage on a scale how large?
12. An unruly tongue can become the instrument of what forces?

7 For every kind of beasts, and of birds, and of serpents, and of things in the sea, is tamed, and hath
been tamed of mankind:
8 But the tongue can no man tame; *it is* an unruly evil,
full of deadly poison.
9 Therewith bless we God, even the Father; and
therewith curse we men, which are made after the
similitude of God.
10 Out of the same mouth proceedeth blessing and
cursing. My brethren, these things ought not so to
be.
11 Doth a fountain send forth at the same place sweet
water and bitter?
12 Can the fig tree, my brethren, bear olive berries? either a vine, figs? so *can* no fountain both yield salt
water and fresh.

Lesson 18

The Untamable Tongue

The tongue as a beast. The overriding purpose of the Epistle of
James is to help believers get beyond religious posing—going to
church with a clean face and a smile, spouting Christian lingo,
promising to pray for everybody and everything—to real spirituality.
A central message has been that real spirituality requires control of
the tongue. The tongue, as James said in the previous passage, is "a
fire, a world of iniquity" (v. 6). It not only defiles the whole body, but
sends wickedness to wherever it is heard in the world beyond. The
tongue is the chief tool the heart uses to make trouble, the chief
weapon that people employ to destroy their families and friendships,
the chief source of problems in the church, even the chief cause of
evil twists and turns in the course of history.

In the next block of verses, James continues his lament for the
tongue when used as an instrument of sin. He calls us to notice how
hard it is to tame the tongue. It is harder to manage than a monstrous wild animal (v. 7). He points out that no kind of beast has escaped being subjugated by man. In his list of animals he uses the
same categories that we find in the account of creation. He mentions
beasts, birds, serpents, and sea creatures. In Genesis 1:26, we read
that when God created man, He bestowed upon him dominion over
fish (an example of sea creatures), birds, cattle (an example of a land-

dwelling beast), and creeping things including serpents. Therefore, in affirming that man has tamed all these creatures, James wants us to see that man's power over nature has attained the level of dominion intended by God from the beginning. James does not mean that man has made pets out of all these animals, or domesticated them for some economic use. Rather, he means that no kind of animal can prevail against man if man hunts it down, whether to kill it or capture it.

But the little tongue, a hardly significant bit of flesh compared with a lion, for example, has been tamed by "no man" (v. 8). The statement is absolute. No one is perfect in his speech. James is repeating the sober warning given earlier in the chapter, "For in many things we offend all" (v. 2).

The tongue as a source of venom. To enlarge his picture of how wicked the tongue is, James says it is "an unruly evil, full of deadly poison" (v. 8). He has already told us that it is evil and unruly, but now he adds that it is like the fangs of a poisonous snake. The reader should allow James's words here, as elsewhere in the book, to paint a picture in his mind. He gives us one striking image after another so that we will not only hear the truth as conveyed by words, but also see vivid pictures illustrating the truth. The picture in this verse is a man lunging like a serpent and biting his enemy, using his tongue to inject deadly venom. James is teaching that although hate and anger seldom lead to actual murder, they often lead to deadly violence of another kind—to the use of words that assassinate another person's reputation or demolish his self-respect or trash his desire to be loved rather than hated.

Blessing or cursing. Next, James reworks this picture of man's wickedness by adding some even darker hues (v. 9). The same man who employs the tongue to destroy also uses it to bless God. So, besides being cruel, he is false and deceptive. When it suits him to seem religious, he will intone words that make him look like a saint. But as soon anyone stands in his way or makes him feel the pinch of opposition or criticism, he casts off pious pretense and stands forward in his true character as a vindictive sinner. He takes his tongue out of its velvet sheath, where it could only speak words of blessing, and uses it as a steel sword to slash and strike his enemy with injurious words, words of cursing rather than blessing. Such a man in his essence is a hypocrite. All the evidence needed to convict him of hypocrisy is furnished by his tongue.

But, sad to say, we are so accustomed to bless and curse with the same tongue that we do not see the glaring self-contradiction. If we bless God, how can we curse a man? Man is God's creature made in God's image (v. 9). There is consequently so much value inherent in one soul that when we look upon a wicked man, or a man we think is wicked, we should desire only his salvation, preserving his soul from eternal destruction. However wicked a man may be, he is not beyond hope of redemption until he dies. When we curse a man, we become, as it were, cheerleaders for the destruction of his soul.

If we use the tongue to curse a fellow believer, our offense is even greater. The person we are targeting is not only made in God's image; he is also God's child. Thus, if we feel that he has wronged us, we should have no desire to retaliate with harmful words. Far from it. Our only desire should be that he will repent of his sin and regain the path of God's blessing. To curse him is a terrible sin, for it puts us in league with the lion who is seeking to devour him (1 Pet. 5:8).

Now James comes down from the heights of generality and makes the necessary application (v. 10). He again addresses his readers as "my brethren." This term introduces love to soften the rebuke that follows: "These things ought not so to be." In other words, fellowship among brethren in Christ should be free from the monstrous kind of hypocrisy that employs the tongue for both blessing and cursing.

Harmony in nature. Such a mixture of uses is so bizarre and inexcusable that even the world of nature witnesses against it. A mere fountain can be depended on to always provide the same kind of water (v. 11). It does not gush sweet water for a while, then bitter water for a while.

When James repeats the same thought in the next verse, he explains the intended contrast (v. 12). He is referring to fresh water and salt water. For a given fountain, either its underground sources have been invaded by brackish water from the sea or they have not. Salty outflow from contaminated springs represents nasty speech from a hateful heart. The imagery is appropriate because salt water is a disappointing find when looking for pure water, good for drinking and other uses that meet human needs. If put to any of these uses, it is harmful in its effects, not helpful. Likewise, just as drinking too much salt water can sicken the body, so listening to evil words can damage the soul.

The world of nature gives many other examples of things consistent in what they produce. Any natural tree, for instance, always bears fruit true to type, an olive tree olives and a fig tree figs. James's view does not take in horticultural novelties, such as a tree with branches of one kind grafted into the rootstock of another. In the works of God, there is always a harmony between the various parts. The fruit always maintains the identity of the whole plant. So in our speech, our words should always express our identity as children of God. From our mouths should come only words of blessing. Words of cursing should be utterly foreign to our lips.

Self-Test

The self-test in the previous lesson has already covered the evil uses of the tongue, so this self-test will concentrate on the good uses.

1. When someone frustrates me or does me harm, how do I react?

Do you strike back like a snake, delivering venom with your tongue, or do you make your tongue an instrument that returns good for evil? Even under the greatest provocation, the tongue should be a fountain of blessing, not cursing. In the Sermon on the Mount, Jesus said, "Love your enemies, bless them that curse you, do good to them that hate you, and pray for them which despitefully use you, and persecute you" (Matt. 5:44). Think of the last incident in your life when someone brought you to grief. Did you bless your enemy? Did he hear you bless him? Are you blessing him now in your heart, or are you nurturing bitterness? Bitter thoughts yield bitter words, words which in their essence are curses.

Of course, to have a spirit of blessing and forgiveness when you are hurt does not mean that you must go around all bubbly, with a grin for everybody you meet. To hide emotional pain under a smiley face is not possible unless your emotions are shallow or you are good at putting on a show. But even in the midst of inner suffering, you can let people see that trouble has not destroyed your joy as a heaven-bound child of God (Gal. 5:22), and you can be kind to your enemy. You can even take opportunities to minister to his needs.

Our example is Jesus. At the Last Supper He knew that Judas would go out to betray Him, yet He washed Judas's feet (John 13:4–5). Later, when Judas led a mob through the dark to arrest Jesus, he identified the man they were seeking by greeting Jesus with a kiss. Jesus responded by calling Judas "friend" (Matt. 26:50). But I do not think for a moment that Jesus spoke the word with a smile on His face. No doubt His face showed grief at Judas's decision to throw his life away.

To feel hurt by someone is not a sin. The sin is to be hateful.

2. How do I deal with the wounds of life?

The temptation is to cease blessing God with the tongue and to curse Him instead, as Job's wife prodded him to do after God had allowed tragedy to rain upon his life (Job 2:9). The right response is not to feel mad at God, but to seek God's help. For any hurt, however painful, there can be healing through the Holy Spirit, whose primary role is to serve as the Comforter in a world that is always placing God's children in need of comfort (John 15:25–26; 16:6–7).

How does the Spirit help us with the wounds of life? Back when my wife was going through her battle with cancer, I remember sitting one day feeling rather discouraged. Discouragement is a kind of hurt. I reminded myself of the three secrets to gaining comfort through the Holy Spirit.

1. **Surrender.** We must say to the Lord, "I will accept without complaint whatever trial you have appointed for me, because I know that your will is best." By saying this, we echo Jesus' own prayer in the Garden of Gethsemane (Luke 22:42).

2. **Faith.** We must believe that God's purpose in everything we endure is to achieve something good (Rom. 8:28). It helps to remind ourselves that someday when we see the good that hardship has wrought, we will thank Him that our lives were governed not by chance, or even by our own preferences, but by His wise plan.

3. **Hope.** We must believe that God is a loving Father whose purpose is by no means to make us unhappy. On the contrary, He is helping us to attain real happiness. The full realization awaits our entrance to a better world, but we must always be grateful that even in this world He delights in giving us good things, increasing our joy (Jas. 1:17).

Surrender, faith, and hope are your resources to deal with any hurt, whether the cause is circumstances or people. If it is people, divine comfort through these resources enables you to speak words of blessing rather than cursing.

3. Are words of blessing the normal product of my mouth?

As you go through your day, what do the people around you hear? Do they hear complaining words, belittling words, words driven by selfish desire, words gloomy and hopeless, words of merciless criticism, words that ignore God or even question God, words that seek to escape responsibility, blaming words, slanderous words, nit-picking words, words that justify compromise and obscure what is wrong, vulgar words, words of rejection and disdain? All these verbal expressions of your heart and mind are forms of cursing, since they attack others or attack God Himself.

The alternative is words of blessing. The people in your daily world should hear encouraging words, affectionate words, complimentary words, words praising God, words constructive in solving present problems and hopeful of future remedies, words highlighting the best in others and minimizing the worst, words of willingness to help and work, words of comfort and cheer at moments of trial, words promoting what is right and warning against what is wrong, words of wise counsel, words of unconditional and unfailing love.

What do people hear from your mouth?

Review Questions

1. How bad is unbridled use of the tongue?
2. The tongue is harder to tame than what?
3. How does Scripture shape James's view of the natural world?
4. How great is man's dominion over nature?
5. To what does James compare the tongue?
6. Besides being cruel, what other wickedness marks an unruly tongue?
7. Why is cursing never right?
8. How does James show that it is unnatural to combine blessing and cursing?
9. What then illustrates evil speaking?
10. What shows that in the works of God, there is always harmony between the various parts?

> **13** Who *is* a wise man and endued with knowledge among you? let him shew out of a good conversation his works with meekness of wisdom.
> **14** But if ye have bitter envying and strife in your hearts, glory not, and lie not against the truth.
> **15** This wisdom descendeth not from above, but *is* earthly, sensual, devilish.
> **16** For where envying and strife *is*, there *is* confusion and every evil work.

Lesson 19
Wisdom True and False

Two essential qualities. When speaking to those "among you," James means "among my brethren" (Jas. 3:12), including all who claim to be followers of Christ. Continuing a theme that appears early in chapter one, he again exhorts them to seek wisdom. What is wisdom? As he uses the term, it is the kind of knowledge that enables good moral judgment. We all need it, but we all face the same barrier to attaining it. The barrier is, we think we are wise already (Prov. 21:2). We all without exception attach a great deal of weight to our own opinions and a great deal of doubt to everyone else's. But as we will see in James 3, there is a true wisdom and a false wisdom. Before you boast in your wisdom, you had better test what kind it is.

At the outset of discussing true wisdom, James gives its two essential qualities (v. 13). First, it is productive of "good conversation" full of "works." Back when the KJV was translated, the word *conversation* had a very different meaning than it has today. Today it means "talk," but then it referred to a man's way of conducting himself in society.[53] For "conversation" we could substitute "manner of life" and come much closer to what James intends. He is saying that anyone observing the life of a wise man will see nothing but goodness, especially in the form of good deeds. Yes, the man will use good words, tending to instruct, comfort, and encourage, but even more he will make the effort to help others, though it requires a sacrifice of time and energy. For the sake of assisting the poor or God's work, he will be willing to part with money he had intended for pleasing himself. He will be willing to break out of his own routines and give time to visiting the needy. Indeed, he will be willing to roll up his sleeves and undertake whatever useful work needs to be done.

Thus, James is returning here to one of his major themes—that a good man is a doer and not just a talker.

Paul serves as our example. After his ship wrecked on the Island of Malta, he was willing to join others in gathering sticks for the fire (Acts 28:3). This leader of gentile Christianity was not too important to get his hands dirty.

The second essential quality of true wisdom is meekness. The wisdom that is earthly, sensual, and devilish (v. 15) consists of knowledge that puffs up a man, making him prideful. It is therefore an incomplete knowledge, because it lacks a realistic knowledge of self. A man really knows nothing if he thinks he is something. True wisdom begins in the heart with an understanding that self is nothing before God. If a man wishes to be wise, he must accept that he is a wretched sinner, unworthy to receive any of the good things that God has created. Instead, he deserves only to suffer God's wrath in an eternal hell. This kind of self-knowledge yields a healthy fear of God, which is the foundation of true wisdom (Prov. 9:10).

Because true wisdom is meek, it is not pushy. It is not always seeking to expose the stupidity of others (Prov. 12:23; 17:27–28; 29:11). I have had students who always wanted to contest things that I said or that I wrote on the board. To silence them, it was seldom enough to prove that I was right, if indeed I was right. Pointing out their ignorance merely provoked them to argue, as if the sheer quantity of words is a measure of truth. The only way to stop their counterproductive comments and questions was to deal with the root problem, pride.

Of course, to teach is not being pushy if we have a responsibility to teach. Nor is it ever inappropriate to answer questions or furnish information in reply to someone who is seeking truth. But we do not parade our wisdom or force it on others. What did Jesus do? When challenged by His enemies, He frequently chose to evade the question rather than get into an unprofitable dispute, or he even chose to keep silent (Matt. 21:23–27).

False wisdom. Now turning to discuss false wisdom, James says that it creates "bitter envying and strife," both deeply rooted in the heart (v. 14). From the context, we understand that he is looking especially at relationships within a church. The word "envying" suggests a pronounced resentment toward others, giving rise to hard words or even prolonged war. The word "strife" is similar, although it focuses more on methods than on feelings. It refers to political infighting that uses unscrupulous tactics to gain an advantage. Both envying and strife arise when someone takes such pride in his own opinions that he is willing to assert them at the expense of hurting others. He insists on his own ideas, paints anyone who disagrees as an enemy, attacks his enemy not only with harsh words but also with maneuverings to make him look bad, and finally tears apart the body of Christ.

James warns against two evil results in particular: glorying and lying against the truth. The first, glorying, speaks of offending the truth by boasting a party line that is actually a distortion or violation of the truth. The second, lying, speaks of forsaking the truth deliberately, just for the sake of prevailing over others. Both are serious sins because they are the hallmark of God's chief enemy, Satan. Not only is he the father of lies (John 8:44), but also, like these church members that James is rebuking, he especially gravitates to lies that make him look good.

The Satanic source. Next, James makes explicit the Satanic character of false wisdom (v. 15). It comes not from above. Thus, it is unlike all the good gifts descending from our generous heavenly Father (Jas 1:17), among them true wisdom (Jas. 1:5). Rather, false wisdom comes from three sources that James characterizes as "earthly, sensual, devilish." His wording is the Biblical foundation of an idea familiar to Christians down through history—the idea summarizing the sources of evil as three in number: the world, the flesh, and the devil.

But notice that James's wording is more precise. He tells us exactly what is dangerous in the world. It is anything earthly as opposed to heavenly. In other words, it is anything in the world that comes not from the benevolent hand of the Creator above, but from the polluting touch of Satan below. James also tells us exactly what is dangerous in the flesh. It is the sensual appetites that, in their relentless drive to gain satisfaction, overmaster good moral judgment. These appetites include all the desires of body, soul, and spirit that can lead us to disregard the law of God. Finally, James expands upon the threat coming from the devil. It is not the devil alone who endangers the soul. It is also his host of fellow rebels against God, the army of demons under his control, for the word "devilish" could be translated "demonic."[54]

Fractured churches. The fruit of false wisdom is nothing good, either for the man who has it or for the life of the church. It produces "envying" and "strife," the exact same manifestations of false wisdom given in verse 14, and from these come "confusion and every evil work" (v. 16). "Confusion" suggests the sorry fate of all efforts to continue God's work in an atmosphere of strife. Bickering and feuding waste everyone's energy and derail all attempts to win the lost and edify the saints. United effort behind the leaders dissolves into factions with self-seeking agendas. The church as a whole suffers a loss of laborers for every good cause, as well as a decline in both attendance and giving. A spirit of brother helping brother gives way to nasty indifference. The last result is "every evil work." James may be thinking of what generally happens in the last stages of conflict among members of a local church. All who belong to a combative group go on the attack mode, seeking to take control and force out their adversaries.

From this kind of fighting comes one of two results, both of which I have seen in my experience. The contentious brethren may win. In such a church, torn apart by warring factions and reduced to a remnant who managed to squeeze out everybody else, there is no testimony of God's love and thus no meaningful work of the gospel. The church is dead.

The other result is when the fractious brethren abandon the church, leaving it under the control of the true saints who had war thrust upon them when they desired peace. In such a church, gospel ministry survives, although on a reduced scale through loss of people and financial support. The second result is preferable to the first, but both represent a triumph for evil forces seeking to oppose God's work.

A church's top priority must be to stop any conflict before it gets started. Disagreements and misunderstandings and personal slights must be handled immediately in a Biblical fashion, lest they fester below the surface and finally erupt in damaging conflict.

Self-Test

1. What proportion of my godliness consists of deeds rather than words?

You should speak words honoring to the Lord, but if you wish to truly honor Him, you should also make sacrifices of time and money to help others.

2. Am I too assertive with my own opinions?

You need not always keep them to yourself. It is not out of place to share them in pleasant conversation with friends and family. But do you foist them on people who would rather not hear them? Or even when speaking to a sympathetic audience, do you sometimes keep pushing your opinions to the point of needless argument?

Nothing we are presenting here should be construed as an objection to legitimate preaching, teaching, or witnessing. Still, in witnessing to the lost, you must seek divine wisdom on how much to say. If you encounter hostility, the best course is to back down and go away. Jesus strongly counseled us never to cast our pearls before swine, lest they become enraged and attack us (Matt. 7:6). To unnecessarily put ourselves at risk of persecution serves no good purpose.

When people write to my website just to argue with me, I usually do not reply. I feel that life is too short to spend it debating issues with people who are firmly entrenched in their own thinking. The only people worth engaging in discussion are those truly open to changing their minds.

How do you measure a person's willingness to learn something new? You must be careful not to confuse a willingness to learn with a willingness to talk. Many talkative people, eager to fill your ears with a stream of words, have self-seeking motives. When you knock on doors while canvassing a neighborhood, you can expect a variety of outcomes. Most who answer will be unfriendly or indifferent to the gospel. Yet even among these, some will see you as a good target for their pent-up feelings. Two cases are most common.

1. A person full of self-pity arising from failure or tragedy may pour out his feelings upon you in the hope that you will show concern, perhaps even love. But he does not really want any feedback suggesting that he needs to make changes in his lifestyle. He views the gospel as irrelevant or even as offensive. The best course in dealing with someone who only wants emotional support is indeed to show concern and love, but at the same time to insist that all solutions to life's problems lie in submission to God's will. You should state the gospel, describe Jesus as the great problem solver, and then, if the person seems deaf to the gospel, graciously terminate the conversation.

2. Not infrequently in witnessing, you will meet someone with a grudge against God because of adversities he has suffered, or against religion because of the hypocrisy of some people professing to be religious, or against Bible believers because he sees them as barriers to social progress. He may not be overtly hostile. On the contrary, he may view the witnessing believer as someone he can recruit to his side. Never enter into discussion with such a person. Cut off the conversation as quickly as possible. Why? By attacking God and the work of God he is committing sin. You dare not encourage him to continue. It is best both for his protection and yours—his from sin and yours from the temptation to doubt God—to disengage yourself from all his ranting. Go away nicely, but go away.

3. If I find myself in disagreement with another person, do I make false or exaggerated statements to enhance my position? Or am I scrupulously truthful?

For someone locked in a heated exchange, the goal quickly shifts from defending truth to becoming the winner, and the easiest way to win may be by taking shortcuts bypassing truth. Remember, though, that to win an argument is one thing; to be right is another. In many arguments I have heard over the years, both sides have been dead wrong. The winner achieved nothing except to plague the world with more nonsense.

4. When I win a disagreement, does it make me feel good, even if the other person feels bad?

If you are controlled by love, you will find arguing very unpleasant, and you will avoid it. But often we cannot avoid disagreements. To proceed correctly in some task may require a choice among different opinions. But the right atmosphere for making the choice should be friendly discussion, and afterward, if your opinion prevails, you should not feel smug like a victor, but you should hurry to show respect for everyone else involved in the decision-making process and to soothe the feelings of anyone who might feel set aside like a loser.

5. Do I ever support those responsible for factional debates within the church?

There is a place for defending the fundamental truths of our faith. But most of the strife within churches boils down to competition for power. Strife is usually a sign that the motivation governing interaction between the brethren is not love, but selfish ambition.

Review Questions

1. What is wisdom?
2. What is the first essential quality of true wisdom?
3. What is the second essential quality of true wisdom?
4. What does false wisdom create?
5. What are two evil results?
6. How do true wisdom and false wisdom differ in their sources?
7. How does James define the three sources of evil that we know as the world, the flesh, and the devil?
8. What comes from envying and strife?
9. What may be the last stage of conflict in the church?
10. How can we avoid such a destructive outcome?

✛ James 3:17–18 ✛

> 17 But the wisdom that is from above is first pure, then peaceable, gentle, *and* easy to be intreated, full of mercy and good fruits, without partiality, and without hypocrisy.
> 18 And the fruit of righteousness is sown in peace of them that make peace.

Lesson 20
Wisdom from Above

Attributes of true wisdom. After warning us against false wisdom, James undertakes a full description of the kind of wisdom we should seek. Wisdom deriving from above rather than from this sinful world has eight attributes.

Purity. The first attribute is purity (v. 17). The virtue James intends is not limited to sexual purity, but is purity in a broader sense, referring to freedom from all evil motives. A wise man must not use his brainpower for wicked purposes.

A common figure in popular entertainment is the evil genius, or criminal mastermind. But I have never met a real-world specimen either in my own experience or in the daily news. As a breed, criminals are uncommonly dumb. That is why jails are overcrowded with people wasting the best years of their lives.

Yet it is possible to use wisdom as a tool for taking advantage of other people. A clever salesman can sell worthless products. A sharp politician can manipulate public opinion to gain support for unjust policies. A skillful teacher of false religion can speak impressive words that entice people away from the truth (2 Pet. 2:18–19).

Our supreme example of pure wisdom is Christ. A few years after Jesus died, God sent Peter to the city of Caesarea, where Cornelius, a Roman centurion, and a group of his friends and relatives were waiting to hear the gospel. Never before had Peter sought to win Gentiles. In his message (Acts 10:34–38), he took it for granted that his hearers were already familiar with Jesus' life and ministry. He confidently stated, without any fear of contradiction, that Jesus had devoted Himself to helping the needy. It is evident that His good works were so outstanding that the common people saw them, not anything evil, as the hallmark of His career. Thus, the wisdom shaping His choices must have been pure and, by James's standard, from above.

Peaceableness. Secondly, true wisdom is peaceable (v. 17).

Earthly wisdom engenders strife (vv. 14–16). When Paul lists the works of the flesh, he gives prominence to strife in various forms: variance (heated debate), emulations (rivalries), wrath, strife, seditions (dissensions), heresies (schisms), and envyings (Gal. 5:19–21). When someone thinks he has the correct opinion on some issue, he is tempted to argue with anyone who voices a different opinion. That is human nature, and human nature will have its way unless restrained by humility. But a good rule throughout life is, never argue. In any argument, you are either right or wrong. If you are wrong, you should not expose your ignorance. If you are right, the truth will survive whether or not you defend it. Even if you are trying to convince someone to believe God or to do His will, you accomplish nothing by arguing. As soon as you encounter unyielding resistance, you should back off, recognizing that the working of the Spirit will be more effective than your words.

Gentleness. Thirdly, true wisdom is gentle (v. 17). Time after time, the New Testament gives gentleness as a mark of Christian leadership (2 Cor. 10:1, of Christ; 1 Thess. 2:7, of Paul; Titus 3:2, of all in leadership). One responsibility of leaders is to rebuke any brother who has gone astray. Yet they must deal with him gently, for that is the way of true wisdom (2 Tim. 2:24–26; Gal. 6:1). As the old saying reminds us, "It is easier to catch a fly with honey than with vinegar." If you confront a brother who has fallen into sin or foolish ideas, your purpose is not to antagonize him, but to win him over. Therefore, you avoid exaggerating his guilt. You use pleas rather than threats. You speak kindly, not roughly. You keep a caring face. The visible emotion should be love rather than anger or rejection. If you attack him, he will raise his defenses higher and entrench himself deeper in disobedience. Instead, you must present yourself as his ally and friend, so that he will lower his defenses.

The same tactics should be used in the home. When differences arise, we should seek to overcome them not with heated argument, but with gentle persuasion.

Openness to entreaty. Fourthly, true wisdom is "easy to be entreated" (v. 17). That means "easy to approach" or "easy to talk to." An entreatable person is a good listener. He readily cooperates with reasonable requests. If you disagree with him, he is open to good arguments, and he is capable of changing his mind if he is wrong. He does not resent criticism, and if it is fair, he takes it to heart. In all practical matters, though not in matters of principle—in other words, in all matters of convenience rather than conscience—he is flexible. James says that flexibility in this sense comes with true wisdom.

As you get older, we must be careful to remain entreatable. An older person who refuses to consider advice is a sore trial to his family. If God grants you a long life, the time will come when you should no longer drive. But you may feel as capable then as ever before. So, when your children think you should stop, you had better listen to them. One reason my wife and I had a good relationship with my mother, who lived with us for many years, is that she remained flexible. For example, in her 80's she was still using her own car, but after a few episodes of passing out at home, I told her that she needed to give up driving, and she accepted my advice graciously.

Mercifulness. Fifthly, true wisdom is full of mercy (v. 17). One aspect of intelligence is the ability to spot flaws in the thinking and work of other people. Unless tempered by mercy, an intelligent mind can be severely critical. I had an English teacher in high school who fancied himself to be a literary critic of the first rank. When he graded my essays, he covered them with red ink, showing every minute imperfection, real or imagined. It was a good learning experience for me, I suppose. But when he solemnly pronounced that I would never be a writer, he went well beyond his proper role as a teacher. He made me so afraid of his criticism that I developed a terrific case of writer's block in his class. I managed to get an A only because he did not like anyone else's writing either. His problem? He had no mercy. His ability to pulverize students reinforced his self-esteem as an intellectual. I knew many people like him in the academic world—people who validated themselves by tearing others apart.

But the wisdom of a godly man is merciful. In at least four respects, his mercy is outstanding.

1. He gives criticism only when appropriate. Perhaps his role requires it. For example, a teacher or parent must sometimes find fault with his children. It is not generally my place to criticize somebody else's children, however. Criticism is also appropriate if it is necessary to save someone from harming himself, whether through sin or carelessness. If I see someone about to step in front of a coming car, I will shout at him to stop. If I find a Christian brother looking at pornography, I will exhort him to throw it away and repent of his sin.

2. He sets a realistic standard. It is unrealistic if he faults a toddler for not tying his shoes or a teenager for not wanting to live with his nose to the grindstone, forever deprived of any fun.

3. He does not exaggerate. If the children are raising a commotion in the bedroom, he tells them to quiet down. He does not accuse them of having a bad attitude. And he does not tell them that they never do right. Be careful of terms like "never" and "always" when you criticize. Usually keep your focus on the problem now and forget about yesterday.

4. He balances criticism with praise whenever possible. If you feed a child nothing but criticism—if you never have anything good to say about him—you will crush his spirit. Out of despair he will give up trying to cope with the demands of life, and he will sink into chronic failure.

Fruitfulness. Sixthly, true wisdom bears "good fruits" (v. 17). The natural tendency of a wise man is to sit and think rather than go out and do. It is not an exaggeration to say that thinkers as a group are prone to laziness. But you cannot be an ivory-tower Christian, forever meditating on the finer points of theology. When you stand someday before God in judgment, He will reward you not according to your intelligence, but according to your righteousness. Therefore, a wise man will devote himself to doing good.

Impartiality. The seventh property of true wisdom is lack of partiality (v. 17). It is human nature to prefer associating with people like oneself. Another old saying is, "Birds of a feather flock together." Someone that the world labels "wise" or "smart" is no different. He prefers the companionship of people tagged in the same way, for he expects them to appreciate just how clever he is. He wants friends who will applaud his wit whenever he wishes to flaunt it and who will stroke his ego whenever he feels insecure about his smartness.

What does the Bible say to people who think themselves wise? "Seest thou a man wise in his own conceit? *there* is more hope of a fool than of him" (Prov. 26:12). If you have some knowledge or sophistication, do not take yourself too seriously. You are not as wise as you think. Moreover, "Condescend to [keep company with] men of low estate" (Rom. 12:16). Do not be snobbish. Do not give all your attention to those you consider your equals. Indeed, be friendly to everyone in the church.

Lack of hypocrisy. The eighth and last property of true wisdom is lack of hypocrisy (v. 17). A wise man can use his intellectual skills in the service of error and evil as well as truth and righteousness. Remember Balaam? Here was a man with such a reputation for wisdom that kings sought his counsel. The Moabites summoned him to curse the nation of Israel, but when God forbade him to cooperate and instead required that he bless the nation, he was disappointed. He did not want to lose the gold and great riches that the Moabites offered him in return for his help. Therefore, after pronouncing the blessing God wanted, he counseled the Moabites that the only way to defeat Israel was to draw its people into idolatry and immorality. The result would be that God Himself would destroy Israel. The strategy almost worked. Moabite women enticed thousands of Israelites to commit sin, and God slew the sinners by means of a plague. Yet the leaders of Israel took a stand for righteousness, and for their sake God spared the nation. When He later directed the nation to take vengeance on Moab, they slew all but the youngest girls. Among the casualties was Balaam the prophet. His downfall was the result of hypocrisy. He pretended to be a prophet of God, yet he set a price on his wisdom and sold it to those seeking an advantage against the people of God.

How do we remember Balaam? Three times the New Testament refers to him as the prototype of every false prophet (2 Pet. 2:15; Jude 11; Rev. 2:14). A false prophet is a man who pretends to be a spokesman for God but who serves only his own greed. His wisdom is earthly, sensual, devilish.

True wisdom from above never conceals wicked designs under a mask of piety. Jesus, the man perfect in true wisdom, was unique in being totally the same inside and outside. He never presented a false face to those around Him. The unifying theme of both His public and private character was the determination to do His Father's will (John 6:38).

Summation. James concludes his description of true wisdom by returning to perhaps its most distinctive mark—peaceableness (v. 18). A clearer translation is, "But the fruit of righteousness in peace is sown for those that make peace."[55]   He evidently means that through their peacemaking, the peacemakers sow fruit that they themselves will enjoy. That fruit is the opportunity to live righteously in an environment of peace, without the perpetual antagonism and persecution that make a life of righteousness difficult. James is recalling Jesus' beatitude, "Blessed are the peacemakers: for they shall be called the children of God" (Matt. 5:9). Jesus implies that by building peace in our fallen world, the righteous will earn great respect, to the extent that fellowmen enjoying the peace will call them the children of God. The result will be, as James affirms, that the righteous themselves will be allowed to live in peace.

Self-Test

1. Is my wisdom pure?

The test is whether you use your mind to plot strategies for getting your own way or advancing your own interests. Instead, you should use it to find the right path at every moral crossroads, to devise new ways of helping others, to guide others out of confusion, to manage your God-given responsibilities, and to plumb the mysteries of God's Word. These are the legitimate uses of a good mind.

2. Is my wisdom peaceable?

It is not if you are constantly flaunting your opinions and daring others to disagree. Another test is how you react when others have the gall to disagree with you. Do you use heavy arguments to swat them dead like a pesky fly?

3. Is my wisdom gentle?

It is not if your words have the sensitivity and kindness of a machine gun.

4. Is my wisdom easily entreated?

If you are wise in this respect, people will think of you as a person easy to talk to. They will feel free to come to you with advice or criticism. They will not stay away for fear that you will belittle them in defense of yourself.

5. Is my wisdom merciful?

If mercy shapes your thoughts, you will not expect more of others than is reasonable. Remember, you are not perfect either, and you hardly measure up to the highest standards even from a human perspective. By God's standards, your accomplishments are nothing.

6. Is my wisdom fruitful?

Christian ministry should be the primary focus of your life. Do not deceive yourself that you are doing enough as a Christian when you just sit and think about spiritual things.

7. Is my wisdom impartial?

The test is whether you reach out with love to the unlovely. You are failing the test if you show favor only to people you regard as in your own set and at your own level.

8. Is my wisdom without hypocrisy?

Your pose as a wise man is hypocritical if you employ clever devices to make yourself look more spiritual than you are, or if the religion on your face and in your mouth is not the same as the religion in your heart.

Review Questions

1. What is the first attribute of wisdom from above?
2. Who is our chief example of wisdom in every respect?
3. What is the second attribute of wisdom from above?
4. What is the third?
5. What is the fourth?
6. What is the fifth?
7. What is the sixth?
8. What is the seventh?
9. What is the eighth?
10. Who was a prime example of false wisdom?

> **1** From whence *come* wars and fightings among you? *come they* not hence, *even* of your lusts that war in your members?
> **2** Ye lust, and have not: ye kill, and desire to have, and cannot obtain: ye fight and war, yet ye have not, because ye ask not.
> **3** Ye ask, and receive not, because ye ask amiss, that ye may consume *it* upon your lusts.

Lesson 21

Wars and Fightings

War in the church. The next subject James undertakes is a natural outgrowth of his long discourse on speech, contrasting the evil uses of the tongue with uses controlled by true wisdom. He now turns to consider the most destructive kind of speech within the body of Christ (v. 1). To unmask its true nature, he calls it "wars and fightings." He is talking about the verbal feuding that may intrude upon a church and tear it apart. This kind of speech is like warfare not only in its intent to do harm, but also in its unwillingness to stop without total victory. The emotional engine that starts the fighting, or that eventually emerges to prolong it, is hatred. Because hatred speaks to the heart in a roar that drowns out the still, small voice of conscience, each group of combatants easily yields to the temptation to carry on their campaign without restraint or pity.

James asks the obvious question, "What causes heartless conflict of this kind within the church, which is supposedly a showcase of love?" The answer is that outward war always starts with inward war. War between brothers is always an outgrowth of war within themselves, as they struggle unsuccessfully to manage their own lusts. The Greek word translated "lusts" signifies the desire to please self.[56] Failure to control this desire can quickly bring brothers into conflict. In church settings, the root of most battles is ambition, whether for recognition or power. But all objects of ambition are in limited supply. One man cannot be promoted to teach a class, for example, without demoting another, or at least without denying another the same promotion. The other forms of privilege also resist being shared equally. Ambition is therefore a breeding ground for wars and fightings. It is not an exaggeration to say that somebody's self-seeking desire, usually in the form of ambition, is at the bottom of every dispute in the church.

Murder in the church. James now shows the precise connection between desire and fighting (v. 2). The general opinion of scholars is that verse 2 should be rendered in the following manner: "You lust and have not, and so you kill. You desire to have and cannot obtain, so you fight and war. You have not because you ask not."[57] Clearly, then, desire leads to fighting because a man's own power to change his world may be insufficient to satisfy his heart's desire. He cannot get what he wants because he wants things beyond his reach. The result is frustration, prompting him to more desperate attempts to gain the prize that has so far eluded him. Such attempts may bring him into competition with others, and from competition comes war.

James makes the shocking assertion that in striving to satisfy desire a person may commit murder. He says, "Ye kill." This statement has provoked endless discussion. What does James mean? After all, he is talking to believers. Surely he does not mean that in the churches he was addressing, people were killing each other. No, he does not mean that. I have never heard or read about a dispute within a local church that led to fatalities. Yet James is not using murder as a mere figure of speech for doing great harm. He is not saying that when believers fight, what they are doing is so bad that it amounts to killing.

Then what does he mean? Perhaps he is looking down the corridors of distant church history and anticipating all the wars that would erupt between different branches of Christendom, such as between Catholics and Protestants in the years following the Reformation. This interpretation is untenable, however, because throughout his epistle James is talking to "my brethren" (Jas. 1:2; 16, 19; 2:1, 5, 14; 3:1, 10, 12; 4:11; 5:7, 9, 10, 12, 19). If we examine the religious wars in the past, we find that the leaders on both sides were seldom, if ever, true brothers in Christ. Generally, power hungry rulers were fighting each other under a religious pretext, or authorities allied with a corrupt church were wreaking violence against those seeking to rebuild the New Testament church.

So, what does James mean? He must mean that fighting can kill people indirectly. How? It can happen in many ways.

1. If you raise your voice at another believer—especially if you engage him in a shouting match—what might happen? You might raise his blood pressure high enough to precipitate a stroke, and he dies. Then before God, you will be guilty of murder.

2. To keep on fighting with another believer could have serious consequences in another way. If he is emotionally vulnerable, you could discourage him to the extent that he falls into depression and commits suicide. Then before God, you will be guilty of murder.

3. Even though the fellow believer you have attacked may not become suicidal, the stress you have added to his life may cause or aggravate a disorder that saps his good health and shortens his life.

Stress can be fatal. If anyone dies from a stress-related condition that you have made worse by fighting against him, then before God, you will be guilty of murder.

4. If you bring strife into the church, some churchgoers may become so bitter or disillusioned that they leave. They may forsake Bible-based religion and adopt a less wholesome lifestyle involving more eating and less exercise, or perhaps even involving drink or drugs or dangerous companions or crime. Their new way of life apart from God may well lead to premature death. Then before God, you will be guilty of murder.

5. The same disaster could overtake members of your own family if the strife you have nurtured causes you to leave the church and to remove them as well. Any of them who subsequently follows the way of the world could become a victim of early death. Then before God, you will be guilty of murder.

6. Besides all these ways of killing the body, there are also ways of killing the soul—of committing spiritual murder. Your wars and fightings make you guilty of spiritual murder if they keep anyone from coming to Christ.

Obviously, there are many ways to commit murder that we refuse to acknowledge, lest we see the despicable selfishness and hellish blackness of our own behavior toward people who are targets of our disdain solely because they keep us from pleasing ourselves.

The power of prayer. James next reminds his reader that there is a right way to gain our desires. Instead of fighting to fulfill them, we should take them to God. Just ask, James says, and expect God to answer. James is harking back to the Sermon on the Mount, where Jesus gave His disciples a blank check to cash in the bank of heaven (Matt. 7:7–12). Jesus promised that whatever they sought, the Father would provide. Of course, James is taking for granted that his readers have not forgotten his earlier admonition to ask in faith (Jas. 1:6–7). Faith is the first key to successful prayer.

When prayer fails. James knew full well, however, that some among his readers would protest, "I tried that, and it didn't work. I asked God to give me my heart's desire, and it never came." James replies by giving the clearest and bluntest explanation in all Scripture for unsuccessful prayer (v. 3). He says simply that many prayers go unanswered because they are motivated by lust. As we noted earlier, the Greek word translated "lust" just means desire. So, the desire prompting the request may not seek anything actually sinful. Yet the request fails because the petitioner wants something with no purpose or value except to please himself. In other words, the prayer is selfish. The point James is making is that in our prayer life, we should be mainly seeking good things for others. What will meet their needs and bring them joy should be our emphasis. Therefore, the second key to successful prayer is unselfishness.

Is it wrong to seek good things for ourselves? No, the Bible authorizes a believer to pray for his spiritual and material needs (Matt. 6:11–13). But as a rule, he is wise not to beseech more from God unless he is expressing a desire that the Holy Spirit has placed on his heart. We must remember that God is already generous before we pray. On His own initiative, He lavishes pleasurable things upon us. Is He not the source of "every good gift and every perfect gift" (Jas. 1:17; 1 Tim. 6:17)? We need not ask Him for good things any more than a child needs to ask his father for Christmas presents. God's gifts are more precious to us, and our gratitude is more pleasing to Him, if we have not pestered Him for the things He gives, but have been content to let Him provide as He sees fit. And it always turns out that His choices give us far more satisfaction than we would derive from many of our own choices.

Self-Test

1. Have I ever participated in fighting or feuding within the church?

Can you now see that your basic motive was self-seeking, in pursuit of a selfish desire? In other words, do you understand that the conflict arose from lust in your heart?

2. Do I realize that by raising strife in a church, I could kill someone by bringing about his premature death?

As we have said, you can kill people just by raising their stress level.

There is also the danger of making someone suicidal. We must recognize that the church is a refuge for all kinds of people, including many who are weak, although in time by the grace of God they will become strong. Yet at first when they receive Christ, they are emotionally vulnerable.

Most of our churches include members who suffer or who have suffered from depression. One component of the treatment they receive should be Biblically-based counseling. Yet many churches fail to provide it for two reasons: first, because they fear legal liability and, second, because they have unwisely yielded to the view of modern society that depression is a medical condition manageable by pills alone. It is undoubtedly true that pills give symptomatic relief, but symptomatic relief is not a solution. A person whose mind is oppressed by sadness needs to learn effective life-changing dependence on the sweet influence of the Holy Spirit. He does not need to attend a church where feuding prevails, putting him at risk of serious or even life-threatening discouragement. The church should be a place where the afflicted find an atmosphere of healing, not hatred.

Another danger of strife is that it might drive spiritually weak people wholly out of the church, into circumstances that will shorten their lives. We dare not be numbered among those responsible for the strife that proved fatal.

3. Do I realize that by raising strife in a church, I could destroy my own family members?

James says that self-centered ambition leads to killing (v. 2). One tragedy he foresees is the destiny of children dragged from church. Case histories abound of young people formerly in church who later fell into wretched and unhappy lifestyles, or who went to jail for committing felonies, or who even killed themselves. In some instances the root cause was a decision by parents to leave a church because they had become embroiled in strife. When they broke away after losing some battle, they hoped to find something better, but instead brought disaster to their own home. They ended up killing their own children, either their bodies or their souls.

4. Do I realize that if I engage in fighting and feuding, I could block someone from receiving Christ, and that as a result I would be guilty of spiritual murder?

How much evangelism is accomplished when a church is fighting? Virtually none. All those responsible for the fighting are therefore guilty of withholding life-saving truth from lost people. Perhaps the lost who were left unreached will never have another chance to hear the truth. They will die in their sins, and the bickerers and backbiters who kept them out of the Kingdom will be parties to soul murder.

5. Is the focus of my prayer life on myself or on others?

It is of course proper to pray for your own needs. God wants you to pray for them, so that you will see His answering provision and love Him still more. But your main subject should be the needs of others. Indeed, God wants you to learn the discipline of unselfishness.

6. Do I pray improperly for God to increase my pleasures?

Instead, you should be content with those He provides, and you will find that He will provide even your heart's desire (Ps. 37:4), assuming of course that you let Him shape your heart's desire so that it seeks what is truly good.

Review Questions

1. What is the most destructive kind of speech within the church?
2. What is always the source of wars and fightings?
3. What is the causal chain leading to war?
4. To whom is James speaking throughout his epistle?
5. What does James mean when he says, "Ye kill"?
6. In what six ways can feuding lead to murder indirectly?
7. What is the right way to gain our desires?
8. What is generally the reason God does not grant a request?
9. What should be the emphasis of our prayers?
10. Why is it unnecessary to ask God for good things beyond our needs?

> 4 Ye adulterers and adulteresses, know ye not that the friendship of the world is enmity with God? whosoever therefore will be a friend of the world is the enemy of God.
> 5 Do ye think that the scripture saith in vain, The spirit that dwelleth in us lusteth to envy?
> 6 But he giveth more grace. Wherefore he saith, God resisteth the proud, but giveth grace unto the humble.
> 7 Submit yourselves therefore to God. Resist the devil, and he will flee from you.
> 8 Draw nigh to God, and he will draw nigh to you. Cleanse *your* hands, ye sinners; and purify *your* hearts, ye double minded.
> 9 Be afflicted, and mourn, and weep: let your laughter be turned to mourning, and *your* joy to heaviness.
> 10 Humble yourselves in the sight of the Lord, and he shall lift you up.

Lesson 22

Friendship with the World

Spiritual adultery. Although it may not be apparent to a casual reader, the flow of thought in this passage follows a logical train. Throughout an earlier passage spanning many verses, James dealt with sins of the tongue (chap. 3). Then he turned to the worst of these sins—the kind breeding wars and fightings in the church—and showed that they are rooted in selfish desires impossible to fulfill (vv. 1–3). Now he digs a little deeper (v. 4). What is the source of the lusts that can provoke conflict even among believers? The answer is worldliness.

In this answer, exposing what lies at the bottom of the lusts that produce combative speech, James agrees with John, who wrote that "all that is in the world, the lust of the flesh, and the lust of the eyes, and the pride of life, is not of the Father, but is of the world" (1 John 2:16). The world system teaches men that the purpose of life is to please self. It promotes lust by misrepresenting it as the proper driving force in human relationships. According to the world, a person works to become successful, accumulate money, and buy possessions. A person marries to acquire a mate who will satisfy his or her needs. A person goes to church to take advantage of its programs. Yet all this sort of thinking is a distortion of the true purpose of life. The Westminster Catechism framed its true purpose in the eloquent words, "The chief end of man is to glorify God and enjoy Him forever." The proper center of life is God, not self.

In an attempt to rescue those who have adopted the world's philosophy, James gives their sin a name unmasking how serious it is. He calls it adultery. Those who follow the way of the world he calls adulterers and adulteresses. He is reminding them that membership in the body of Christ brings them into a relationship with God so warm and intimate and all-consuming that the only suitable comparison is marriage. Hence, when they prove themselves false to God by drawing close to the world that hates Him, they are like a man unfaithful to his wife or a woman unfaithful to her husband. James warns them that they have a choice. They can either be friends with the world or friends with God. They cannot be both. If they choose friendship with the world, they make themselves enemies of God.

Next comes a verse that some expositors have described as the most difficult in the New Testament (v. 5).[58] In many translations, the second part is a quotation introduced by the first part, but the words of the second part do not correspond to any text in Scripture. So, why does James imagine that Scripture is their source? Some expositors have come to the reasonable view that the two parts of the verse are separate thoughts, only the first expressing a question, which should be rendered, "Or think you that the Scripture speaks in vain?" In their view, the Scripture James intends is not the following statement but the previous statement, marking friendship with the world as enmity with God. Furthermore, he is referring not necessarily to a specific text, but to a general theme of Scripture as a whole.[59]

In Scripture we do indeed find the pervasive teaching that man has a choice either to serve God or serve the world. But we need not dismiss the possibility that a specific text is in the forefront of James's mind. Perhaps here as in many other verses he is alluding to the Sermon on the Mount. The relevant portion is where Jesus declares the impossibility of serving both God and Mammon, a term identifying the world system as a false god (Matt. 6:24).

The role of the Spirit. James's next statement has spawned a great variety of conflicting translations (v. 5b). Many expositors take the view that the spirit must be man's, for the Holy Spirit appears nowhere else in the epistle.[60] But His absence elsewhere does not forbid us to find Him here. James certainly had a mature knowledge of the Holy Spirit. A better approach to James's remark is to let Scripture explain Scripture. Since all of Scripture has one Author, we may even seek illumination of James's words in the writings of Paul (Gal. 6:16–17). Paul sees the Holy Spirit as intensely desiring to subdue the sinful part of a man. A simple extension of this thought is that He is jealous to secure a man's loyalty to God. Understood in this way, the statement by James could be translated, "The Spirit that dwells in us jealously desires us." In other words, with a possessiveness comparable to a human lover's, He wants us to scorn any rival tempting us to commit spiritual adultery. One rival is the world.

Worldliness in the contemporary church. Just how dangerous is it to be worldly? This is an especially important question to consider in our day, when the church in America is not growing. The last growth spurt throughout the fundamental-evangelical wing of Christianity was back in the '70s, in the years before the election of Ronald Reagan. In the '80s and '90s, further growth seemed confined mainly to megachurches. Since then, Bible-believing churches have been in decline, and the rate of decline is accelerating. The American church seems to be hurrying down the same slope taken by the church in England after World War I. If present trends continue, little vital Christianity will remain in America after a few more decades.

Why are we going downhill? Are we failing to reach out and witness to the lost? Certainly we need to work harder at bringing new people into our churches. But who in Jesus' day excelled at winning converts to their religion? It was the Pharisees (Matt. 23:15). The religion of the Pharisees was in some measure based on the Scriptures. Was Jesus therefore pleased with them because they were aggressive in spreading their doctrines? No. He disapproved of their success because they accomplished nothing except to turn converts into replicas of themselves, and Jesus in the same passage goes on to show that the Pharisees were hypocrites.

God intends our churches to be nurseries for spiritual babes, providing the nurturing they need to grow into the likeness of Christ. The reason God is not giving growth to the churches in America is that He cannot trust them to perform their function. Instead of turning converts into replicas of Christ, contemporary Christians are, like the Pharisees, turning converts into replicas of themselves.

What is God's complaint against Christians today? They are too worldly. That is why the churches in America are not growing. Worldliness takes many forms.

1. One that we see in today's churches, both in the people who attend and in their leaders, is materialism.

2. Another is addiction to forms of entertainment that corrupt the soul.

3. Yet another, perhaps less obvious but pervasive in its destructive effects, is erosion of good character. Under the influence of today's culture, which teaches that self-interest should be the bedrock of moral judgment, many contemporary Christians are living by the dictates of pragmatism rather than principle. Some years ago the famous preacher Warren Wiersbe warned of this trend in his book *The Integrity Crisis*.[61] Prophecy warns that in the Last Days, people who profess true religion will be as morally twisted as godless people

(2 Tim. 3:1–5). In today's world, dominated by a popular culture that is discarding not only the forms of duty but even the word itself, we see the fulfillment.

4. The world shapes our behavior in even more subtle ways. The figures we see in the media, in all the sitcoms and dramas and talk shows, model ways of treating each other that are an offense to God. Their speech tends to swing between the extremes of sarcasm and flattery. If it is not rude or abusive, it is wheedling or flirtatious. At either extreme it is calculated to gain some selfish purpose. The social behavior of these people on the screen is just playacting designed to manipulate. Its purpose is not to help or teach or edify others, but to make others tools of personal ambition.

Victory through grace. Next, after James alerts us to the great danger of loving the world, come words of great assurance (v. 6a). He wishes us to understand that it is possible to make the right choice. We can indeed renounce the world and cling to God. How? God furnishes the necessary grace, and not just grace, but "more grace"; literally, "greater grace."[62] Greater than what? Perhaps the meaning is that when a believer is imperiled by greater enticements to worldliness, God furnishes him greater grace to resist.[63] Grace is the force always sufficient to counteract the world, however compelling its influence may be.

Humility as the key. But how can we obtain this grace? How can we be victors in our battle against the world? How can we escape being casualties of worldly lust and instead survive spiritually with an acceptable love for God? James answers by reminding us that we can unlock divine grace with the key of humility (v. 6b). He is merely recalling a familiar proverb (Prov. 3:34) remembered also by Peter (1 Pet. 5:5). It is a wonderfully brief statement of a truth that ranks very high in significance, a truth so important that we might call it the secret to understanding much of human experience. We might reword it as follows: humility is the way up, whereas pride is the way down. A proud man, despite abilities that make him proud, always finishes in the depths, because God, who determines his fate, resists him. A humble man, despite inabilities that keep him humble, always finishes in the heights, because divine grace carries him upward.

The path to humility. To renounce pride and embrace humility should therefore be our chief priority, for what man in his right mind would suffer God's disfavor when it is possible to enjoy His favor? What sane man would remain mired in the swamp of this world when he can rise to the beauty of Paradise? James gives a series of ten commands for those who wish to prove themselves humble. These commands take the form of imperative verbs.

1. "**Submit** yourselves therefore to God" (v. 7). Our only real choice is whether we will submit now or later (Phil. 2:10). It only

makes sense to submit now, while we can still gain blessings in return, the greatest being life forever.

2. **"Resist** the devil, and he will flee from you" (v. 7). The devil is not omnipotent. He has limited resources to invest in his war against God. Therefore, he will not waste them in what seems to be a losing battle. If he senses that he cannot overcome you, he will go away and engage a more promising target of attack.

3. **"Draw nigh** to God, and he will draw nigh to you" (v. 8). Drawing nigh to God is an overture of love. To receive our love was precisely the reason that God created us. He wanted our love so that He might love us in return. As a God of love (1 John 4:8), He did not choose to exist alone, but made creatures with whom He could be united in love. Indeed, His love preceded ours (1 John 4:19). If we draw nigh to Him, it is because He has already drawn nigh to us.

4. **"Cleanse** your hands, ye sinners" (v. 8). The great barrier between God and man is man's sin. Before we can draw nigh to God, we must therefore remove the barrier. We do so through repentance. James devotes several commands to explaining what repentance means. First of all, it means to stop the performance of sin. Since the hands are the chief tool we use in carrying out our will, James chooses them to represent all of our conduct. We must, he says, clean up our conduct in the world.

5. **"Purify** your hearts, ye double minded" (v. 8). Behind sinful conduct lie the sinful motives residing in the heart. True repentance involves a change not only in what we do, but also in what we want to do. "Double minded" here is the same word used in James 1:8 to describe a man torn by conflicting motives.[64] To please God, we must sift through the motives in our hearts and discard all those tending to sin. That is, we must purify our hearts.

6. **"Be afflicted"** (v. 9). Another translation is, "Be wretched."[65] Some people erroneously imagine that repentance can be a purely intellectual decision. "O.K., I will stop sinning," and that's it. But in true repentance we take God's view of our sin, and there is more to His view than just an intellectual labeling of our sin as wrong. He hates it with a fierce wrath. Therefore, we should also see it with a strong emotional aversion. We should see it as not only wrong, but as hateful, and the fact that it lodges in our hearts should bring us to great sorrow (2 Cor. 7:10), even to a state of wretchedness. To put it plainly, we should feel terrible about our sin.

7. **"Mourn"** (v. 9). James alludes to the proper mindset of a sinner, as described by Jesus (Matt. 5:4).

8. **"Weep"** (v. 9). The outward sign of mourning is tears. By combining the commands to mourn and weep, James emphasizes that a real sorrow will appear on both the inside and the outside.

9. "Let your laughter **be turned** to mourning, and your joy to heaviness" (v. 9). Here we have a clear allusion to the Beatitudes as they are recorded in Luke (Luke 6:21, 25). Often Scripture speaks of

the saints weeping. Seldom does it speak of them laughing. Many times it speaks of our Lord weeping. Never does it speak of Him laughing. We find an explanation in Ecclesiastes (Eccles. 7:2–6). Laughter is not wrong. We need laughter to make life bearable, and it is especially appropriate as an expression of simple joy, although it easily slides into mockery, vulgarity, and other forms of sin. Yet sorrow is better. Why? Because it reminds us of our true condition—that we live in an evil world which we will not escape until we die, and that we will never know genuine happiness until we come to a better world.

10. "**Humble** yourselves in the sight of the Lord, and he shall lift you up" (v. 10). This summation of the whole discussion states the obvious application of the principle given at the outset, in verse 6. If God resists the proud and gives grace to the humble, then we must humble ourselves to be exalted.

Self-Test

1. Whom do I love more—the world, or God?

One of the best ways to assess whether God is your choice is to ask how you spend your free time. Do you ever welcome it as an opportunity to help others, to read godly books, to study the greatest book of all, God's own Word, or to meet with God Himself in personal fellowship? Do you relish times when you can get alone for communion with God?

The next questions explore whether worldliness has infiltrated and corrupted your values and your behavior. We said that worldliness takes many forms.

2. Am I materialistic?

Do possessions dominate your life? How much time do you fritter away on daydreaming about things you want to acquire? How much time do you spend shopping? What portion of your free money goes to build your collection of junk that you will sell at your next move?

3. Do I love worldly entertainment?

Your standard when choosing entertainment should be simply this: what would I do or watch if I could see Christ next to me? Of course, you cannot apply that standard correctly unless you understand that Christ is the Holy One, absolutely intolerant of sin.

4. Do I lack integrity?

Where on a scale of one to ten would others place your personal integrity? There is no better test of which side you are on. God is truth. Fudging truth for personal gain is the hallmark of God's enemy, Satan.

5. Do I ever hurt others with abusive speech?

Do you bully fellow church members, throw your weight around, raise a fuss when you are slighted, and generally make yourself a nuisance in the body of Christ? Are you always complaining or criticizing? Do you make fun of people in ways that are thoughtless and unkind? If you have fallen into any of these sins, it is not surprising in today's world. You are following the examples you see in the media, where nearly everyone has a bad mouth.

6. Do I ever use manipulative speech to gain my objectives?

Do you use flattery and half-truths to win the support of others? Such tactics for getting ahead come not from God, but from this godless world.

The last questions deal with every man's never-ending battle with pride.

7. Am I proud?

What you think is less important than what others think, because a proud person seldom admits to pride. Do others think you are proud? Of course, you must consider the source. Someone jealous of you might think you are proud, just because he feels insecure. The best people to ask whether you are proud are those who have known you longest and who can be trusted to tell you the truth as they see it, someone like a sibling or a spouse.

8. Do I see that I have an enemy who is waging a war against my soul?

Do you consciously resist him? The right strategy to adopt against his onslaughts is fully explained in Ephesians 6 (Eph. 6:10–18). The best defense is always faith. All his threatenings and accusings and enticings melt under the sunlight of faith.

9. Have I dealt with my own sin by putting it away through genuine repentance?

Has the change been both internal and external? That is, are you as much a new person inside as you seem to be on the outside?

Have you felt a sorrow for sin? You need not suppose that repentance is invalid unless the sorrow coming from it is vehement and inconsolable. But if sorrow was absent from your repentance, you should question whether you truly repented.

Review Questions

1. What is the source of lusts that provoke conflict in the church?
2. What does the world say is the purpose of life, but what is its true purpose?
3. To what does James compare worldliness?
4. What is the Spirit's role in our battle against the world?
5. Why is the church in America not growing?
6. In what four ways is the world corrupting the church?
7. By what means can we achieve victory over the world?
8. What is the key to unlocking divine grace?
9. What are the ten commands that will lead us down the road to humility?
10. What is better than laughter, and why?

---

11 **Speak not evil one of another, brethren. He that
speaketh evil of** *his* **brother, and judgeth his brother,
speaketh evil of the law, and judgeth the law: but if
thou judge the law, thou art not a doer of the law,
but a judge.**
12 **There is one lawgiver, who is able to save and to destroy: who art thou that judgest another?**

Lesson 23

Judging the Law

Evil speaking. After James's fervent appeal for humility as the
only way to win divine favor, he returns to the main idea controlling
the middle portion of his epistle. It is as if he is writing a symphony
and the time has come to restate a main theme so that we will hear
the music as a unified whole. This theme is given out in the words,
"Speak not evil one of another, brethren." Literally in the Greek, he
says, "Speak not against one another, brethren."[66]

The first statement of the theme was back in chapter one, where
he warned us against an unbridled tongue (Jas. 1:26). Then in
chapters three and four it became the principal subject of an entire
movement, as he displayed the iniquity of the tongue in all its varia-
tions, including the following:

1. false or unprofitable teaching (Jas. 3:1–2);
2. words defiling the body or the course of history (Jas. 3:3–6);
3. cursing directed against fellow creatures of God (Jas. 3:7–12);
4. earthly, sensual, and demonic wisdom (Jas. 3:13–18);
5. lust-driven speech leading to wars and fightings (Jas. 4:1–3);
6. speech seeking friendship with the world (Jas. 4:4–5);
7. words serving as the vehicle of pride (Jas. 4:6–10).

When at last he came to pride, he touched the first and fundamental
sin. All sin proceeds from the prideful illusion that self has the
authority to determine right and wrong. This illusion is equivalent to
putting self in the place of God, the same course chosen by Satan
when he rebelled, and therefore it is pride of Satanic proportions.

In all these sins we both corrupt ourselves and offend God. But
also we victimize a brother. As James brings his discussion of
speech to a close, he focuses on the kind of speech that does the
greatest damage to others. His purpose in coming to this climax is to
show how the central message of his epistle applies to speech. The

message prominent throughout is that genuine faith produces a life full of good works, bringing blessing to others rather than harm. Thus, a heart alive with faith should never use deadly words.

As examples of especially harmful speech, he gives two: speaking against a brother and judging a brother (v. 11a). The first, speaking against a brother, refers to any faultfinding with an evil purpose. It is one thing to confront a brother with criticism for the purpose of helping him. Indeed those with spiritual discernment are commanded to help any fellow believer ensnared by sin (Gal. 6:1–2; Jude 22–23). But it is another thing to use criticism as a weapon to tear down a brother. Scripture clearly lays out the difference between the two kinds of criticism. The kind that can rightly be called constructive respects the six rules we gave earlier (see discussion of James 1:26) for any personal confrontation, including Christian counseling. It is (1) private, (2) just, (3) humble, (4) unhypocritical, (5) resistant to being recruited to the same fault, and (6) gentle.

To these six we will now add some others that are more fundamental. Paul said, "That we *henceforth* be no more children . . . ; But speaking the truth in love, may grow up into him in all things, which is the head, *even* Christ" (Eph. 4:14–15). From Paul's description of proper dealings between brothers in Christ, we derive two rules for criticism.

1. It is true. Yet much of the criticism that passes through our minds is simply nonsense! We are quick to find evil motives where none exists. For example, if someone walks by without greeting me, I had better be sure that the slight was deliberate before I decide that I have been snubbed. Maybe the person was too preoccupied to see me.

2. Above all, it proceeds from love and uses loving words. Love is the motive, the method, and the outcome.

Any critical speech that does not meet these eight criteria is exactly what James condemns as speaking against a brother.

Judging. The second kind of evil speaking that he mentions is judging. Again, he is alluding to the Sermon on the Mount. He is recalling Jesus' solemn warning, "Judge not, that ye be not judged" (Matt. 7:1). Judging is basically hostile. It takes criticism a step beyond mere faultfinding to the stage of passing sentence, as in a court of law. It not only holds the offender guilty, but also decides that he should suffer evil consequences. Perhaps this sense of what justice requires will foster attempts to punish the offender, whether by cutting him off from friendship, or running down his reputation, or driving him from the church. Judging is therefore always a sin.

James teaches us exactly why it is a sin. It is a violation of the law (v. 11b). The law he has in mind is undoubtedly the same law that he has previously upheld as the ultimate standard for Christian conduct, calling it the perfect law of liberty (Jas. 1:25; 2:12) and the

royal law (Jas. 2:8). It is the same law that Jesus cited as the summation of all duty to our fellow man (Matt. 22:37–40). The requirement that it lays upon us is to love our neighbor as ourselves, and
our neighbor certainly includes our brother. When we make our
brother the target of judgmental criticism, we are treating him the
opposite of how we wish to be treated. Therefore, we are depriving
him of real love and breaking the royal law.

But James wants us to understand that evil speaking is not just
a violation of the law. It is far worse than that. It is a blatant attempt to undermine the authority of the law and to cast it aside. The
evildoer is not only attacking his brother; he is attacking the law itself. He is speaking against the law in the sense that he is denying
that the law is good, and he is judging the law in the sense that he is
trying to overthrow it. When James says to the evildoer, "If thou
judge the law, thou art not a doer of the law, but a judge," he means
that whereas the evildoer should willingly remain under the law, he is
trying to lift himself above it—to make himself the final arbiter of
right and wrong—to stand in judgment of what God has decreed as
though he were a being superior even to God.

God's supremacy. James rebukes such arrogance in words that
are decidedly sarcastic (v. 12). He says that there is only one qualified source of law: God. He alone is qualified because He alone has
power of enforcement. He can give life or death as He chooses. A
man, on the other hand, is a mortal being with no power over His
own destiny or anyone else's. He is a cosmic weakling. Any attempt
to make himself a lawgiver higher than God, with the right to judge
God's laws, is folly beyond measure. So, James concludes, "Who art
thou that judgest another?" In other words, "You who take it upon
yourself to set aside the law of God, who do you think you are? Are
you above God?"

We derive the same perspective from Aesop's fable of the lion and
the hares.

> King Lion was fair-minded as well as mighty. He saw that
> the strongest animals did as they pleased, often hurting the
> weaker ones, and he felt this was wrong. So he issued a decree:
> "Might does not make right. While I am King, it shall be the law
> that everyone—big or little—must do what is fair."
>
> This Law of Fairness was popular with most animals. But
> one day the hares marched to the palace to protest. "We de-
> mand a turn on the throne! The law says, 'Might does not make
> right.' Therefore you have no right to be king all the time, just
> because you're stronger than we are."
>
> "Chatter, chatter," said the lion in disgust. "One reason I am
> King instead of you is I don't chatter." Suddenly he stood up,
> showing his teeth and claws. "What I do is ROAR!" All the ani-
> mals in the kingdom heard that roar. Even tigers, far off in the
> jungle, heard it, and remembered the law.
>
> The lion returned to his throne. "The Law of Fairness did not

make me King. Rather, I made it the law. What's more, I can make it stick. Can you?"[67]

When we question the law of God, we are like the hares who thought they could rule better than the lion.

Self-Test

1. Am I guilty of speaking against a brother, or of judging a brother?

You might do this either openly to others or privately within your own mind.

Recruiting others to hear your evil speaking and judging is gossip, a sin we have already dealt with in detail. Because I teach strongly against gossip, no one ever gossips to me or my wife. In every church where we have ministered, we have seldom heard news through the grapevine. It is hard to hear through a channel you are not connected to. Generally we do not hear news until it appears in the prayer bulletin. But how does the old saying go? Ignorance is bliss.

The second kind of evil speaking and judging—within your own mind—is simply hatred. Before you give place in your thoughts to hatred, you had better ponder the warnings in First John (1 John 3:15; 4:20). If you hate, you are a murderer; you cannot love God at the same time; and your faith is pretense rather than real.

2. Do I slip into evil speaking when I pray?

Once in days past, while my wife and I were praying together, I was waxing eloquent as I poured out my complaints against a brother in the church who was causing me great trouble. I will call him Brother Smith. Something happened to interrupt us—whether the phone rang, I cannot remember. Afterward, I said to my wife, "Now, where was I?" She replied, "You were telling God about Brother Smith." All at once we both burst into laughter, as we realized how dumb I was in trying to inform God about anything. How much of our prayer life consists of pointless complaints about people or circumstances, as if we needed to bring God up to date with the bad news?

3. Do I practice constructive criticism?

We said that there is a place for constructive criticism. But do not attempt it until you have carefully reviewed the criteria setting it apart from evil speaking. The safest course is never to voice criticism unless you have first filled your heart with love for the person you are criticizing.

4. Do I recognize and accept my smallness in the scheme of things?

Do you understand that the only rational response to a god as mighty as the God who exists is to bow the knee? Do not doubt Him, or question Him, or quibble with Him, or fuss at Him, or resent His decrees. Just accept who He is and do your best to earn His smile. Nobody but a fool would do otherwise. Of course, what He wants from you first is to admit that you are a sinner undeserving of His favor: second, to recognize that His favor is available only through Christ; third, to receive Christ as Savior; and fourth, to become His servant working under the direction and power of His Holy Spirit.

Review Questions

1. How does James restate one of his main ideas?
2. Why is pride the first and fundamental sin?
3. What two forms of speech are especially harmful to others?
4. What are the marks of constructive criticism?
5. What teaching found in the Sermon on the Mount does James restate?
6. How does judging go beyond criticism?
7. What law does judging violate?
8. Any attack against a brother is also an attack against what else?
9. Who alone is a qualified source of law?
10. Why does He alone hold this privilege?

✛ James 4:13–17 ✛

> 13 Go to now, ye that say, To day or to morrow we will
> go into such a city, and continue there a year, and
> buy and sell, and get gain:
> 14 Whereas ye know not what *shall be* on the morrow.
> For what *is* your life? It is even a vapour, that ap-
> peareth for a little time, and then vanisheth away.
> 15 For that ye *ought* to say, If the Lord will, we shall
> live, and do this, or that.
> 16 But now ye rejoice in your boastings: all such rejoic-
> ing is evil.
> 17 Therefore to him that knoweth to do good, and
> doeth *it* not, to him it is sin.

Lesson 24
Presumptuous Planning

God's control of tomorrow. A major objective of James throughout his epistle is to stop evil speaking. In his crusade against it, he winds through many arguments and illustrations until he comes to the fundamental issue: a man's attitude toward the law of God (Jas. 4:11). James shows that a man who breaks the law by speaking against a brother is doubly guilty. First, he is guilty of act-ing contrary to the law, and second, by casting the law aside, he is guilty of holding the law in contempt. In essence, he is denying that God has a right to define his behavior as sin. Thus, by judging God's law, he is placing himself higher than the lawgiver, God, and making law for himself. But what folly (Jas. 4:12)! A rough translation of James's rebuke of such a man is, "Who do you think you are?" James points out that God has ultimate power, even over life and death, whereas we are nothing. His power to destroy us if we fail to obey Him should give us, if we have any common sense, a healthy respect for His law.

The next verses continue the comparison between man's weak-ness and God's strength. The enormous gulf between creature and Creator exists not only in God's ability to declare what is right, but also in His ability to control the future. Everything that happens is the direct outworking of God's will. He is the One who ordains the course of history. Man, however, has no control of the future beyond his ability to make plans and preparations that may never come to fruition.

Before drawing out the implications of God's sovereignty over tomorrow as well as today, James says, "Go to now"—literally, "Come now" (v. 13).[68] These are words calling for close attention. He is saying, "Listen to me, for I will show you how misguided you are, you who take seriously your attempts to plan your lives." He addresses especially those traveling merchants whose normal practice is to map out a strategy for making money in the months ahead. For the sake of illustration, he describes a typical strategy that they might conceive. They might decide to leave today or tomorrow for another city, with the intention of staying there and conducting profitable business for a whole year. James characterizes their plans as presumptuous (v. 14). They are making unfounded assumptions about what will happen. Everything they confidently expect is a matter of speculation—whether their final balance sheet will show a profit, whether they will be able to remain in the city a full year, even whether they will reach the city. They really do not know what tomorrow will bring.

Doubt attaches even to whether they will live another year. James reminds them that life is like a vapor that, after suddenly appearing, quickly disperses and fades away, becoming undetectable. He is thinking perhaps of a wisp of smoke, or of an odorous exhalation from a jar of perfume, or of a slight breath of fresh air. Such a vapor is now here, now gone, just like a human life—now here, now gone.

The proper lens for seeing the future. In view of how uncertain the future is, we should look upon our plans as mere guesses. We should acknowledge that whether our plans come to pass depends strictly on whether God allows them to prosper (v. 15). To every thought of what will happen, we should attach the condition, "if God wills." James does not mean that it is a sin to omit this wording whenever we speak of the future. Rather, he means that in our hearts we must never fail to recognize that the future depends on God. Though we do not actually say "God willing," this proviso should be fundamental to our outlook on things to come. We must always understand it to be true whether or not we say it. Yet there are times when it is good to hedge a promise by stating outright, "God willing." We find many examples in the New Testament (Acts 18:21; 1 Cor. 4:19; 16:7; Heb. 6:3; Phil. 2:24). It is always good to speak these words if the people hearing us might build up expectations that come to nought, leaving them disappointed.

Making plans. If "the best laid schemes o' mice an' men gang aft a-gley" (or, go often awry), as the poet says, should we make plans at all?[69] When criticizing the merchants who lay out a strategy for making money, did James mean that a businessman is wrong if he looks ahead? Planning is normal practice in every realm of life—not only in business, but also in education, family affairs, even the work of the church. Is it wrong? Should we simply live day by day without giving any thought to the future? No, that is impossible. Whatever we do is governed by some picture of what will happen. Any purchase, for example, assumes that we will live to use it. Any departure from home assumes that we will arrive somewhere else. No, it is not possible to exclude planning from our lives.

Lest we make wrong applications of his teaching, James tells us exactly what is objectionable (v. 16). It is sin to "rejoice [or glory[70]] in your boastings," an unmistakable allusion to Proverbs 27:1: "Boast not thyself of to morrow; for thou knowest not what a day may bring forth." Here we have another reminder that the Epistle of James falls in the tradition of Jewish Wisdom Literature. James is identifying two things as evil. The first is to make plans that ignore the hand of God ("boastings," which refers to plans assuming that oneself can really see the future). The second is to glory in those plans; in other words, to congratulate oneself for skill in managing the details of to-morrow. The second evil follows from the first because to exclude God from our picture of life's outcomes creates a vacuum that human pride rushes to fill. If we do not see that the future depends on God, we will imagine ourselves to have power over the future. In essence, we will make ourselves gods. Presumptuous plans, forgetting that God can overrule, are therefore a form of idolatry.

When doing nothing is sin. In conclusion, James presents an important principle in the clearest and most succinct terms we find in Scripture. He says, "To him that knoweth to do good, and doeth it not, to him it is sin" (v. 17). Many other texts build important conclusions on the same principle, although without making it explicit (Luke 12:47; John 9:41; 2 Pet. 2:21).

James's formulation may be a lesson that he drew from Jesus' parable of the two sons (Matt. 21:28–32). Their father directed them to go work in the vineyard. One refused, but later changed his mind and obeyed. The other agreed to go, but stayed away. His failure to do right was sin.

Or what James says may be his application of the so-called Golden Rule: "Therefore all things whatsoever ye would that men should do to you, do ye even so to them: for this is the law and the prophets" (Matt. 7:12). Notice that Jesus' actual words are far more demanding than the familiar words. He does not command, "Do unto others as you would have them do unto you." So stated, the rule merely prohibits things that we ourselves would not like to suffer. Rather, Jesus commands that we do every good thing we can imagine. To fall short of doing every good thing we can imagine is therefore sin, as James reminds us.

In context, the good that James is urging upon his readers is to heed his instruction in verse 15, where he told them to add, "If the Lord will," whenever they spoke of their plans. But he is also referring more generally to everything he has said so far in his epistle. He has offered many ways to do good. We should seek wisdom (Jas. 1:5), rejoice in humble circumstances (Jas. 1:9), visit the fatherless and widows (Jas. 1:27), etc. To neglect any of these admonitions is sin. We prefer to think of sin as a deliberate trespass of a negative law, such as "Thou shalt not kill." But our duty goes far beyond the mere avoidance of evil deeds. It takes in every good deed fulfilling a positive law, such as the preeminent requirements to love God with our whole being and to love our neighbor as ourselves.

Self-Test

1. When I consider any human reckoning of the future, do I understand how shaky it is?

Do you leave room for other possibilities if God overrules? It is always wise to plan for the unexpected. When in years past the American government urged citizens to prepare for the next flu pandemic or the next terrorist attack, did anyone pay attention? We are all too preoccupied with making ends meet today to consider tomorrow, and if we consider tomorrow, we inevitably view it as a simple extension of today, making no allowance for any fundamental or radical changes.

But the Bible teaches that we are entering a period of history when there will be momentous wars and disasters on a scale people today can hardly imagine, and therefore the prediction seems like fantasy. But the truth is that God Himself will soon upset all human reckoning when He puts His hand into history again as He last did at the resurrection of Christ. Then He raised one man from the dead. Soon He will take living saints out of this world.

2. Have I learned from experience that reality may spoil all my plans?

Young people immersed in today's media and public schools have learned the politically correct motto, "You can be whatever you want to be. Just pursue your dreams and you will see them come true." Suppose a young man decides to pursue his dream of becoming a nuclear physicist. Unfortunately, he cannot get passing grades in either algebra or geometry. He cannot even recognize an obtuse angle if it is turned slightly so that neither side is horizontal. The plan he has laid out for himself is nothing but empty boasting. If he sought the mind of God, he would discover a more realistic future.

It is important that children receive competent career guidance so that they will make plans based on their real gifts and abilities. The future within their reach depends on God's endowment rather than personal fancy.

3. Do I make plans that leave God out of the picture?

In every decision about the future, you should seek guidance from the One who holds the future, and to discover His will you should consult the teaching of Scripture and the inner witness of the Holy Spirit. If you shape your plans accordingly, submitting to God's sovereignty with a glad rather than a begrudging spirit, you are declaring that you wish His will to prevail. Thus, you are in effect stamping your plans with the proviso, "God willing."

How often do we create problems for ourselves by forging down a certain path without consulting God first! David failed to ask God how to transport the ark, and a man died (2 Sam. 6:1–8). We can all think of illustrations from our own lives.

One in my own life a few years ago was useful as comic relief. Because it was nothing of serious consequence, it gave both me and my wife something to laugh about. Every morning for over a year I was going through a time-consuming ritual to obtain an allergy pill. Each was individually encased in a plastic cover, so I was using scissors to remove it, often crushing it in the process. After becoming very frustrated, I shared my problem with the Lord, adding some words that were not very complimentary to the manufacturer. It seemed to me that He said, "Have you looked at the directions?" I do not mean to be irreverent, but it almost seemed as if He spoke with a smile in His voice. When I took His advice, I discovered that all I had to do was push the pill on one side and it would pop out on the other. Instead of fuming and complaining, I should have been praying.

4. Do I faithfully remind myself and others that what happens depends on God?

It is especially important for our children to hear that God is in control. Otherwise, they develop anxieties about the future. It gives them a great sense of security if they feel that they can trust the future to God. I remember a famous preacher describing how much he worried as a young man that his best option for a wife would be dowdy, dumpy, and dull-witted. When God gave him the dream of his heart, he learned that the cure for worry was to wait on God's will.

5. Do I ever take pride in detailed planning, as if this proves how well I can control my world?

In an age when nearly everybody has a pocket planner or day-timer or similar device to organize his future, it is easy to fall into this kind of pride. One test is whether you resent interruptions of your schedule. You cannot deny that these interruptions come from God. Therefore, if you resent them, you are criticizing His judgment and imagining that yours is superior.

6. Do I see failure in positive duty to be as sinful as any violation of a prohibition?

By this standard, we can hardly live or breathe without falling into sin. How much time do we give ourselves that we could give to helping others?

Review Questions

1. In what other respect is God vastly superior to His creatures?
2. What does James give as his example of presumptuous planning?
3. How uncertain is life itself?
4. What condition should we attach to every thought of what might happen?
5. Is it wrong to make plans?
6. What is the first thing that is wrong?
7. What is the second thing that is wrong?
8. What important principle does James state in conclusion?
9. From what source did James derive this principle?
10. How does he want us to apply it?

> 1 **Go to now, ye rich men, weep and howl for your miseries that shall come upon you.**
> 2 **Your riches are corrupted, and your garments are motheaten.**
> 3 **Your gold and silver is cankered; and the rust of them shall be a witness against you, and shall eat your flesh as it were fire. Ye have heaped treasure together for the last days.**
> 4 **Behold, the hire of the labourers who have reaped down your fields, which is of you kept back by fraud, crieth: and the cries of them which have reaped are entered into the ears of the Lord of sabaoth.**
> 5 **Ye have lived in pleasure on the earth, and been wanton; ye have nourished your hearts, as in a day of slaughter.**
> 6 **Ye have condemned *and* killed the just; *and* he doth not resist you.**

Lesson 25

Destiny of the Rich

Their coming miseries. In chapter five, James leaves his discussion of a living faith evident in good works and returns to another major theme of his epistle, a theme he touched on both in chapter one, where he advised the rich man to humble himself (vv. 10–11), and in chapter two, where he denounced the rich for oppressing the poor and blaspheming God (vv. 6–7). Now he issues the rich a chilling prophecy of what their future will be.

He begins by summoning them to hear his words. He calls out, "Go to now, ye rich men" (v. 1a). As in the previous usage (Jas. 4:13), the opening words are better translated, "Come now."[71] In other words, stop whatever else you are doing and listen closely. He immediately justifies his claim on their attention by telling them bluntly that they are headed for disaster (v. 1b). They face such miseries that, if they could now see them in all their horrible detail, they would not be able to contain their grief. They would be helpless to hold themselves back from utter despair. Indeed, James advises them to "weep and howl." Both are strong words, referring to vocal expressions of grief in extremity.[72] A translation giving a better idea of the anguish suggested by these words is, "Wail and scream."

Why does James urge the rich to distress themselves about

miseries they will not face until sometime in the future? Because now is the only time they can change their destiny by repenting of their sins. James hopes that they will repent if they look with realistic fear and sorrow at the future awaiting them.

In his appeal he seeks to counter the two reasons that the rich continue in sin. First, as they lie on their beds of ease and drink in all the pleasures that money can buy, they are satisfied with life as they know it. They see no incentive to change. To unsettle their apathy and contentment, James reminds them that their life of pleasure will not last. Soon it will be gone, and then they will suffer misery and loss. After death, they will enter into a different sort of life, not really life at all, but a state of consciousness that they will express through weeping and howling. Therefore, if they wish to get a taste of their coming experience, they should start even now to weep and howl. This way of facing the stark reality of future miseries will, if they are wise, move them to repent.

The decay of their possessions. The second reason that the rich continue in sin is that they are entranced with the beauty of their riches, so entranced that they cannot see anything else. James tells them that they are wearing blinders. They do not see the true condition of all the wealth around them. He says, "Your riches are corrupted, and your garments are moth-eaten. Your gold and silver is cankered" (vv. 2–3a).

James is showing the transitory nature of three specific kinds of wealth. Because "corrupted" is the word for rotted,[73] many expositors agree that the first kind James has in view is perishable foodstuffs, which in antiquity were a valuable commodity that the rich sought to acquire (Luke 12:16–21).[74] The word translated "cankered" refers to rust.[75] Also, each verb signifies an event already past.[76] Thus, a more illuminating translation of James's warning is, "Your foodstuffs have become rotten, your garments have become moth-eaten, and your gold and silver have become rusted."

In summary, as the rich survey all their accumulation of property and rejoice in its eye-fixating glamour, James says, "Look, it is already starting to decay." Jesus pronounced a similar verdict: "But lay up for yourselves treasures in heaven, where neither moth nor rust doth corrupt" (Matt. 6:20). Indeed, nothing in this world is exempt from deterioration. Nothing lasts but a moment in a perfect state. The point James is making is that it is folly to pin one's happiness upon possession of things that are wasting away and will soon vanish. When they vanish, so will any happiness they provided.

Why James supposes that gold is vulnerable to rust is a question long debated. Perhaps he is using "rust" as a generic term for every form of metallic decay. Although gold is not subject to oxidative corrosion, it yields to the corrosive effects of various other agents, such as fluorine, chlorine, and aqua regia (a mixture of hydrochloric and nitric acids).[77] The other precious metal he names—silver—is prone to the type of oxidative corrosion known as tarnish.[78]

Their sins requiring punishment. Why do the rich deserve the terrible fate that God has ordained? James next proceeds to give the answer, listing four grievous sins that they have committed.

1. The very decay that is eating away at their wealth witnesses to their first sin (v. 3b). They have devoted their lives to what is worthless. Instead of seeking eternal reward by doing works of eternal value, they have collected pretty junk, here today and gone tomorrow. As a result, they have wasted their time, their talents, and everything else God has entrusted to them for accomplishing good.

James continues, saying literally, "Ye have treasured up in the last days." He means that they have done nothing better than to amass troves of fleeting treasure, even though they should have known that they were living in the last days: that is, in the days right before they would face God in judgment.

They will pay an awful price for their love of corruptible wealth. James says that corrosion ("rust") will "eat your flesh as it were fire." It is a law of human existence that every man is destined to be molded in the image of whatever god he chooses. As believers in the true God, we assume His attributes and change into His likeness, which is the summit of every virtue. An idolater, however, replicates his lifeless gods, for his destiny is death, when he too will be unable to speak, see, or walk (Ps. 115:4–8; 135:15–18). The rich worship money. Mammon is their master and god. Hence, just as material wealth succumbs to irreversible decay, causing its substance to crumble and scatter, so the worshipers of wealth will waste away forever. The processes of decomposition, which James calls "rust," will degrade their bodies without relief, yet without ever destroying them completely. As Jesus says, they will go to the place "where their worm dieth not, and the fire is not quenched" (Mark 9:48). Their most terrifying prospect is that they will perpetually feel the corrosion at work upon their bodies. It will burn like fire.

2. James indicts the rich with a second grievous sin (v. 4). "By fraud" is not actually in the original, but without it the text is still clear. As employers, the rich have cheated their employees out of rightful compensation. James refers specifically to day laborers hired to assist in the harvest of crops. It was the custom for a landowner to visit the marketplace early in the morning and pick out workers for the coming day. When he hired them, he promised certain wages. Yet at the end of the day, when the work was done, an unscrupulous employer might pay less than he promised, or he might pay nothing at all. What recourse did the laborers have? Virtually none in the ancient world. There was seldom a legal remedy. Judges were reluctant to hear complaints against a leading citizen, and any accusation that he failed to keep a verbal agreement was hard to prove

anyway. Besides, a rich man could use bribery to secure a favorable ruling.

James warns the rich that there is a judge who cannot be bribed and who is not indifferent to the complaints of the poor. He is the Lord of "Sabaoth," transliteration of the Hebrew word for hosts.[79] The title "Lord of hosts" is of course common in the Old Testament (e.g., Ps. 24:10; 84:1; Isa. 1:24; Jer. 32:18). James is saying that although the poor appear weak and defenseless, in fact they have on their side the most powerful defender of all, the very God who can summon all the forces of heaven to do His will.

Down through history, the rich have exploited the poor, and the poor have resented the rich. In the last few centuries many political movements promised to wrest power from the rich and give it to the poor. The most important was Marxist Communism, which promised to organize society under the dictatorship of the proletariat (the working class), but in reality merely succeeded in creating new oppressors. The wealthy capitalists at the top of society were replaced by wealthy Communists, who expanded the power of the ruling elite at the expense of everyone else's freedom. While promising liberation, Communism brought the iron grip of tyranny. Who is the only advocate and defender of the poor who can be trusted? James gives the answer. It is the Lord of Sabaoth.

3. The third grievous sin of the rich is that they wallow in self-indulgence (v. 5). This has taken two forms. First, they have "lived in pleasure," which might be translated, "lived delicately."[80] That is, they have furnished themselves with every manner of comfort and convenience as a buffer against anything unpleasant. Second, they have "been wanton." The Greek word speaks of carrying self-indulgence to the point of riotous living.[81] But to what purpose have they nourished their lusts? James says, "Ye have nourished your hearts, as in a day of slaughter." Here, James offers us two distinct pictures of the rich man. The day of slaughter suggests an overfed cow ready for butchering. ·The overnourished heart suggests a heart so fat with sin that it is insensitive to the gentle touch of conviction, and thus God can do nothing with the rich man except bring him into judgment. The image of a fat heart derives from Isaiah's famous denunciation of the godless in Israel (Isa. 6:9–10), twice quoted in the New Testament (Matt. 13:15; Acts 28:27).

4. The last grievous sin of the rich is murder (v. 6). In an effort to multiply wealth, they have not scrupled to kill good men. Perhaps the specific instance James has in mind is the evil that came from Ahab's greed. He framed Naboth on a charge of treason so that he might put him away and take possession of his vineyard (2 Kings 21:1–16). History is replete with other examples. It would not be an exaggeration to say that human life is cheap in any society where greed reigns supreme.

What does the just man do in self-defense? James takes it for granted that because he is just, he will not resist the evildoer. Again we see James's debt to the Sermon on the Mount, where Jesus commands, "Resist not evil" (Matt. 5:39), but rather, "Love your enemies" (Matt. 5:44). By resistance, Jesus means stooping to your enemy's level, returning gibe for gibe, sneer for sneer, and blow for blow. The mark of a good man is that he seeks his enemy's welfare. Thus, even when under an attack that could take his life, he will strive to spare his attacker.

I do not believe that either Jesus or James means that we should never protect ourselves from violence or oppression. The scenario James implies is a rich man manipulating the justice system to destroy someone standing in his way. In that situation, providing no legal refuge, a man seeking to honor the Sermon on the Mount can do nothing but submit.

Self-Test

The first questions address whether you are devoting your life to corruptible things. To be specific, where does gaining money and possessions fall on your scale of priorities?

1. How do I spend my free time?

Do you use it for improving your money-making skills, planning out new money-making strategies, poring over your accounts, shopping, basking in the luxuries money can buy, and daydreaming about new luxuries to acquire? It is not wrong to shop, for the alternative is to make hasty purchases soon regretted. And it is not wrong to practice money management, for God expects us to be good stewards of whatever wealth he has given us. The question deals with your priorities. Your use of free time should testify that for you, serving God is more important than self-enrichment.

2. How do I spend any extra money?

Does it go to pad your investments? Do you spend it on increasing your collection of bric-a-brac and your arsenal of toys? God may choose to bless you with some nice things that you do not really need. But still, if you have surplus funds sitting unused, you would be well advised to invest them in God's work.

3. When I make major life decisions, what is my overriding goal?

Are you trying to become a more fruitful servant of God, or are you positioning yourself to make more money? This is a critical question for young people as they take steps that will shape the rest of their lives—steps determining their education and career, as well as whom they will marry and where they will live. But the question also applies to older folks, for they are not exempt from life-shaping decisions. Perhaps you receive an offer of a better job, but it requires that you move to a place lacking a sound Bible-believing church. What should you do? If money and career are most important to you, you will move, after convincing yourself that the available churches are good enough. But in response to your declaration of priorities, God will not bless your family. They will suffer spiritually. Your children will probably copy your priorities and devote their lives not to pleasing God, but to promoting themselves and gaining worldly riches.

Remember Lot (Gen. 13:5–13; 18:20–21; 19:1–38). He went to live in the wicked city of Sodom because he wanted to make money. But the city corrupted his children. When the angels came to bring him out of Sodom before God rained destruction on it, he begged his married children to leave, but they refused and died in the fiery catastrophe that reduced the city to a perpetual ruin. The unmarried daughters who accompanied Lot proved to be women of poor character.

Are there any Sodoms today? Yes, there are many. Any city that fails to pass the following tests may prove as dangerous as Sodom:

- Does it provide a good church?
- Does it allow children to receive a Christian education?
- Does it furnish employment that will not require the employee to hide his identity as a Christian or to conduct himself in a morally compromising manner?

The remaining questions deal with the other sins that James charges against the rich.

4. Have I increased my wealth by defrauding others?

The person most vulnerable to this sin is a businessman. A Christian in business must renounce sharp practices, such as false advertising, price gouging, price fixing, cost-cutting measures that reduce products and services to inferior quality, high-pressure salesmanship, refusal to honor legitimate complaints, exploitation of employees by routinely demanding overtime or by denying reasonable pay and benefits, etc.

5. Have I spent money to provide myself with sinful pleasure?

Money naturally gravitates to the providers of sin. I remember reading about a respectable, churchgoing man who won a major lottery. Before another year had gone by, he was frequenting places of wicked pleasure. The story of the prodigal son is a picture of the ruin that threatens any man with a big bankroll in his pocket. Ask yourself whether having some extra money has ever been the lure that led you into compromise or corruption.

6. Have I harmed any just man?

James's exposé of the sins committed by rich men was written not to exhort believers, but to warn the wicked. It is most unlikely that you, if you are a believer, have ever killed a just man. Yet perhaps you have sometimes been so distracted by riches that you have failed to serve his welfare. Your brothers and sisters in Christ need your encouragement, your help, your friendship, your cooperation in carrying on the work of the church. Therefore, your presence in the church and in their lives must be dependable. You cannot be constantly skipping town for the sake of selfish pursuits made possible by your money.

Review Questions

1. To what theme does James now return?
2. What is the first incentive that James gives a rich man to examine his way of life ?
3. What is the second?
4. What are the three categories of wealth, and to what is each prone?
5. What is the first grievous sin of the rich?
6. What is the punishment befitting their sin?
7. What is the second grievous sin of the rich?
8. Who is the poor's defender?
9. What is the third grievous sin of the rich?
10. Whom do the rich resemble?
11. What is the fourth grievous sin of the rich?

> **7** Be patient therefore, brethren, unto the coming of the Lord. Behold, the husbandman waiteth for the precious fruit of the earth, and hath long patience for it, until he receive the early and latter rain.
> **8** Be ye also patient; stablish your hearts: for the coming of the Lord draweth nigh.
> **9** Grudge not one against another, brethren, lest ye be condemned: behold, the judge standeth before the door.

Lesson 26

Imminence of the Lord's Return

Two consolations. James has been enumerating some of the sins that will bring rich men to a frightful judgment (Jas. 5:3–6). The last he mentioned was that they have "condemned and killed the just; and he doth not resist you" (v. 6). As soon as James remembers how cruelly the privileged have sometimes treated the righteous, compassion stirs his heart and turns his attention from the victimizers to all of God's people who might become their victims. He addresses his fellow saints in loving terms, calling them his own "brethren" (v. 7), and, to help them cope with persecution, he exhorts them to be patient. He reminds them that this present world, so grievous for the godly, will not go on forever. Whereas the miseries of rich men will be unending in an eternal place of punishment, the sufferings of good men cannot last beyond the coming of Christ. His descent to the earth will be the grand moment when good triumphs visibly and decisively over evil. He will deliver the just from every oppression and usher them into a life of permanent joy.

Yet James is not content with one reassuring promise. He gives two. The second is that the coming of the Lord is drawing nigh (v. 8). Our wait for deliverance will be short, at least from an eternal perspective. Soon the strong hand that evil extends to do us harm will be crippled, cut back, and consumed. It brings hard blows upon us now, but in a little while it will disappear, and God will heal all injuries.

These verses furnish an important prophecy. It belongs to a class of three prophecies foreseeing the future spread of the gospel and growth of the church.

Parable of the Mustard Seed. In this parable appearing third in the Parables of the Kingdom (Matt. 13:31–32), Jesus predicted that in the historical period preceding His return, something exceedingly small, like a mustard seed, will grow to be exceedingly large, like a mustard plant towering above the other plants of the garden. What is this organism of phenomenal growth if not the church? The church indeed began exceedingly small, as only 120 in the Upper Room (Acts 1:15). Yet the church—or, more precisely, nominal Christianity—has become the largest religion in the world. According to statistics compiled in 2005, the people in the world today who name Christianity as their religion amount to about one third of the world's population. Their number is about the same as the sum of adherents to the next two largest religions, Islam and Hinduism.[82] Thus, the Parable of the Mustard Seed is a remarkable prophecy. Two thousand years ago, before the church even existed, Jesus knew that He was founding a religious movement that would continue and prosper until it overshadowed all rivals.

Jesus' last instruction. In His last words before His ascension, Jesus explained how the professing church would become so large (Acts 1:8). The dominance of Christianity over other religions would come about through worldwide evangelism. When He said, "Ye shall be witnesses," He used the future tense in the indicative mood,[83] signaling that we should understand His words as a statement of fact. He was clearly prophesying that before He returns, the gospel would reach the uttermost part of the earth.

The prophesy can be interpreted in two ways: as referring simply to general expansion of the church to every place, or as referring to something more specific. Where was Jesus when He made the prediction? He was on the Mount of Olives outside Jerusalem. In relation to that specific location, where is the uttermost part of the earth? It is the directly opposite point on the globe. That point lies in the South Pacific Ocean, and the closest inhabited island is Rapa-iti. Although small and remote, it was not overlooked in the early years of the modern missionary movement. The first preacher to land there was John Davies of the London Missionary Society. Soon after his arrival in 1826, all of the island's inhabitants adopted Christianity as their religion.[84]

Yet as we said, Jesus' instruction could be understood more generally as a prediction that the gospel would go everywhere in the world. This too has been fulfilled. The modern era since 1800 has been an age of great missionary enterprise, pushing the gospel to every nation under the sun. Statistics compiled in 2001 show that the church's goal of reaching the whole world has been substantially attained.

1. Radio with evangelical programming reaches 99% of the world's population in a language they can understand.
2. About 94% of the world's population lives in a culture with an

indigenous witnessing church, and another 4% has a resident witness provided by outsiders.

3. In the 1990s, a broad-based initiative by American evangelicals to reach groups who had not yet heard the gospel was dramatically successful. This initiative, called The Joshua Project I, put church-planting teams in a thousand unreached cultures, about two thirds of those identified, and started churches of at least one hundred members in about half of the cultures where the teams had penetrated.[85]

We should not overstate the progress, however. Although the gospel today is available to nearly everyone in the world, personal evangelism has confronted only a small minority, and still a large percentage of the world's population has never actually heard the gospel.

Yet what has been accomplished so far seems in itself a fulfillment of Jesus' prophecy that the gospel would go to the uttermost part before He returned. Within my lifetime, virtually all the last places deprived of the gospel have finally heard it. Today's global culture held together by mass communications has spread so aggressively that it has probably reached or will soon reach any remote tribes overlooked by missionaries. Thus, no uncompleted task prevents Christ from returning now. The worldwide embrace of the church is a major sign that the end is near.

The patient husbandman. The third major prophecy concerning future growth of the church is our text here in James (vv. 7–9). The author's use of a developing crop to picture church history is reminiscent of Jesus' Kingdom Parables, especially the Parable of the Wheat and the Tares (Matt. 13:24–30, 36–43). Just because the patient husbandman is a poetic image, we should not, from an outlook that sees poetry as vague and imprecise, assume that his story is meaningless except as an illustration of patience. On the contrary, when we approach the compositions of great poets—the Miltons and Shakespeares of our world—we expect to find design in details. After all, depth and density of meaning are proofs of genius. Why should we expect anything less than genius in the Word of God? In every speck of matter that comes from the same creative source, we find design too intricate for human comprehension. It is therefore wise to assume that when James, the divinely inspired author whose work is infused with meaningful imagery, uses a farmer to represent Jesus waiting to return, he intended even the details of the image to be true prophecy.

When we view this text with eyes open to larger meaning, we find it highly significant for three reasons.

1. It agrees with several others that Jesus would return only after some delay. In the Parable of the Talents, where Jesus compares Himself to a man who returns home from a far country and rewards

his servants according to their work while he was gone, He says that the man returns "after a long time" (Matt. 25:19). In a similar vein, Peter teaches that in the Last Days, men will arise who scoff at Jesus' promise to return. Why will they see it as a false promise? Because so much time has elapsed and still nothing has happened (2 Pet. 3:3–4). Likewise, James compares Jesus to a husbandman who wants to harvest the fruit of his garden, but who chooses not to come for it immediately. Rather, he waits with long patience until the fruit is ready.

2. James says that the fruit will not be ready for His return until it has received both the early and the latter rains. Most commentators view the two rains as merely a way of describing a full growing season. But as we argued, a better approach is to look for specific prophetic meaning. Rain is probably a metaphor referring to the Holy Spirit, whom Jesus likened to living water (John 7:37–39). Whatever the rain represents, its indisputable effect is to spur growth. So, James is clearly saying that the Church Age will continue until there is a final period of growth to balance the growth at the beginning.

The prophecy has been fulfilled. Expansion in the church has been mainly confined to two historical periods. In its infancy the church spread like wildfire despite fierce opposition by the Roman government. Countless believers were martyred, yet the church thrived. This was the time of early rain. Vigorous growth of the church has also taken place during the modern era, since 1800. For the first time in history, the church has carried out Jesus' command to spread the gospel to the uttermost part of the earth. This has been the time of latter rain.

3. James tells us what will happen after the latter rain. The waiting will be over and the husbandman will come. Where do we stand in history? The latter rain has now fallen for generations, but it is subsiding. Missionary work is being scaled back. The churches in many countries are at some stage of drift into the waters of unbelief and corruption. Since Scripture places no more rain after the second outpouring, the apostasy we see all around us in our day must be the final apostasy foreseen in many prophecies (2 Thess. 2:1–3; 2 Tim. 3:1–5, 13; 4:3–4; Luke 18:8; etc.). Exactly how long this retreat from vital faith might continue, we have no idea. Nevertheless, we can be sure, as James says, that "the coming of the Lord draweth nigh."

A side benefit of our investigation of James's seemingly simple exhortation is the discovery of a double sign that the Lord's return is near: first, that the latter rain has fallen; second, that it is stopping.

Two applications. Before closing his words of prophecy, James makes two key applications.

1. He stresses again that the imminent return of Christ makes it easier for us to endure the troubles of life in a wicked world (v. 7).

The confidence that He is coming soon is the secret to waiting for Him with a patient heart. It removes the anxieties that would otherwise keep us unsettled and sad.

2. The imminent return of Christ is another incentive to guard our tongue (v. 9). James warns, "Grudge not one against another, brethren." "Grudge" renders a word suggesting complaints spoken with a sigh or groan. It could be translated "grumble."[86] He evidently is not referring to passing frictions of a minor sort, soon forgiven and forgotten, because the consequence is severe—to be condemned at the Judgment Seat of Christ. There, although a believer will not have his salvation taken away, he may incur penalties. The kind of offense in James's mind is probably a chronic resentful attitude toward a brother—a simmering bitterness verging on hate—that leads to the wars and fightings he discussed earlier (Jas. 4:1–2). The danger in holding on to such an attitude is that our lives on earth might come to an end at any moment, perhaps through sudden death or even perhaps through the surprise return of Christ. In either event, there will be no chance to put away sin before we see our Judge. If we wish to protect ourselves from His displeasure, we must deal now with any wrong spirit that is poisoning our love for the brethren. Lest we balk at correcting ourselves, James reminds us that the Judge stands before the door. As we said once before, the image has two meanings. Christ is standing at the door of heaven, ready to pass through into our realm and steal away His people. He is also, figuratively speaking, standing at the door of the courtroom, ready to enter and conduct our trial. Let us therefore live as though we might at any moment receive a summons into His presence.

Self-Test

1. Am I truly aware that Christ might appear at any moment?

Within my lifetime, there has been within Christianity a sharp decline in looking for His return. The fundamentalist movement was born in Bible conferences urgently organized to affirm Biblical doctrines that liberals were aggressively denying. Often the main or exclusive subject was prophecy, especially the doctrine of Christ's premillennial return.[87] The liberals wanted the church to concentrate on reform of society. They felt that the Second Coming was a pie-in-the-sky hope weakening the social gospel. In our day a similar pragmatism, viewing Bible prophecy as a distraction from the work of building churches, has swept through the evangelical realm. The result is that fewer and fewer believers are consciously anticipating the return of Christ—exactly the state of affairs that He said would emerge just before He returned (Matt. 24:44).

2. Do I allow the promise of Christ's imminent return to serve the spiritual purpose that God intended?

In the midst of trial and suffering, do you look to this promise for comfort?   Do you take it as encouragement to be patient?   Many hymns give voice to the wonderful consolation that it affords.   For solace and spiritual refreshment, try meditating upon the words of "Is It the Crowning Day?," "Christ Returneth," or "Some Golden Daybreak."   It is sad that so many of these hymns are fading out of use in churches.

3. Does the prospect of standing soon before my judge deter me from sin?

In particular, does it motivate you to settle differences with your brothers and live with them in peace?   There are times when it is well to picture spiritual realities in your mind.   When you are tempted to sin, just imagine the Judge standing at the door.   Though your thoughts are woefully inadequate to reckon or represent heavenly glory, try nevertheless to see Christ in all His magnificent splendor, perhaps taking as your guide His portrait in Revelation 1:13–17.

Review Questions

1. What first consolation does James offer the poor under oppression?
2. What second consolation does he offer them?
3. What does the Parable of the Mustard Seed foresee?
4. What does Jesus' last instruction reveal?
5. How has His prophecy been doubly fulfilled?
6. How does James picture the Church Age?
7. What is the first prediction hidden in these words?
8. What is the second?
9. What is the third?
10. What help do we derive from the prospect of Christ's return soon?
11. What strong incentive do we derive from it?

> 10 Take, my brethren, the prophets, who have spoken in the name of the Lord, for an example of suffering affliction, and of patience.
> 11 Behold, we count them happy which endure. Ye have heard of the patience of Job, and have seen the end of the Lord; that the Lord is very pitiful, and of tender mercy.

Lesson 27

Patience in Adversity

Encouragement for sufferers. To comfort those under persecution, James has been exhorting them to look for Christ's return (vv. 7–8). The imminence of this event reminds suffering saints that their siege of trouble cannot go on forever. It will end soon when they pass out of this world either by death or by the rapture of the church. James now marshals two more arguments to encourage them in patient endurance.

The first is that the possibility of patient endurance has already been demonstrated by their godly forerunners (v. 10). He points out in particular the example of "the prophets, who have spoken in the name of the Lord." James's use of the prophets to illustrate how to handle persecution recalls the last of his brother's Beatitudes: "Blessed are ye, when *men* shall revile you, and persecute *you*, and shall say all manner of evil against you falsely, for my sake. Rejoice, and be exceeding glad: for great *is* your reward in heaven: for so persecuted they the prophets which were before you" (Matt. 5:11–12). Even though the prophets stood as spokesmen of the King of kings, they did not escape rejection and retaliation by sinners, infuriated that anyone should dare to question their evil practices. The wicked, desperate to stop the words stinging their hearts, did not tremble to lash out against the prophets. But even as these men of God were engulfed by violence, they stood fast in their faith, leaving us timeless illustrations of two virtues: "suffering affliction" (a single word implying a deliberate choice to accept suffering[88]) and "patience," which means to keep an unwavering heart through severe trials.

The second argument designed to encourage those under affliction is that they have blessings awaiting them. What did the prophets accomplish by enduring pain rather than denying God's message? James alerts us to the answer. He says, "Behold." In other words, shift your gaze from the scene of suffering to another scene I will show you. What is that? He says, "We count them happy which endure" (v. 11a). That is, we know what happens to them after all their trials, so bitter and heartbreaking while they last, finally come to an end. They leave this world to receive their reward, which is an everlasting state of being "happy," or "blessed." Looking back, they rejoice at God's leading, though it took them through perilous paths. Could they live again, they would not choose any other course. An easier life would diminish the suffering, but also the victory and the rewards for victory.

Suffering of the prophets. The New Testament frequently pays tribute to the prophets for their bravery in the face of persecution (Matt. 23:29–37; Acts 7:51–52; Rom. 11:3; 1 Thess. 2:15; Heb. 11:32–38; Rev. 16:6). Who were these prophets that wicked men tormented and killed? The sufferings of many are remembered in the Old Testament. Others are memorialized in Jewish tradition.

We know, for example, that the wicked Jezebel, wife of King Ahab of Israel, slew many prophets (1 Kings 18:13). She would have killed Elijah, except that he fled into the wilderness.

Every one of the major prophets underwent great hardship. Isaiah had a long career, stretching more than fifty years from the reign of Uzziah probably to the reign of Manasseh, the vilest of all the kings of Judah (Isa. 1:1; 2 Kings 20:21). According to a pre-Christian Jewish tradition, Manasseh killed Isaiah by having him cut in two with a wooden saw.[89] Doubtless Isaiah is the one remembered in Hebrews 11:37 as the martyr who was "sawn asunder."

Jeremiah was constantly in danger of his life throughout the closing years of his ministry. Zedekiah, the last king of Judah, allowed the prophet's enemies to cast him into a miry dungeon, where he would have starved except the king relented and imprisoned him instead in a courtyard above ground (Jer. 38:1–13). Later, after Nebuchadnezzar destroyed Jerusalem, the Jewish remnant took Jeremiah to Egypt against his will (Jer. 43:1–7). One tradition says that while there he was stoned to death.[90]

We do not know how Daniel died, yet as a youth, after he was taken to Babylon, he was willing to defy the king and face death rather than disobey God. He refused to eat the food and to drink the wine that the king provided because the food was forbidden by the dietary laws of Moses (Lev. 11) and the wine was forbidden by a divine command preserved in the Book of Proverbs (Prov. 23:31–35). If God had not stirred up sympathy in the heart of Daniel's overseer so that he made an exception for the Jewish boys, Daniel would certainly have lost his life (Dan. 1:5–16). Many years later, when Daniel came to the end of his career, the king decreed that for thirty days, no prayers should be raised except to himself, and Daniel again risked his life by doing what was right. He continued his practice of praying to God three times a day. As a result, he was arrested and cast into a den of lions. For a whole night he sat in foul, dark confinement surrounded by hungry beasts, yet an angel of God protected him. In the morning, the king found him unharmed (Dan. 6:4–23).

In Jesus' estimation, the greatest of all the prophets was John the Baptist (Matt. 11:11). Yet his greatness did not bring him the acclaim of men counted great by the world, but rather their hatred. When John denounced Herod for marrying his brother's wife, Herod imprisoned him. Later, at the instigation of this woman, named Herodias, Herod had John beheaded. He was killed while Herod was entertaining guests at a banquet, and his head was delivered to Herodias on a platter, as if it were just another course in the meal (Mark 6:21–28).

The sinner's hardness of heart. Why were the prophets hated? Because they told the people that God was angry with them. They challenged the self-satisfaction that all human beings use as a defense against guilt. The main message of the prophets was that Israel had angered God by forsaking Him and embracing the idols of the heathen. But the people were impressed by their heathen neighbors. They replied, why not worship gods that made their followers rich and strong? Besides, Jehovah was too demanding. Life was more fun without Him. When the prophets threatened judgment, the people rose up in rage against them and killed them. Usually among the chief instigators were the false prophets, who viewed their godly rivals as a threat to their lucrative business, pulling in good revenue by telling people what they wanted to hear.

The mentality of these people is exactly described by the title of a best-selling book some years ago: *I'm OK, You're OK.* To escape God's opinion of their sin, many men wrap themselves in denial and turn their fury on anyone who tells them the truth. They do not necessarily deny God's existence. Yet if they believe in God, they will recreate Him as a soft-hearted grandfather who thinks whatever they do is cute, or as a jolly Santa Claus who winks at whatever gives them pleasure. They set their own reflection in the place of God and give it a smiley face. They sing, "God bless America" when their wickedness has forfeited God's blessing. They reject any suggestion that God is holy, beyond compromise with sin, beyond sympathy with man's selfish ways. And anyone who tells them what God is truly like becomes a target.

How can any mortal man find the strength to stand in a prophet's role, in which he will inevitably suffer scorn, rejection, perhaps even death? John Bunyan, author of *Pilgrim's Progress,* was such a man. For him, the price of preaching the truth was to spend many years in jail, separated from his beloved wife and family. Let me quote one of Bunyan's poems illustrating how he encouraged himself in the Lord.

> Who would true Valour see
> Let him come hither;
> One here will Constant be,

Come Wind, come Weather.
There's no Discouragement,
Shall make him once Relent,
His first avow'd Intent,
To be a Pilgrim.

Who so beset him round,
With dismal Storys,
Do but themselves Confound;
His Strength the more is.
No Lyon can him fright,
He'l with a Gyant Fight,
But he will have a right,
To be a Pilgrim.

Hobgoblin, nor foul Fiend,
Can daunt his Spirit:
He knows, he at the end,
Shall Life Inherit.
Then Fancies fly away,
He'l fear not what men say,
He'l labour Night and Day,
To be a Pilgrim.

The example of Job. In commenting on all the terrible calami-
ties that befell the prophets, James says, "Behold, we count them
happy which endure" (v. 11a). Yet in any story of persecution to the
point of martyrdom, we find no evidence that the victim achieved
happiness. He suffered distress and pain even to the last moment of
life. If he won happiness by his endurance, he must have found it
beyond the grave. Then how can we know that happiness was indeed
his reward? Recognizing that our view is limited to this life, James
helps us to see the end of patient suffering by presenting the example
of Job (v. 11b). Here was a man who kept his heart right with God
even in the midst of heavy blows. God allowed Satan to cut off from
Job everything dear to him except his wife. In one day, Job lost all
his wealth to robbers and all his children to a great storm (Job 1:7–
22). Then a short time later, he succumbed to a horrible disease,
subjecting him to unrelieved pain (Job 2:1–8). Yet although his wife
tempted him to curse God and die, he refused (Job 2:9–10). At the
height of his troubles, he declared, "Though he [God] slay me, yet will
I trust in him" (Job 13:15). God was so pleased with Job that instead
of prolonging his ordeal until he died, He delivered and rewarded Job
while he still had many years of life remaining. Besides taking away
Job's disease, He replaced all his losses, to the extent of doubling his
material possessions and granting him and his wife as many new
children as the number who perished (Job 42:9–17).

God's purposes in suffering. James says that the case of Job demonstrates "the end of the Lord"; in other words, "the final result that the Lord intends when He permits a saint to go through suffering." For Job, the final result was to receive an outpouring of God's blessing. Every other saint going through a hard trial can look forward to the same outcome. When God is done accomplishing His purposes in the suffering, blessing will take its place.

What are God's purposes in allowing His children to suffer? He has many. Among them are the following:

1. Because the saints here below could not endure their suffering except by His grace, their endurance glorifies Him before the angels and the saints above.

2. Their endurance also silences the accuser, Satan, who argues that God's children love Him with a love too shallow to survive any hardship from His hand.

3. Trials refine the character of His children by increasing their patience and trust.

James reveals that in accomplishing all these purposes, God shapes our experience so that we come to a proper view of His character (v. 11c). We learn that although He has taken us through tough lessons good for us, He is not a grim schoolmaster, but a loving God. We see His love in two ways.

1. We see it when, either in life or in death, He delivers us from trouble and afterward heaps upon us great reward.

2. We also see it in the measure of suffering. He does not give us all the trouble that might serve a good purpose irrespective of our pleasure, but He cuts it short. He withholds the worst. Why? Because, "Like as a father pitieth his children, so the LORD pitieth them that fear him" (Ps. 103:13), or, as James says, "the Lord is very pitiful, and of tender mercy." Love shapes and limits and directs His intervention in our lives.

Self-Test

1. When I find myself in the midst of suffering, do I help myself endure patiently by studying and following the good example set by many saints of old?

The best place to look for these examples is in Scripture, which is profitable for "instruction in righteousness: That the man of God may be throughly furnished unto all good works" (2 Tim. 3:16–17). But also it is very helpful to read Christian biographies, especially those written in past generations. The subject of many recent biographies,

such as you find in a Christian bookstore, is not a real saint who exemplified a holy and sacrificial life, but a modern celebrity outstanding for fame and fortune rather than spirituality. Dig into older
Christian books if you want to be sure of spiritual blessing rather
than froth.

2. Do I measure my sufferings on the right scale—a scale comparing myself with past saints and martyrs?

On such a scale, do you see that God has visited others with far
greater suffering than you must endure? Do you praise Him for His
mercy to you? Whenever you feel sorry for yourself, try reading
Foxe's *Book of Martyrs.* Then you will see that the suffering God has
required of you is small change.

3. How well have I endured testing and trouble?

No doubt they have not destroyed your faith, or you would not be
reading this lesson. But have the troubles of life robbed you of the
enthusiasm you once felt for the things of God? Are you more distant
from God than you used to be? Do you fault God for weighing you
down with a greater burden than you can bear? Then stop trying to
carry it. Remember that He is willing to carry it for you. As the
psalmist says, "Cast thy burden upon the LORD, and he shall sustain
thee: he shall never suffer the righteous to be moved" (Ps. 55:22).

4. To encourage myself, do I keep my eyes on the rewards for endurance?

Whether we will receive them in this life or in the life to come, we
do not know. Scripture certainly authorizes us to hope and pray that
we, like Job, will see our sufferings lifted before we die (Ps. 90:14–16;
27:13). We should therefore comfort ourselves with the thought that
we may yet find a little space of peace and rest in this world, another
Beulah like the pleasant land that Pilgrim in *Pilgrim's Progress* en-
joyed before he crossed the great river. But even if we must fight the
good fight until the moment of death, we know that rewards await us
in the realm of the blessed. Besides saying much about God's goodness to His children in this world, the psalms also say much about
the delights we will know when we dwell in His presence forever (Ps.
16:11; 17:15; 30:5; 73:24–26). Consider also many other promises of
Scripture that our future beyond the grave will bring us happiness
worth any price of suffering now (Isa. 35:10; 25:8; Rev. 21:4).

5. Have I ever seen God's pity hold my trials in check?

In my wife's bout with cancer some years ago, we marveled at
how God strictly limited her ordeal. The cancer was found early

enough to be removed with little risk of recurrence. She escaped the need for chemotherapy. Before discovery of the cancer, she had gone on Medicare and supplemental health insurance that fully paid her expenses. God directed us to a surgeon who was a Christian. Though we lived in a rural area, a world-class radiologist was available nearby. The church volunteered to supply meals while she was undergoing radiation treatments. The list goes on. God is a merciful God even when our troubles rise to full measure.

Review Questions

1. What is James's first encouragement to people going through suffering?
2. What is his second encouragement?
3. Who are notable examples of endurance through suffering?
4. Tell what happened to Isaiah, Jeremiah, Daniel, and John the Baptist.
5. Why were the prophets hated?
6. Who suffered more than most and remained true to God?
7. What followed his suffering and follows the suffering of every saint?
8. What are three purposes in suffering?
9. What additional purpose does James emphasize?
10. In what two ways do we see God's love?

+ James 5:12 +

12 But above all things, my brethren, swear not, neither by heaven, neither by the earth, neither by any
other oath: but let your yea be yea; and *your* nay,
nay; lest ye fall into condemnation.

Lesson 28
Truthfulness

A truthful heart. At the outset of his epistle, when he is preparing us for the subjects he will treat, James makes it clear that one
of his chief objectives will be to draw the line between true religion
and hypocrisy. He wants those who claim the name of Christ to have
a religion that is not lip service, but heart devotion. They should not
only hear the Word "able to save your souls" (Jas. 1:21), but also put
it into practice by renouncing dead profession and embracing living
testimony (Jas. 1:22). He declares that one of the marks of hypocrisy
is an unbridled tongue (Jas. 1:26). In the main body of the epistle,
warnings against sins of the tongue are a main theme.

Then right before bringing his epistle to a close, James treats another form of sinful speech. He has not previously considered it, but
since his epistle draws heavily from the Sermon on the Mount, we are
hardly surprised that before finishing, he gives his attention to one of
its prominent topics. Jesus, in His exposition of the Ten Commandments, addresses the question of whether it is right to take an oath
(Matt. 5:33–37). His answer is the basis of verse 12, which is
James's nearest approach to an actual quotation from the Sermon on
the Mount. Although James gives us Jesus' teaching in a condensed
form, he exactly repeats some of the key wording.

Rather than comment on what James says, we will shift our attention to the fuller teaching that he summarizes. Jesus was shedding light on the Third Commandment: "Thou shalt not take the
name of the LORD thy God in vain" (Exod. 20:7). In Old Testament
times it was permitted to certify words of promise or testimony by
means of an oath. The primary meaning of the Third Commandment
is that an oath in the name of the Lord must be honored. To break a
solemn promise sealed with an oath or to give false testimony despite
an oath is to take His name in vain.

The Third Commandment is similar to the Ninth: "Thou shalt not
bear false witness against thy neighbor" (Exod. 20:16). Both prohibit
false statements: the first, any false statement backed by an oath; the
second, any false statement made to harm another person. The

Third and Ninth Commandments converge in condemning a witness in a formal judicial proceeding who tells lies after he has sworn to tell the truth. The fact that two of the Ten Commandments deal with truthfulness shows how important it is to God.

In recalling the teaching of the Old Testament (Matt. 5:33), Jesus chose not to quote the Third Commandment itself. Instead, He referred to some of the secondary laws intended to define specific violations. Yet what He said is not an exact quotation of any one in particular. Rather, He melded several (Lev. 19:12; Num. 30:2; Deut. 23:21) into a single concise prohibition. The mere fact that He freely edited the wording of the law was a claim of high authority.

In His treatment of the Third Commandment as in His treatment of the Sixth and Seventh (the commandments forbidding murder and adultery), Jesus sought to illumine the underlying moral principle. The principle obliging us to perform an oath is that we should be honest through and through. What God wants, Jesus implied, is truthfulness deeply lodged in the heart. Every small word we utter should be gold-plated truth. As Jesus said, our "yes" should mean "yes" and nothing else, and our "no" should mean "no" and nothing else (Matt. 5:37). If our promises are well known to be absolutely dependable, an oath adds nothing to what we say. Indeed, an oath cannot give us credibility if we have a reputation for lying.

Sticking to promises. The way of truthfulness often winds through tricky dilemmas. For example, what if you give your word, then change your mind? To say one thing today and another tomorrow is a form of dishonesty, even though what you say today is sincere. To change your mind after giving your word turns your word into a lie. You should be willing to keep your word despite the cost (Ps. 15:4).

Is it ever right to break a promise? We must define a promise. It is any commitment that, if not kept, will cause others to lose something. Asking the seller at a garage sale to hold an item until you come back with payment is a promise, because he may lose money if you fail to keep your word. Telling children that you will take them to the park on Saturday is a promise, because if you do not go, you will deprive them of a good time. But mentioning to your neighbor that you plan to shop for groceries tomorrow is not a promise, because whether you follow through has no effect on him.

So, we repeat. Is it ever right to break a promise? The most solemn of all, a vow to God, is inviolable. Scripture says plainly that if we make such a vow, we dare not fail to perform it; also, that to refrain from making it may be a better choice, because the vow will put us in a position of danger (Eccles. 5:1–7). If, in our feeble humanity, we forget it and let it go unfulfilled, we will offend God. Yet to shun vows altogether is not a good policy. The proper foundation of marriage, for example, is a vow of faithfulness.

What about a promise that is not a vow, strictly speaking? Is it ever right to break it? One kind should never be honored. You should never keep a promise that requires you to transgress the law of God. The need for this rule becomes obvious when we consider specific cases. If anyone agrees to help evil companions commit murder, he had better withdraw from the plot. If a young person is enticed by friends to swear that he will join some pursuit of sinful pleasure, he had better not go along with them. But if you break a promise to do wrong, you avoid the wrongdoing only by reneging on your word. You avoid the greater sin only by committing a lesser sin. You lose either way. So watch what you say.

How binding are other kinds of promises? Promises in the form of contracts are often necessary in the realm of work and business. What if the circumstances of life intervene and make it impossible for you to fulfill a contract? For example, a teacher who signs a contract for the coming year might be stricken by an illness that will sideline him before the year is finished. If the contract is well-written, such a contingency will be taken into account. But it may not be. Generally among Christians it is understood that contracts expire when over-ruled by events beyond anyone's control. The same escape clause may be explicit or implicit in many secular contracts. But to be safe—to protect yourself from falsehood when you sign a contract or give any other formal promise—sometimes the best solution may be to fill in the missing language; in essence, to attach the qualification, "Lord willing" (Jas. 4:15).

What about the lesser promises common to everyday life, such as the one we mentioned before—telling children that you will take them to the park on Saturday? What if the weekend brings severe weather? You should stay home, of course. It is then acceptable to go back on your word. Why? Because a promise of this kind should not be construed as an obligation to do what is unsafe or unwise. It is not a promise in the sense of a binding vow. It is really just a hopeful plan. Your children should be taught early in life that any such plan will be canceled if circumstances under God's control make it too risky or costly. Still, do not withhold something you promised your children just because it turns out to be inconvenient.

If we do not have moral freedom to change our word, what must we conclude? That we must be careful in giving our word. Do not bind yourself to any promise, do not give any advice, do not render any judgment, and do not make any commitment without first thinking through all the implications. Think before you speak. Do not say anything today that will make you uncomfortable tomorrow. Engage your mind, especially your common sense, before you limit your future to a course that can never be undone. In making deci-sions, do not let guesses and impressions and momentary feelings take the place of sound reasoning based on solid information.

The sins in swearing. Jesus did not teach that we should shun oaths as a matter of preference. Rather, He forbade them outright.

He said, "Swear not at all" (Matt. 5:34). He prohibited all swearing for several reasons including the following:

1. An oath in the form "by God" is presumptuous. It is essentially a plea that God will witness the oath and punish us if we do not keep our word. Children make the true meaning of their oaths explicit. They say, "Cross my heart and hope to die." But God does not want any man to ask for his own condemnation. We are to seek God's mercy.

2. An oath's wording is also a call for God to serve as witness. Thus, if we swear to a promise that is false or never fulfilled, we are lying to God Himself and inviting His judgment. The devil, knowing that failure to honor our word may bring us under divine wrath, seeks to trap us into oath-taking. This tactic of our enemy explains why Jesus said that anything more than "yes" or "no" comes "of evil" (Matt. 5:37); that is, from the evil one.

3. Jesus wanted us to distance ourselves from the Pharisees, who used oaths as a cover for lying. They taught that whether failure to perform an oath is a violation of the Third Commandment depends on the name called upon to witness and enforce the oath. It is a violation if the oath taker referred to God. It is not a violation if he referred to heaven, earth, Jerusalem, or one's head. Jesus pointed out that all these lesser things belong to God and are subject to His control (Matt. 5:34–36). Therefore, to name any of these in an oath is the same as naming God Himself.

Some Christians concerned to obey the prohibition against oath-taking have decided that in good conscience they cannot give pledges, such as the Scout pledge, the Pledge of Allegiance, or a pledge of marriage. But a pledge does not invoke the name of God. It is merely a solemn promise that we should not make unless we intend to keep it.

Even more Christians historically have refused to do the swearing required in certain legal ceremonies, such as the induction of a witness or juror to a trial in process or the inauguration of a government official. But the traditional form of the oath taken on these occasions sets it apart from a real oath. It is not a promise "by God" but "so help me God." This is merely a prayer for God's assistance in performing the promise.

Deception in warfare. Now that we have built a strong case for telling the truth, some reader might wonder whether Rahab, the harlot of Jericho, sinned when she lied to protect the two Israelite spies from being discovered and killed (Josh. 2). The short answer is that God has on occasion specifically authorized the use of deception in prosecuting a just war (Josh. 8:11–29; Judg. 7:15–25; 1 Chron. 14:13–16). It would be nonsensical ethics that permitted killing an enemy but forbade lying to him. Imagine saying to your enemy, "I cannot hurt you by telling you a lie, but I <u>can</u> shoot you."

Self-Test

1. Is my word so dependable that no one doubts it?

Or do you have a reputation for skimping on the truth? You may think that no one suspects you are a liar. But a law of human psychology is that a liar never recognizes the man who recognizes a liar. Just because a man does not call you to account for your lying does not mean that you have fooled him. A wise man in this sinful world learns to protect himself from liars by pretending not to notice, unless he can respond effectively. Indeed, a wise man follows God's example (Ps. 18:26). That is, although a wise man will not lie, he will not tell all his thoughts to someone he believes is a liar. Certainly he will not share his estimate of the other person unless such candor will accomplish something good.

To present a balanced picture, we must add that although you are responsible for your word, you are not responsible for whatever people might read into it. Others are sometimes not content with the ordinary meaning of what we do or say, so they imagine some additional meaning hidden below the surface.

Examples are a routine part of life. A girl thinks a boy is in love with her because he happened to say, "Hi." Before a church service, a boy thinks his two friends are trying to exclude him when they come in and sit by themselves on the other side. Actually, they do not see him.

There are two problems with reading motives into outward behavior. First, with no concrete supporting evidence, you have a flimsy case for assigning motives that you fear based on evil suspicion or that you desire based on wishful thinking. So, you are being unfair. Second, people are complex beings. Like everyone else, I have thoughts that others would never guess. The only way to discover them is by talking to me. The devil is a master of mind games, and the only way we can counter his constant work of creating false impressions and misunderstandings is through communication.

2. Do I keep my promises?

Or do you forsake them if they prove hard to carry through? Or do you conveniently forget them, so that your word changes from day to day? It is vital in dealing with children to keep your word so as to build their trust. The same is true for the adults you know. To gain their trust requires that you consistently follow up your promises with action.

3. Do I excuse myself for little white lies, so-called?

When someone you dislike calls on the phone, do you plead that you are just going out the door? White lies of this kind are commonplace because there is little fear of detection or reprisal. But besides being wrong in themselves, they corrupt your soul. They deaden your conscience against lying, and make it easier to tell big lies.

As we have said before, however, saying nice things to people about their appearance or performance is never lying if they are doing their best. Complimenting them is taking God's point of view. By human standards they may fall short, but God grades only for effort.

4. Do I cheat?

One form of cheating common in the world of professional writing is plagiarism. It is even more common in student papers. A typical student is so foolish as to assume that a veteran teacher cannot tell the difference between the prose of a published author and the prose of a C student in English. Even at the college level, I was continually catching students at plagiarism. Dealing with it wasted a considerable amount of my time.

5. Do I exaggerate?

I must confess that much of my humor, such as it is, is based on exaggeration. So I warn people, "The one time you need not believe me is when I am trying to be funny." Bending the truth to make a joke is known as comedic license. Exaggeration is not a form of lying so long as everyone understands that it is not meant to be taken seriously.

The time we are most inclined to exaggerate is when we are telling about our accomplishments. This kind of lying is called boasting, a sin that Scripture severely condemns (Rom. 1:28–30). Scripture says also that it will be a characteristic sin in the Last Days even among people who pretend to be religious (2 Tim. 3:1–2).

Some people doctor the facts on a resumé so they will appear more qualified for a job they are seeking. Resumé inflation has become a serious problem in America. The lesson for us? Never take a resumé at face value. Also, when you prepare a resumé, it is best to avoid suspicion by understating your credentials. Make no claim about yourself that cannot be documented.

6. Am I forthright?

If a man fails to tell his fiancée that he has been married before, he is lying to her, although she never dreams to question him about his marital history. It is lying to withhold information that someone has a right to possess.

7. Do I take oaths?

From the Sermon on the Mount, we learn that all oath-taking, as distinguished from a solemn pledge or a solemn request for God's help, is illegitimate. In our culture, oath-taking has become a rare practice except among children. Still, never let yourself be trapped into swearing on a stack of Bibles or anything else of like character.

8. Do I use minced oaths?

Minced oaths include all those expletives that appear to be innocuous in meaning, but derive from blasphemous expressions. "Gosh," "golly," "goodness," and "heaven" (as in "heavens" and "for heaven's sake") originated as substitutes for "God." "Oh dear," "dear me," "my," "oh my," and many others originated as substitutes for longer phrases containing His name. (My use of these terms is not immoral because, as a teacher of right conduct, I must make its boundaries clear.) "God damn" has become "goldarn" or just "darn." "Hell" has become "heck." The name of Jesus has been transmuted into such forms as "jee," "jeepers," "jee whizz" (which probably means "Jesus' wounds"), and "jiminy crickets" (which probably means "Jesus Christ"). It would not be edifying to list all the words people have invented in an attempt to swear in a socially acceptable manner. You may easily verify what I am saying by consulting a dictionary of slang.[91]

All these minced oaths seem to be disappearing, not because people today are more scrupulous, but because, on the contrary, people today have no qualms about using the real words instead of their substitutes. They feel no need to disguise holy or solemn words when they abuse them.

It is important to understand exactly why minced oaths are wrong. Most have nothing to do with oath-taking itself and are therefore not violations of Jesus' command, "Swear not at all" (Matt. 5:34). The term "swearing" expanded long ago to take in all foul language.

Some of the foulest language resorts to obscenities, perhaps in modified forms. These we have not included in our list, and we need not consider them, except to point out that Scripture forbids all manner of filthy speech (Eph. 5:4).

Terms like "hell" and "damn" and all their substitutes pronounce a curse, and cursing is wholly improper for God's children (Matt. 5:44; Jas. 3:8–10).

The most common use of minced oaths employing God's name in disguise is to express surprise or dismay. Yet to serve the same purpose, many people habitually speak His true name, whether in a proper form or in a cheapened form such as "Lordy." Such interjections are not swearing in the strict sense. Nor are they obscene. Nor are they cursing. Yet they are wrong, because they refer to God flippantly, with no real intent to give Him honor or to address Him in reverent and loving prayer. So they demean God's name by using it in vain, which is forbidden by the Third Commandment.

Review Questions

1. What teaching of Jesus does James virtually quote?
2. What shows the importance of truthfulness?
3. What is the moral principle underlying the Third Commandment?
4. What is the proper definition of a promise?
5. Is it ever right to break a promise?
6. What does Scripture teach concerning a vow?
7. What lesson should we draw from the necessity to keep our promises?
8. What is the first reason that swearing is wrong?
9. What is the second reason?
10. Why is the oath taken on certain formal occasions not a violation of Jesus' teaching?
11. Why was Rahab's lie justified?

13 Is any among you afflicted? let him pray. Is any merry? let him sing psalms.
14 Is any sick among you? let him call for the elders of the church; and let them pray over him, anointing him with oil in the name of the Lord:
15 And the prayer of faith shall save the sick, and the Lord shall raise him up; and if he have committed sins, they shall be forgiven him.
16 Confess *your* faults one to another, and pray one for another, that ye may be healed. The effectual fervent prayer of a righteous man availeth much.
17 Elias was a man subject to like passions as we are, and he prayed earnestly that it might not rain: and it rained not on the earth by the space of three years and six months.
18 And he prayed again, and the heaven gave rain, and the earth brought forth her fruit.

Lesson 29

The Prayer of Faith

Wholesome speech. Toward the end of his epistle, James abruptly shifts gears. He has brought his reader through several scathing attacks on ungodly and abusive speech. Now, as a sort of counterweight to all he has said before—as an addendum obviously intended to leave us with a balance of positives and negatives—he shows us the right way to use the human tongue. He recommends four kinds of speech in particular, all meeting God's approval because they are clean in their content and constructive in their effects. Each has a place in our lives, depending on the circumstances.

The first kind of wholesome speech is prayer for relief and deliverance when either oneself or one's brother is troubled by an affliction (v. 13a). The second, appropriate for expressing a glad heart bubbling over with merriment, is singing (v. 13b). The third is confession of sin (v. 16), and the fourth is godly counsel (vv. 19–20), which will be the subject of our next lesson.

Singing psalms. Let us take a closer look at each kind of speech pleasing to God. The second he introduces but the first we will consider is to "sing psalms" (v. 13). These two words in English render a single Greek word that in the New Testament refers generally to the singing of sacred songs, whether or not they are psalms in the strict

sense (1 Cor. 14:15; Eph. 5:19).[92] So, here is another instance of
James agreeing with Paul, who also urges the saints to sing. Singing
is so important that Paul wants the music to continue in their hearts
even when their lips are silent (Eph. 5:19; Col. 3:16). The command
to sing is prominent throughout the Psalms (Ps. 92:1–4; 147:1, 7).
Why does Scripture so strongly encourage singing? The basic reason
is that God Himself likes to hear it. Many activities that engage people now will cease when this world comes to an end, but singing will
go on forever. One of the few things we know about heaven is that
the saints will sing (Rev. 5:9; 14:3; 15:3). Their singing will be an
eternal delight to God, because it will render praise and love through
a mode of expression that is at once thoughtful, creative, and harmo-
niously beautiful. A singing congregation or choir is an exquisite
picture of relations within the body of Christ. Each voice submits to
a large plan for the smooth functioning of the whole. Yet the whole
derives its perfection from the unique contributions of individual
singers.

The church today is embroiled in controversy over what kind of
music is appropriate for Christian songs and hymns. We cannot
delve into a detailed discussion of music standards. But we can say
emphatically that the chief test of whether something is right is always how God Himself views it. When we discussed entertainment,
we said that our standard when evaluating a book or program or
movie should be whether Jesus would enjoy it. Likewise in the realm
of music, we need to seek God's opinion. He certainly has an opinion, for He is a musician and music critic of the highest order. Indeed, He is the very creator of music. Therefore, as far as we are
concerned, the right music should be whatever He likes. We can list
three kinds of music that unquestionably must be an offense to Him.

1. We can be sure that He does not like so-called Christian music
written primarily to make money rather than to glorify Him. When
Jesus found that commercialism had invaded the Temple, He drove it
out (John 2:13–17). Like all servants of God, a Christian musician is
entitled to support for his ministry. "The labourer is worthy of his
hire" (Luke 10:7). But accepting support is not the same as chasing
profits. Money-grubbing is the lifeblood of all contemporary Christian music (CCM) put out by secular corporations under the control
of unsaved board members.

2. We can be sure that God does not like music that denies truth
or debases things that are holy. In CCM, much is either doctrinally
off-base or morally off-color, and the name of Jesus is disappearing.
He is seldom if ever called Christ or Son of God.

3. We can be sure that God does not like music in a style derived
from nightclubs and other places where people gather for drunken
revelry in celebration of fleshly lust. That's the devil's music, not His.
The devil is also a musician (Ezek. 28:13–16). His music includes
anything that can be readily classified as jazz, pop, or rock.

Prayer for the afflicted. In verse 14, James returns to the first kind of wholesome speech, the kind seeking divine help when either oneself or one's brother is "afflicted." He now tells a believer what he should do if he is suffering one of the most common afflictions, which is bodily sickness. Here is a topic of great importance. Sickness plagues all mankind. Whatever sickness we have suffered in the past, we may suffer worse in the future. We need to know how to respond.

James advises any sick person that he should summon the elders of the church to pray over him and anoint him with oil in the name of the Lord. The grammatical construction suggests that the anointing should precede the praying. Several historic controversies have arisen from this verse. First, is James describing a procedure that the Lord intended for the church universal? In other words, are all churches everywhere and in every age obliged to handle sickness exactly as James prescribes? Second, what is the purpose of anointing with oil? Third, is it essential for success?

Some bodies of churches as well as some churches acting alone have decided that in cases of severe illness, they should follow the exact procedure laid out by James. The elders gather around the bed of a sick brother and pray for him after anointing him with oil. Most churches, however, have viewed James's procedure not as an obligation, but as an option. They reason that if it were an obligation, the New Testament would refer to it more than once. But Paul, the founder of the gentile churches, says nothing about it, although his letters are full of instruction spanning the whole gamut of doctrine and practice.

The impasse for most churches is the requirement to anoint with oil. James himself makes it quite clear that such an anointing is not what produces healing. Rather, healing comes by "the prayer of faith" (v. 15). So, if anointing is not the real instrument of healing, what is its purpose? We gain insight on the practice by looking at other Biblical references to it. Mark records that Jesus' disciples anointed the sick with oil before they healed them miraculously (Mark 6:13). Why did they do this? As the story of the Good Samaritan illustrates (Luke 10:30–36), anointing with oil was in Jewish culture considered a form of medical treatment.[93] We also find mention of the same practice in sources outside the New Testament.[94] We now understand why it was customary even for the disciples. In the work of healing, they relied both on natural remedies and on supernatural grace. That is, they took as much help as they could from ordinary medicine and called upon God to accomplish the rest. In this respect, they did just as we do today. We do not shun doctors and human devices. We use them, while depending on God not only to make them effective, but also to carry the healing beyond the best outcome possible by purely natural means.

Viewed in this way, the procedure James describes was

appropriate for the Jewish churches he was addressing, but it is not binding on us all. There is no harm in using it, especially if it tends to encourage faith. But it is better to draw from James's advice the appropriate application to our culture—that while relying upon prayer as the real instrument of healing, we should also use the best of modern medicine.

In the next verse, verse 15, James makes another statement which has fostered much controversy. He says, "And the prayer of faith shall save the sick, and the Lord shall raise him up." But the universal experience of Christians is that some of the sick among God's children will remain afflicted even after the church prays for them. So have we found a contradiction between promise and fact? No. The promise of healing here in James is not intended to be absolute. God has always performed mighty miracles of healing in response to prayers of faith, and he still performs them today, but whether He grants healing is subject to four conditions. What are they? The first two we surmise from James's own discussion.

Confession of sin. James says that if the sick person "have committed sins, they shall be forgiven him" (v. 14). Steeped in the Old Testament, James knows that sickness is often God's tool of judgment in the lives of believers as well as unbelievers. King Ahaziah, a rebel against the God of Israel, did not recover from his sickness because he sought help from the false god Baal (2 Kings 1:16). But also King Uzziah, a follower of the true God, was stricken with leprosy because he tried to usurp the privileges of a priest (2 Chron. 26:16–21). In the New Testament, Paul reaffirms that a believer's sickness may come from God's chastening hand (1 Cor. 11:29–30).

Yet every sickness is not the result of sin. James agrees, for he says, "if he have committed sins" (v. 15), implying that sin might or might not be at the root of the sickness. It was the habit of the Jews to see divine judgment behind all the troubles of life, but Jesus rebuked them for being simplistic (John 9:2–3). He pointed out that these troubles can have other causes, such as God's intent to glorify Himself by showing His hand of deliverance.

But if sickness comes as a punishment from God, the church cannot reasonably expect Him to heal the sick person so long as he persists in his sin. Any prayer for healing, however fervent and full of faith, will be ineffectual. James therefore says, "Confess your faults one to another, and pray one for another, that ye may be healed" (v. 16). He is stating the first condition for healing. If the sickness is God's chastening for sin, the sin must be confessed and put away.

Confession of sin is the third kind of wholesome speech. Why does James specify confession "one to another"? Is it not enough to confess our sins to God? James is holding to the perspective expressed elsewhere in his epistle. Often he has reminded us that many sins characteristic of believers are violations of the royal law, the law requiring us to love our brother as ourselves. When we sin against our brother, we cannot make it right just by apologizing to God. We must exercise some practical humility by going to our offended brother and apologizing to him. We must confess our fault to the one we have harmed.

Energetic prayer. In verse 16, James states a second condition that must be met before God will consent to a prayer for healing. It must be "the effectual fervent prayer of a righteous man." This condition combines two requirements.

1. The prayer must be "effectual fervent." The translation here rests on a single Greek word, which is the root of the English word *energy*.[95] Prayer will avail only when it is energetic both in intensity and in perseverance.

2. The prayer must rise from the lips of a righteous man. The futility of prayer when the petitioner has sin in his heart is a common teaching of Scripture (Ps. 66:18; Isa. 59:1–2; Mic. 3:4).

Thus, to pray successfully for healing, we must first cleanse our hearts of sin that will obstruct our access to God, and we must dedicate ourselves to praying with energy. The casual prayer of a carnal Christian will bounce off the ceiling.

It may seem to us that God is asking more than we can do. He wants energetic prayer, yet, like the disciples who went with Jesus to the Garden and fell asleep instead of praying for Him, we are lacking in energy. As Jesus said to them, "The spirit indeed is willing, but the flesh is weak" (Matt. 26:41). James therefore reminds us of Elijah. Although he too was a creature of flesh, "subject to like passions as we are," he met the requirements of effective prayer (vv. 17–18) and through prayer accomplished great wonders. He stopped rain from falling upon Israel for three and a half years. Then he made the rain to resume. His human limitations did not keep him from being righteous enough and fervent enough to win God's assent to his requests.

When reminding us of how Elijah stopped the rain, James's point is not that we should wield the power of faith as a weapon against our enemies. The New Testament gives us no warrant to call down divine judgment upon them. Rather, we should ask God to bless them, and the blessing we seek should be broad in scope. We should want them to enjoy not only spiritual enlightenment, but also provision of material needs. If we make rain an issue of prayer, we should seek it for all men, thus emulating God Himself, who "sendeth rain on the just and on the unjust" (Matt. 5:44–45).

Thorn in the flesh. By comparing Scripture with Scripture, we learn the third condition for healing. God will not remove an affliction that yields spiritual benefits. He left the thorn in Paul's flesh to keep him humble and to assure his dependence on divine power (2 Cor. 12:7–9). Because he had been granted visions of Christ and heavenly glory, Paul was vulnerable to pride, and because of his natural abilities, he was tempted to serve God in the power of his own flesh.

If you read Christian biographies, you will discover that many other giants of the faith also suffered a chronic affliction which God refused to take away. C. T. Studd, pioneer missionary to Africa, endured chronic and severe gall bladder attacks even as he tramped through the jungles. He never learned the cause until a doctor diagnosed his condition as he lay on his deathbed.[96] Amy Carmichael, rescuer of so many abused children in India and founder of the mission work known as the Dohnavur Fellowship, spent almost twenty years as an invalid, seldom leaving her room.[97]

Why did God so limit her life? I think the reason is that she was an outstanding poet.[98] Although her work never won general acclaim even among Christians, God must have liked it, else why did He confine her to a life that did not permit her to do much except write poetry?

Thorns in the flesh are seldom fatal. Their purpose is not to shorten life, but to guarantee useful, God-dependent service. So, their ultimate effect may be to lengthen life.

Sickness unto death. There is yet a fourth condition for healing. None of us can escape the last sickness in life, the one leading to death. Death is an inescapable curse upon sinful humanity. Before we pray for a Christian on the verge of death, we should examine his prospects in the light of Paul's dilemma described in Philippians 1:23–24. Paul knew that it was better for the churches he founded if they remained under his care, yet it was better for him to depart and be with Christ. The lesson for us is that if age and infirmity have so impaired a saint that he has neither the power to serve God in an active ministry nor the capacity to enjoy his days on earth—or if there is another consideration perhaps known only to God that overrules prolonging his life—then it is better for the saint to graduate to a higher existence, surrounded by light, bathed in love, and filled with joy. We can pray for his healing, yet we should leave the decision with God, for only He can calculate whether it is better for the saint to stay or to depart.

For a saint of God, death comes when God determines that the time is right. It does not simply depend on the person's state of health. It depends rather on what God decides is best for him and for the work of God. Matters of life and death always show His boundless wisdom.

Self-Test

1. When I am happy, do I sing praise to God?

Happiness might be defined as joy not confined to a moment, but prolonged, and joy might be defined as a feeling generated by pleasant thoughts, such as a coming marriage or the nearing birth of a child. One of the benefits in joy is that pleasant thoughts are not only its input, but its output as well. Always the thought that should chiefly issue from joy is gratitude for the goodness of a loving heavenly Father.

Always a good way to express joy is through singing. But many do not sing when they are happy because they never sing. What a shame to miss the gladness in singing! To sing, you need not be especially musical. The great blessing in lack of musical talent is that you will never know just how bad your singing sounds to a fussy musician. Be assured, though, that it sounds good to God, because he judges us not by our talent but by our heart attitude.

2. When I am overwhelmed by affliction, do I pray?

Or does the affliction so absorb your thoughts that you forget about God. It is true that when pain strikes, it is hard to think about anything else. But then, when you need God more than ever, do not push Him away. Rather, bring Him close through earnest prayer. It is always appropriate to pray for your own needs (Phil. 4:6,19).

3. Do I pray fervently for the healing of other saints when they are overtaken by sickness?

James commands, "Pray one for another, that ye may be healed" (v. 16). The prayer list at church has a purpose. You are expected to take it home and use it as a guide to your prayers.

4. When I am sick, do I inform the church so that they can pray for me?

The church wants to know. You may dislike attention because it makes you feel embarrassed, but do not deprive the church of an opportunity to pray for you. Helping you through prayer and other kinds of ministry is good for the church and good for you, because it strengthens ties in the body of Christ.

5. Do I wrestle with God to show me the reason for my sickness?

Unless you do, you will not discover whether it is a judgment upon sin.

6. If I learn that I have contracted a sickness because I have

stubbornly refused to deal with sin, do I take the right steps to clear myself?

Do you seek God's forgiveness and forsake the sin? If you have offended a brother, do you seek to mend the torn fabric of your relationship

7. Do I have a thorn in my side?

If you do, do you accept it as graciously as Paul did? Do you have his determination to reap the spiritual benefits, such as humility and dependence on God?

Review Questions

1. What is the first kind of wholesome speech?
2. Why is singing important?
3. What kind of music does God not like?
4. What is the second kind of wholesome speech?
5. Why did James advise anointing with oil?
6. What is the first condition that must be met for healing?
7. What is the third kind of wholesome speech?
8. What is the second condition that must be met for healing?
9. What is the third?
10. What is the fourth?

✛ James 5:19–20 ✛

> 19 Brethren, if any of you do err from the truth, and
> one convert him;
> 20 Let him know, that he which converteth the sinner
> from the error of his way shall save a soul from
> death, and shall hide a multitude of sins.

Lesson 30
Converting a Brother

Fourth kind of wholesome speech. In the closing verses of his epistle, James ceases to warn against worldliness, love of riches, destructive speech, and other evils. Instead of chiding hypocrites for all the sins showing that their faith is dead, he describes how believers can demonstrate that their faith is alive. Since speech has been one of his themes, he concentrates on speech again, this time by urging spiritual uses of the tongue. Four in particular he recommends: praying when we are afflicted, singing when we are merry, confessing our faults when we have sinned, and, in the last verses, converting a brother when we find that he has gone astray (vv. 19–20).

The term "convert" in the KJV does not bear the familiar modern sense. We limit its meaning to winning a soul for Christ. But the Greek word that James uses means simply to "turn around."[99] The scenario he has in mind is a brother who wanders from the truth until another brother turns him back onto the right path. By "brother," James means, of course, either a brother or a sister. Likewise throughout his epistle, the brethren are the whole family of God, both men and women.

To the believer who is willing to neglect his own affairs so that he might restore his brother at whatever cost of time and loss of convenience, James offers two great rewards. Both raise significant questions, which have divided commentators down through the centuries.

Saving a soul from death. The first reward he promises is that the helpful brother will "save a soul from death" (v. 20). Clearly, the wayward person is a believer also, for James says, "Brethren, if any of you do err from the truth." What then does he mean by death? Jesus said, "And fear not them which kill the body, but are not able to kill the soul: but rather fear him which is able to destroy both soul and body in hell" (Matt. 10:28). Based on this and similar texts, we normally equate death of a soul with eternal condemnation. So, is James teaching that a believer can lose his salvation if he continues unrepentant in sin and rebellion? The answer must be, "No," for regeneration and the other consequences of salvation are irreversible. The impossibility of losing salvation is affirmed by the doctrine known as eternal security, commonly summarized as, "Once saved, always saved." Since many have cited this text in James when arguing against eternal security, we will briefly show that the doctrine has a solid Biblical basis.

We cannot doubt that God has promised to save all who believe. This is the message of more texts than we could list here, the most familiar perhaps being John 3:16: "For God so loved the world, that he gave his only begotten Son, that whosoever believeth in him should not perish, but have everlasting life." Notice that all who believe "have [present subjunctive[100]] everlasting life." Everlasting life is the present possession of anyone who meets the condition of believing. In other words, if you believe in Jesus, you have unending life now. But to say that you have it now would not be true if you could lose it in the future. If you could ever cross over some boundary of permissible sin into impermissible sin, causing you to forfeit your salvation, then all the benefits you enjoy now, including new life in Christ, might be of temporary duration. They could not be described as everlasting. But since your life now is nothing other than everlasting, you know that your salvation is secure forever.

The permanence of salvation is a corollary of the power and love of God.

God's power. To comfort His disciples lest they fear for their eternal security, Jesus taught them, "My sheep hear my voice, and I know them, and they follow me: And I give unto them eternal life; and they shall never perish, neither shall any *man* pluck them out of my hand" (John 10:27–28). His sheep clearly represent all who believe, including ourselves. The promise means that He holds us with a determination never to let go, and with a strength that cannot be overcome by anyone who might want to snatch us away. "Man" is italicized because it is not in the original. Our chief enemy is not a man but Satan, so Jesus was assuring us that we are safe even from Satan's power. No one, not even Satan, can rob us of our salvation.

Then Jesus said, "My Father, which gave *them* me, is greater than all; and no *man* is able to pluck *them* out of my Father's hand" (John 10:29). Who then is holding us, the Son or the Father? Jesus' answer was, "I and *my* Father are one" (John 10:30). In other words, they are one God. The persons of the Trinity, each being infinite in power and knowledge, cannot do otherwise than work together in perfect cooperation. Thus, we are held jointly by the Father and the Son. The wording suggests that when the Father gave us to the Son, He Himself did not let go of us. We are now in the hands of both.

Jude also speaks of God's power to guard our salvation, but he is primarily thinking about His power not against our enemies, but against our own weakness and frailty: "Now unto him that is able to keep you from falling, and to present you faultless before the presence of his glory with exceeding joy" (Jude 24). The writer assures all among "you" that God will keep them from plunging into soul-damning sin. Exactly who belongs to this group? Jude begins his epistle by addressing "them that are sanctified by God the Father, and preserved in Jesus Christ" (Jude 1). "Sanctified" means set apart unto holiness through the work of the Holy Spirit at salvation.[101] Then he says that he is writing to them "of the common salvation" (Jude 3), thus emphasizing that salvation is what he and his readers share. So, the promise of security from falling that we find in verse 24 applies to all who are presently saved. Verse 1 reinforces this conclusion by treating preservation as the natural, inevitable consequence of sanctification.

From Jude we therefore gain a fuller understanding of Jesus' promise that once we are in the hand of God, no one can remove us. The potential threats He considered must have included the believer himself, for Jude teaches that we cannot remove ourselves from God's hand. We are not strong enough to get out. Thus, we cannot lose our salvation even if we sin.

God's love. If we could lose our salvation, God would be a poor father even by human standards. We as human parents do not disown our children should they happen to disobey us. If we did, the streets would be full of homeless urchins. Instead, we persist as long as possible in every measure that might help our children do right.

What we can do for our children is limited, however. What God can do for His children is unlimited. There is no sin that a wayward child of God can commit that his infinite, all-powerful Father cannot correct and eliminate by means of chastening. Thus, since God our Father is perfect in love (Ps. 103:13; Heb. 12:6), He will, if we do wrong, chasten us rather than eject us from His family. We cannot do anything foolish or sinful enough to forfeit our salvation.

The death facing the sinner. Then what does James mean when he says that someone who graciously intervenes to restore a sinning brother will save a soul from death? We must remember that behind James's words lies the background of his own experience. He was one of the original members of the church in Jerusalem. In its early days, God was jealous of its purity and took strong measures against sin. He struck down both Ananias and Sapphira when they had done no worse than exaggerate the generosity of their giving. After selling a piece of land, they said they contributed the entire proceeds to the church when in fact they contributed only a portion (Acts 5:1–11).

God's stern policy toward stubbornly wayward believers prevailed also in the churches that Paul established. Paul informed the Corinthians that God had dealt death to some who came with frivolous and unworthy hearts to the Lord's Supper (1 Cor. 11:29–30).

How thankful we can be that God is seldom so severe in our day!

Yet even now, God may take the life of a believer who commits gross sin or who refuses to repent of lesser sin. James undoubtedly saw death in this sense as the ultimate result of being disobedient. Therefore, the kind of death that he intends in verse 20 is cessation of life in this world. He calls it the death of a soul because the term "soul" is simply a common synonym for "living being" (Rom. 13:1; Acts 27:37; 2:41; etc.). John, another apostle of the early church, also viewed bodily death as a judgment that may befall a believer (1 John 5:16–17).

Covering a brother's sins. The second reward James promises to the helpful brother is that he "shall hide a multitude of sins" (v. 20). "Hide" is better translated "cover," with the meaning that he secures forgiveness for them.[102] The debated question is whether the helpful brother covers his own sins or the sins of the erring brother. The best answer is that James is primarily referring to the sins of the brother he has just called a sinner. Such a man cannot return from his wrong direction except by repentance, and one assured result of his repentance will be the forgiveness of his sins. James sees this as a benefit not only to the sinner, but also to the brother who assisted him, for indeed his act of love will earn an eternal reward. Scripture teaches that special rewards await anyone who has turned "many to righteousness" (Dan. 12:3).

Our interpretation of James's second promise finds support in other Biblical texts. The wording "hide [or cover] a multitude of sins" recalls Proverbs 10:12: "Love covereth all sins," or, as restated by Peter, "Charity shall cover the multitude of sins" (1 Pet. 4:8). Doubtless this is the source of James's words at the close of his epistle. The original proverb has several levels of meaning. One is that love is willing to overlook great imperfection in its object—that love is not conditional upon its object being sinless. Another is that love is always ready to forgive. Either way, the sins under consideration belong not to the loving brother, but to the sinning brother. We may assume that when James recalls this proverb, the sins he has in mind preserve the same sense.

The last two verses of James are in many ways a fitting climax to the whole epistle. One of its themes has been the proper use of our tongues. Another has been the royal law, the law requiring that we love our neighbor and our brother as ourselves. Now, at the end of his discourse, he promotes the use of our tongues that most directly fulfills the royal law. What is the occasion? It is a brother straying from the truth. What is the purpose? It is to save him from terrible consequences, even death. What is the right method of help? It is speech, specifically in the form of exhortation. What is the motive? It is love and only love, for without love there would be no reason to help him. Such speech is therefore a perfect illustration of the brotherly love that is a special virtue of the church and of believers filled with the Holy Spirit.

The last verses are a fitting climax also because the author here unwittingly proves the great value of the book he has written. What has James been seeking to accomplish throughout his letter if not to turn sinners from the error of their way? Down through the centuries, the number who have read his warnings and taken them to heart must be legion. Therefore, the blessings that he promises the person who restores a fallen brother or sister have accrued perhaps in greatest measure to James's own account. Yet we need not suppose that James means to congratulate himself. The reason he appeals so effectively for humility is doubtless that he was a humble man (Jas. 4:6). So, it is most unlikely that when he wrote the final verses, he saw himself as the best example of the good deed he commends. In fact, however, the verses are nothing less than a tribute to James. They appear as the closing benediction in his epistle because the Holy Spirit who inspired it wanted to exalt in our eyes the sweet and selfless younger brother of our Lord.

Self-Test

1. Have I ever interrupted my own life in order to rescue a fallen brother or sister?

When you notice that someone has stopped coming to church, do you—by a call, visit, e-mail, text message, or note on Facebook—encourage him to return? If you hear that a fellow believer is on the verge of a major life decision that will lead to disaster, do you offer loving counsel to trust not in human judgment, but in God's plan for his life? Our example for loving intervention is the woman who swept her house for the lost coin and the shepherd who left the ninety and nine in search of the lost sheep (Luke 15:4–10). Although these two parables primarily show God's diligence to reclaim a child gone astray, they are equally fitting as stories of a Christian who serves as God's instrument in the same noble work. At the climax of both, Jesus reminds us that when a sinner is converted, the very halls of heaven ring with rejoicing.

Yet although we are to intervene to help a wayward brother, we are not to be busybodies (1 Pet. 4:15). Where exactly is the line between helpful involvement and counterproductive interference? You are a busybody if your initiative fails any of the following tests:

1. Is your involvement based on gossip or guessing rather than certified truth? You always need to start with a sympathetic hearing of your brother's side of the story.

2. Does your involvement cause you to violate a confidence?

3. Will you approach your brother with a judgmental, Pharisaical

spirit? You cannot help him unless you first humbly recognize that you too are a sinner.

4. Are you presuming to know God's leading in another person's life? The principle of soul liberty, widely held by modern Bible-believing churches, affirms that every believer has the right to determine God's will for his own life. The reason is that God guides a mature believer by speaking to him, no one else. The only time you have a right to challenge another person's leading is when it clearly violates Scripture or mature wisdom. For example, back in the '70s I went to a Christian school convention where I met a man who belonged to a Christian commune. It was entirely proper for me to point out that what they were doing was not, as they believed, the practice of the early church.

2. Have I ever doubted my salvation?

When you fail God, the first fiery dart Satan will throw at you is the accusation that you are not saved, for how could a child of God behave so miserably? Just do what you would do if you deeply offended your human father. You would, I hope, go to him with remorse on your face, and you would profusely apologize. So also when you have scorned the will of your Heavenly Father, you should go to Him with sincere sorrow for your sins and ask His forgiveness. His smile of love will then drive away all doubts of your salvation.

3. Do I comprehend how bad sin is—that in a believer it can bring the judgment of death?

Read the sobering account of Ananias and Sapphira's sin (Acts 5:1–11). It will startle you into intensifying the war against your own sins.

4. Do I have enough love in my heart to fulfill Peter's recommendation to forgive the multitudinous sins of others?

When you view these sins, do you minimize them, or do you maximize them? It always helps to realize that people looking at you probably also see a multitude of sins. Why should you, a capital sinner yourself, get huffy when you notice that others are not perfect either? If you graciously overlook their imperfections, perhaps they will overlook yours as well, and the result will be an atmosphere of forbearance and love that makes the church a delightful place for everyone.

5. Have I learned to fully appreciate the authority of James's epistle?

Aside from Mary and Joseph, the person best acquainted with Jesus during His earthly years was probably James. James's epistle displays a striking familiarity with Jesus' mind and a profound grasp of Jesus' teachings. Even his style, beautifully concise and poetic, is modeled after Jesus' sayings.

This should come as no surprise. James was the slightly younger brother of Jesus. For years they were companions in work and play and every other realm of life. They slept near each other on the same floor, sat together when the family gathered in a circle on the mat where they shared meals, washed with water from the same pitcher, and kept each other's company when the family traveled to feasts in Jerusalem. Hardly a day passed when James did not walk in Jesus' footsteps and listen to the words coming from His mouth. The truths that Jesus taught later in life were no doubt taking shape throughout His childhood, and James may often have been the first to hear them. Perhaps on occasion he and his brother discussed privately what Jesus was thinking.

For a while in his adulthood, James turned away from following Jesus, perhaps because he had always been a little jealous of his older brother so free of faults, and this jealousy suppressed faith, but when Jesus came to him personally after the Resurrection and cast His divine love upon him, James's natural affection for Jesus was restored in full measure and given another dimension, as he gladly accepted his new role as Jesus' humble servant.

Review Questions

1. What is the fourth kind of wholesome speech?
2. What does Scripture mean when it speaks of converting a brother?
3. How does John 3:16 promise eternal security?
4. What is the first guarantee of eternal security?
5. How do John 10:28–30 and Jude 24 provide the same assurance?
6. What is the second guarantee of eternal security?
7. From what death can a wayward brother be saved?
8. What sins are covered by helping a wayward brother?
9. For what first reason is the promise of covering sins a fitting climax to James's epistle?
10. What is another reason?

+ Appendix 1 +

The Cornerstones of Modern Thought

The three cornerstones of modern thought—evolutionism, pragmatism, and relativism—are all equally impossible to maintain in the light of logic and evidence.

Evolutionism is broader than just the theory of evolution. It involves also the idea that man is progressing to a higher level, and that more advanced beings already exist out in the universe. The theory of evolution is, of course, nothing but mythology for the masses. The really smart people in the world, especially in fields based on biochemistry, have known for at least forty years that complex life forms did not arise by chance. They may believe in some sort of evolution, but they know that evolution by chance is impossible. They are not broadcasting their conclusions to the general public, however, either for fear of censure by their colleagues or for fear of provoking a revival of old-fashioned religion. In their personal views, most have retreated to a worldview that recognizes some sort of higher being or beings.

We mentioned in lesson 8 that the British philosopher Antony Flew, long a well-known spokesman for atheism, abandoned this position some years ago in light of modern discoveries showing the complexity of the living cell. But instead of becoming a Christian, he at first, as we said, "resurrected the eighteenth-century philosophy known as deism, which believed that after God created the universe, He took no further interest in it." But deism is riddled with so many problems that after it arose in the eighteenth century, it did not last long as a popular philosophy. For example, it is naïve to suppose that a universe whose origin depends on a Creator could continue to exist without the Creator's sustaining power.

Another famous scientist who scorned evolution by chance was the physicist and cosmologist Sir Fred Hoyle. His close associate Chandra Wickramasinghe, also a physicist, said, under oath at a trial concerning the constitutionality of a law requiring balanced treatment of evolutionism and creationism in public schools, that the probability of life accidentally emerging from nonlife was comparable to the probability of a tornado sweeping through a junkyard and assembling a Boeing 747.[103] In a book coauthored by Hoyle and Wickramasinghe, they pointed out that the chance development of even a single polypeptide useful to life is absurdly small.[104]

As a scholar whose professional publications are in the field of statistics, I wholeheartedly agree. Origin-of-life studies have failed to demonstrate any natural process for building proteins. Besides, all viable proteins contain only left-handed amino acids. I have written a paper showing that the chance of nature constructing any single viable protein is therefore virtually zero, even if a natural process for building proteins existed. The chance of getting two proteins compatible with each other is incalculably even smaller, and the chance of getting a whole workable unit is, well, so ridiculously small as to confound measurement. And even if the impossible happened and such protolife emerged somewhere in an otherwise dead world, it would be quickly destroyed by natural processes of degradation.[105]

But Hoyle, although he saw the foolishness in chance evolution, was another scientist who did not turn to Bible religion as the obvious alternative. Instead, he offered a theory called Panspermia to explain life in our world. This theory is not science, however, but essentially a retreat to Eastern mysticism. We might even characterize it as a Westernized form of Hinduism or Buddhism. Wickramasinghe, Hoyle's coauthor for the book presenting Panspermia, came from a Buddhist background.[106] The worldview of these two physicists is Western in the sense that they imagine an ascending series of intelligent beings above man with God at the highest level, yet Eastern in the sense that they define God as the universe itself.[107] Use of the personal name "God" strongly suggests that they regard the universe as a person, at least to the extent of possessing a mind. Given Hoyle's long commitment to steady-state cosmology, which views the universe as essentially unchanging, we may suppose that he and his colleague believe that this divine person is eternal and self-existing, like the God of Christians. One critical difference is that whereas the god of Hoyle and Wickramasinghe is identical to the universe, the Christian God exists above, before, and beyond it as well as within it. He is both transcendent and immanent.

The most glaring implausibilities in how Hoyle and Wickramasinghe conceive of God are these:

1. To imagine that the universe has always existed neglects the overwhelming observable evidence that it is in decay.

2. If the universe is a person, we cannot reasonably account for its behavior. It has a moral complexity never found in the character of a single being. Both good and evil exist in extremes pointing to sources who passionately love the one and hate the other. But to simultaneously bear intense love and intense hate for the same object is impossible for a single person.

Still another scientist who turned against old-fashioned Darwinian evolution, supposing that the only creator is natural forces, was Francis Collins, for many years the head of the Human Genome Project. In his book discussing the significance of recent advances in knowledge, he admitted that anything as complex and sophisticated as the genetic code could not originate by chance. It is essentially a language, whose inventor must be an intelligent being. Indeed, he felt constrained by common sense to describe the genetic code as the language of God.[108] But although Collins rejected the gods of deism and mysticism, he could not bring himself to recommend the God of the Bible. Instead, he adopted the position known as theistic evolution, which affirms that the ascent of life forms from simple to complex took place through long ages, just as evolutionists have always believed, but which also affirms, contrary to their belief, that this ascent was not simply the work of chance. It was the fulfillment of a divine plan. God made it happen.[109]

But my reply is to warn you of the alarming implications if theistic evolution is the right interpretation of the world's past. It leaves us with a god whose idea of a good world is one of constant violence, bloodshed, and suffering. (The rich and powerful have no trouble drawing out the lesson for them—that bloodshed and violence are legitimate tools for advancing their agenda). But to conceive of god in this manner creates a huge problem. My own conscience tells me that constant violence, bloodshed, and suffering are not good. They are not the natural features of a good world, but the symptoms of an evil world. Where did my conscience come from? If this universe is under divine management, as Collins admits, my conscience must come from God, my Creator. Why would He give me a conscience that finds fault with His own idea of what is good? No, the more logical position is that my conscience reflects God's character. It is therefore impossible that the true God would have used the ruthless mechanics of evolution to accomplish His purposes.

All these alternatives to Darwinian evolution that we see emerging among well-informed scientists today are just as untenable as the theory they reject. In their desperation to escape from Christianity, they are running to worldviews full of contradictions and wild fantasies. Against evolutionism, the Bible teaches that God created the universe a few thousand years ago. If you are swift to hear, you will open your mind to this teaching. It is all right to respond with many questions, but then it is your duty to do the necessary reading and research to find satisfying answers, and I guarantee you that they exist.

The second cornerstone of modern thinking is pragmatism, which is the belief that nothing in itself is absolutely right or wrong. It depends on the situation. Of course, pragmatism is a simple deduction from evolutionism. If there is no God and man is basically an animal, moral values reduce to self-interest. The only right thing is whatever you can get away with in defense of your own survival or in pursuit of your own happiness. The funny thing about pragmatism is that nobody believes it. If you take any self-proclaimed pragmatist and step really hard on his toes, what will he do? He will loudly protest, in no uncertain terms, that you did wrong, meaning "wrong" in an absolute sense.

The third cornerstone of modern thinking is relativism, the belief that all truth is relative. From this belief comes the claim that all religions are equally valid.   The problem in this claim is that the different world religions all contradict each other.   None agrees with the fundamentals of Christianity.   So are these fundamentals true or false?   You cannot have it both ways.   Either Jesus rose from the dead or He did not.   If He did not, there is no reason to be a Christian.   If He did, there is no reason to be anything else.

+ Appendix 2 +

The Sins in Gossip

In lesson 11 we outlined the right way to deal with problems. Here let us consider further a wrong way that is sadly very prevalent: gossip. True gossip, lurking in the shadows with evil accusations, is wrong for many reasons.

1. It is unloving. As we have already stressed, the Lord has told us exactly what to do if we spot a flaw in a fellow believer. The course of love in compliance with the Lord's guidelines is to confront our brother with a gentle and kind rebuke. Then he can defend himself if he is innocent or correct himself if he is guilty. If he refuses to correct himself, we can bring in others to help us deal with his sin. But he should always be the first to hear our criticism. Never should we who are adults go instead to a third party, even a pastor. And never should we soak up and circulate a complaint about our brother that he himself has never heard. These violations of the Lord's guidelines are simply gossip, and gossip is unloving, because it treats someone in a way that we ourselves would never want to be treated. It trashes the Golden Rule.

2. It is probably untrue. It tells only one side of the story, so it is not free of the accuser's own bias. Indeed, even though it sounds absolutely convincing, it may be altogether false, perhaps because it springs from a hidden agenda. Whether it is no worse than being one-sided, or at the other extreme it is nonsense from start to finish, or it is something in between, gossip is nearly always a form of lying.

When doing marital counseling, I never ceased to marvel at the different pictures a husband and wife might give me of their marriage. Each one might be a saint in his own eyes, a monster in the eyes of the other. Who was telling the truth? Often both were lying for selfish purposes.

Sometimes untrue words have a less sinister origin. They may, for example, be words of rumor, full of wild distortion because they were born in imagination and slightly modified at each retelling. Some years ago on a night set aside at our church for family fun, we were forced inside by rain, and one of my little grandsons cuddled up to me and began to cry. He had heard from some other child that a tornado was coming. It was a false report with no basis whatever, so I used the incident to warn him against rumors.

In matters of public opinion, skepticism is often the shortcut to truth. Yet people when they hear gossip are prone to think that it must have some basis in truth or it would never have begun to circulate. Where there's smoke, there's fire. But that sort of thinking is inexcusably naïve. This is a world whose prince is the father of lies (John 8:44).

3. It is unjust. At the heart of our judicial system are three principles of justice: 1) a man is innocent until proven guilty, 2) a man accused has the right to present the best possible case in his own defense before a neutral judge or jury, and 3) a man accused has the right to confront and cross-examine his accusers. Except where these principles are honored, judgment should be withheld. Yet gossip scorns them all. Needless to say, the standard of justice among Christians should be no less demanding than that upheld by secular law.

Gossip is like a beast lurking in the shadows because there it has the best chance of survival. The accused is so often denied a chance to speak for himself because otherwise the conversational life of many people would suddenly become rather dull.

4. It is destructive. It tramples underfoot a person's valued possession, his good name. It vandalizes his reputation. Moreover, if the gossip is what Christians are saying about a fellow Christian, it may leak beyond the borders of the church and harm the reputation of the church itself, confirming scoffers in their claim that all Christians are hypocrites. They will reach the same conclusion whether or not they believe the gossip. If they believe it, then the accused is a hypocrite. If they do not believe it, then the talebearers are the hypocrites.

5. It is malicious. The motive behind gossip is never love. To speak evil about a brother always arises from love's opposite, malice. To gossip behind someone's back puts you in the same league as the unscrupulous and vicious enemies of Jesus (John 7:45-52).

In conclusion, we see that gossip is a violation of the Sixth Commandment (the commandment against murder), because it does injury to another, and who can say that the injury might not drive him to despair and death, thus becoming actual murder? I recently read a news story about a teenage boy who committed suicide because someone told a lie about him on Facebook. Furthermore, gossip is a violation of the Eighth Commandment (the commandment against stealing), because it is robbery of what rightfully belongs to someone, his good reputation. And it is likely a violation of the Ninth Commandment, because in some measure it may be exactly what the commandment forbids: false witness.

+ Postscript +

The Meaning of "James"

The opening words of James's epistle seem to us like an ordinary greeting, but a first-century Jew might have found them arresting in their implications. The writer says, "James . . . to the twelve tribes which are scattered abroad" (Jas. 1:1). "James" is actually *Iacobos,* Greek spelling of the Old Testament name Jacob, referring to the patriarch also called Israel, who was father of the nation bearing his name.[110] The more exact sense of James's greeting is therefore, "Jacob . . . to the twelve tribes scattered abroad." The twelve tribes were the families of the original Jacob's twelve sons, so a reader in New Testament times might reasonably have suspected an allusion to the original Jacob and all his children.

Was the allusion deliberate? Was James claiming fatherly authority over the Jewish people? The matter justifies a deeper look. I have argued elsewhere that Jesus was not only a son of David, but also the particular son with throne rights.[111] In His day, He should have been king of the Jews. Upon His death, who was next in line? He had no descendants, so the man emerging as His rightful successor was James, the oldest of His brothers. Jesus reestablished His claim to the throne when He rose from the dead, yet James remained the highest ranking figure among mortal men. His pedigree may well have been a factor promoting his rise to leadership in the church at Jerusalem. As the most royal personage among his people, he certainly was in a position to present himself as deserving of their attention, as if he were Jacob himself.

Still, James's outstanding humility argues against any conclusion that he wanted to be seen as kingly. He presents himself as Jesus' servant, not as His successor. The larger implications of his greeting are not his doing, but the doing of the Holy Spirit who inspired him. The Holy Spirit wanted Jewish readers to hear James with deep respect.

In his greeting we also find a profound metaphor. We as followers of Christ are the Israel of God (Gal. 6:16), and our patriarch is God above, our heavenly Father, who is the ultimate source of all Scripture (2 Tim. 3:16). The Epistle of James, as the greeting implies, is God's Word to us, designed to teach us the manner of life that will fulfill His purposes in giving us life both in this world and in the world to come.

✦ REFERENCES ✦

[1]Eusebius *Ecclesiastical History* 2.23.

[2]Josephus *Antiquities* 20.9.1.

[3]Martin Luther *Preface to the New Testament* (1522).

[4]D. Edmond Hiebert, *The Epistle of James: Tests of a Living Faith* (Chicago: Moody Press, 1979), 174.

[5]Many of the returnees could certify their identity as Jews only by naming where in Palestine their ancestors had resided (Ezra 2:1–35). See F. Charles Fensham, *The Books of Ezra and Nehemiah* (Grand Rapids, Mich.: William B. Eerdmans Publishing Co., 1982), 47–52.

[6]Hiebert, 69–70.

[7]Ibid., 85.

[8]Ibid., 87.

[9]Ibid.; W. E. Vine, *An Expository Dictionary of New Testament Words*, reprinted in *An Expository Dictionary of Biblical Words*, by W. E. Vine, Merrill F. Unger, and William White, Jr. (Nashville: Thomas Nelson Publishers, 1984), 326.

[10]Jay P. Green, Sr., *The Interlinear Bible: Hebrew/English*, 3 vols. (Grand Rapids, Mich.: Baker Book House, 1983), 1092, 1391; Hiebert, 87.

[11]Hiebert, 94.

[12]Ibid., 95.

[13]Ibid.

[14]Ibid.

[15]Ibid., 96; Vine, 1215.

[16]Lisa R. Young and Marion Nestle, "The Contribution of Expanding Portion Sizes to the US Obesity Epidemic," in *American Journal of Public Health*, February 2002, Vol. 92, No. 2, 246–248.

[17]"Prevalence of Overweight and Obesity among Adults: United States, 2003–2004," *National Center for Health Statistics*, Web (cdc.gov/nchs/products/pubs/pubd/hestats/overweight/overweight_adult_03), 2007; "Obesity in Youth," *AOA Fact Sheet*, American Obesity Association, Web (obesity1.tempdomainname.com/subs/fastfacts/obesity_youth), 2002.

[18]Hiebert, 98.

[19]Ibid., 99.

[20]Ibid., 101.

[21]George Ricker Berry, *Interlinear Greek-English New Testament* (N.p., 1897; repr., Grand Rapids, Mich.: Baker Book House, 1981), 802.

[22]Hiebert, 112.

[23]Vine, 247; Robert Young, *Analytical Concordance to the Bible*, 22nd American ed., revised by Wm. B. Stevenson (repr., Grand Rapids, Mich.: Wm. B. Eerdmans Publishing Co., 1976), 210.

[24]Hiebert, 118.

[25]Al Barger, "Antony Flew Accepts God," *Blogcritics Magazine: Books*, Web (blogcritics.org/archives), December 9, 2004; Antony Flew, with Roy Abraham Varghese, *There Is a God: How the World's Most Notorious Atheist Changed His Mind* (New York: HarperCollins Publishers, 2007), 156–157.

[26]Hiebert, 128–129.

[27]Ibid., 130–131.

[28]William F. Arndt and F. Wilbur Gingrich, eds., *A Greek-English Lexicon of the New Testament and Other Early Christian Literature.* (Chicago: University of Chicago Press, 1957), 108.

[29]Joachim Jeremias, *Jerusalem in the Time of Jesus*, translated by F. H. and C. H. Cave (German ed., 1962; Philadelphia: Fortress Press, 1969), 114; R. T. France, *The*

Gospel of Mark: A Commentary on the Greek Text (Grand Rapids, Mich., and Cambridge, U.K.: William B. Eerdmans Publishing Company, 2002), 491–492.

[30]F. F. Bruce, _The Hard Sayings of Jesus_ (Downers Grove, Ill.: InterVarsity Press, 1983), 57.

[31]Hiebert, 135.

[32]Berry, 803.

[33]Hiebert, 129–30.

[34]Ibid., 139

[35]Arndt and Gingrich, 237.

[36]F. F. Bruce, _The Acts of the Apostles: The Greek Text with Introduction and Commentary_ (Grand Rapids, Mich.: Wm. B. Eerdmans Publishing Company, 1951), 343.

[37]Berry, 803.

[38]Ibid.

[39]Hiebert, 151–152.

[40]Ibid.

[41]Hiebert, 179.

[42]Arndt and Gingrich, 536.

[43]Luther, loc. cit.

[44]Roger Martin, _R. A. Torrey: Apostle of Certainty_ (Murfreesboro, Tenn.; Sword of the Lord Publishers, 1976) 183.

[45]Arndt and Gingrich, 190; Hiebert, 204.

[46]Arndt and Gingrich, 451; Hiebert, 205–206.

[47]James Smith, _The Voyage and Shipwreck of St. Paul,_ fourth ed., rev. and corrected by Walter E. Smith (N.p., 1880; repr., Minneapolis, Minn.: The James Family Christian Publishers, n.d.), 141.

[48]Hiebert, 213.

[49]Ibid., 216–217.

[50]Berry, 807.

[51]Ibid.

[52]Hiebert, 218–219.

[53]Albert Barnes, _Barnes' Notes on the New Testament,_ complete and unabridged in one volume (Grand Rapids, Mich.: Kregel Publications, 1962), 1026.

[54]Hiebert, 232.

[55]Berry, 808.

[56]Hiebert, 243–244.

[57]Ibid., 244–247.

[58]Ibid., 255; Barnes, 1377.

[59]Hiebert, 254.

[60]Barnes, 1378; Thomas Manton, _The Epistle of James: A Practical Commentary, or an Exposition with Notes on the Epistle of James_ (repr., Mobile, Ala.: R E Publications, n.d.), 348; Matthew Henry, _Matthew Henry's Commentary on the Whole Bible,_ complete and unabridged in one volume (Peabody Mass.: Hendrickson Publishers, 1991), 2416.

[61]Warren W. Wiersbe, _The Integrity Crisis,_ exp. ed. with study guide (Nashville, Tenn.: Oliver-Nelson, 1991).

[62]Berry, 809; Hiebert, 258.

[63]Hiebert, loc. cit.

[64]Vine, 326; Hiebert, 263–264.

[65]Berry, 809; Hiebert, 264.

[66]Berry, 809; Hiebert, 266.

[67]_Aesop's Fables,_ adapted by James A. Hall (n.p.: CBS Records, Inc., 1972), 39.

[68]Hiebert, 273.

[69]Robert Burns, "To a Mouse," in _The Chilswell Book of English Poetry,_ compiled and annotated by Robert Bridges (London: Longmans, Green & Company, 1924), 68.

[70]Hiebert, 279.

[71]Hiebert, 282.

[72]Ibid., 283–284.

[73]Arndt and Gingrich, 756; Berry, 810; Hiebert, 284–285.

[74]Hiebert, 285.

[75]Arndt and Gingrich, 425; Vine, 982; Hiebert, 285–286.

[76]Berry, 810.

[77]"Gold," *Wikipedia,* Web (en.wikipedia.org/wiki/Gold), March 26, 2015.

[78]"Tarnish," *Wikipedia,* Web (en.wikipedia.org/wiki/Tarnish), March 26, 2015.

[79]Arndt and Gingrich, 746; Berry, 810; Hiebert, 290–291.

[80]Hiebert, 291; Arndt and Gingrich, 836; Berry, 810.

[81]Hiebert, 291–292; Arndt and Gingrich, 768; George Ricker Berry, word number 4684, in *Lexicon and New Testament Synonyms,* supp. to *Interlinear Greek-English New Testament* (N.p., 1897; repr., Grand Rapids, Mich.: Baker Book House, 1981), 137.

[82]"Worldwide Adherents of All Religions, Mid-2005," *Encyclopaedia Britannica Online,* Web (britannica.com/eb/article9432620/Worldwide-Adherents-of-All-Religions-Mid-2005), 2005.

[83]*The Analytical Greek Lexicon* (New York: Harper & Brothers Publishers; London: Samuel Bagster and Sons, Limited, n.d.), 168.

[84]Rhys Richards, "The Earliest Foreign Visitors and Their Massive Depopulation of Rapa-iti from 1824 to 1830," *Journal de la Société des Océanistes,* 118, année 2004-1.

[85]Patrick Johnstone and Jason Mandryk, *Operation World: 21st Century Edition* (Bulstrode, Gerrards Cross, UK: WEC International, n.d.), 7.

[86]Vine, 508–509; Hiebert, 300.

[87]David O. Beale, *In Pursuit of Purity: American Fundamentalism Since 1850* (Greenville, S. Car.: Unusual Publications, 1986), 23–67.

[88]Hiebert, 302; Berry, 811.

[89]Homer A. Kent, Jr., *The Epistle to the Hebrews: A Commentary* (Grand Rapids, Mich.: Baker Book House, 1972), 252–253.

[90]Charles L. Feinberg, *Jeremiah: A Commentary* (Grand Rapids, Mich.: Zondervan Publishing House, 1982), 4.

[91]Most of the minced oaths we have listed are discussed in Eric Partridge's *A Dictionary of Slang and Unconventional English,* sixth ed. (New York: The Macmillan Company, 1967).

[92]Hiebert, 317; Berry 811.

[93]Hiebert, 321; Barnes, 1386; Rudolf Stier, *The Epistle of St James,* trans. William B. Pope (Edinburgh: T. & T. Clark, 1871; repr. Minneapolis, Minn.: Klock & Klock Christian Publishers, Inc., 1982), 482.

[94]Hiebert, 321.

[95]Ibid., 327.

[96]Norman P. Grubb, *C. T. Studd: Cricketer and Pioneer* (Fort Washington, Penn.: Christian Literature Crusade, 1972), 232–233

[97]Frank Houghton, *Amy Carmichael of Dohnavur: The Story of a Lover and her Beloved* (Fort Washington, Penn.: Christian Literature Crusade, 1979), 289–290.

[98]Examples appear throughout the work just mentioned; see also, Amy Carmichael, *Gold Cord: The Story of a Fellowship* (n.p., 1932; repr., Fort Washington, Penn.: Christian Literature Crusade, 1974); P. Spencer Palmer, ed., *Wings: A Book of Dohnavur Songs with Music, Part I* (London: S. P. C. K., 1960).

[99]Arndt and Gingrich, 301; Berry, 812; Hiebert, 335.

[100]*The Analytical Greek Lexicon* (London: Samuel Bagster and Sons, Ltd., n.d.; repr., New York: Harper & Brothers Publishers, n.d.), 179.

[101]Henry, 2460; Barnes, 1513.

[102]Hiebert, 336.

[103]Duane T. Gish, "What Actually Occurred at the Trial," in "The Arkansas Decision on Creation-Science," *Impact* 105 (March 1982), 2–3 [*Acts & Facts*, 11 (3)].

[104]Sir Fred Hoyle and Chandra Wickramasinghe, *Evolution from Space* (New York: Simon & Schuster, 1981), 148.

[105]Ed Rickard, "Against Evolution: The Origin of Life," *Bible Studies at the Moorings,* Web (themoorings.org/apologetics/refutations/evolution/origin.html), April 15, 2015.

[106]"Chandra Wickramasinghe," *Wikipedia,* Web (en.wikipedia.org/wiki/Chandra_Wickramasinghe), April 15, 2015.

[107]Hoyle and Wickramasinghe, 143.

[108]Francis Collins, *The Language of God: A Scientist Presents Evidence for Belief* (New York: Free Press, 2007).

[109]"The Language of God," *Wikipedia,* Web (en.wikipedia.org/wiki/The_Language_of_God), April 15, 2015.

[110]Hiebert, 11; Berry, 801.

[111]Ed Rickard, "The Lineage of Christ: Evidence," *Bible Studies at the Moorings,* Web (themoorings.org/apologetics/prophecy/lineage/fulfill.html), May 21, 2015.

+ RECOMMENDED READING +

Primary Source

Hiebert, D. Edmond. *The Epistle of James: Tests of a Living Faith.* Chicago: Moody Press, 1979.

In my effort to illuminate the rich practical guidance in the Epistle of James, I have leaned heavily on Hiebert's commentary for a correct understanding of the Greek text. His work is a superb resource, combining scholarly precision, transparent prose, and godly wisdom. Anyone limited to owning one commentary on James cannot do better than to obtain Hiebert's.

Commentaries

The commentaries I have listed below, besides having a high reputation, meet three additional criteria. They are written in a literate style suitable to their subject. They are not content with superficiality. And they hold staunchly to the high view of Scripture prerequisite to insight granted by the Holy Spirit. My simple test of orthodoxy is whether they grant that the author was the brother of Jesus and whether they affirm that James saw the Lord after a bodily resurrection.

Fausset, A. R. *1 Corinthians — Revelation.* Part 3 in volume 3 of *A Commentary Critical, Experimental, and Practical on the Old and New Testaments,* by Robert Jamieson, A. R. Fausset, and David Brown. N.p.: c. 1870; repr., Grand Rapids, Mich.: William B. Eerdmans Publishing Company, 1990.

Fausset contributed this last portion to the famous commentary traditionally known as Jamieson, Fausset, and Brown. With coverage of the whole Bible, it has usually been printed as three large volumes. Fausset was an Anglican clergyman who began his career as a prize-winning student at Trinity College, Dublin. For the last fifty-one years of his life he was rector of a parish in York, England. His work is marked by incisive, well-crafted comments bringing a godly perspective to the text.

Henry, Matthew. *Matthew Henry's Commentary on the Whole Bible.* Complete and unabridged in one volume. Peabody Mass.: Hendrickson Publishers, 1991.

It has always been the general opinion of English-speaking Bible students that Henry's commentary on the whole Bible is the best by a single author. The evangelist George Whitefield read it four times, the last time on his knees. Although the portion on James was compiled from Henry's notes by fellow pastors after his death in 1714, it still rises to a high level.

Johnstone, Robert. *A Commentary on James.* 2nd ed. N.p.: 1888; repr., Edinburgh: The Banner of Truth Trust, 1977.

After serving as a pastor in the United Presbyterian Church in Scotland,

Johnstone rose in 1876 to the Chair of New Testament Literature and Exegesis at the University of Edinburgh. Spurgeon said of his commentary on James that it was "a very useful, scholarly, and readable book." Although generally lucid and to the point, Johnstone's prose occasionally lapses into an obscure verbosity frustrating to a modern reader, but his insights are worth digging out.

Manton, Thomas. *The Epistle of James: A Practical Commentary, or an Exposition with Notes on the Epistle of James.* Repr., Mobile, Ala.: R E Publications, n.d.

Manton's commentary is still widely read although it dates back to Puritan times. The author, Thomas Manton (1620–1677), was a prominent figure in his own day, serving as a chaplain of Oliver Cromwell and later as a negotiator in proceedings bringing Charles II to the throne. His reputation as a writer survived his death. Spurgeon prized his sermons, saying that none better had come from Manton's contemporaries.

Mayor, Joseph B. *The Epistle of St. James: The Greek Text with Introduction, Notes, Comments and Further Studies in the Epistle of St. James.* 3rd ed. London: Macmillan, 1897; repr., Grand Rapids, Mich.: Zondervan Publishing House, 1954.

Although a commentary, Mayor's work is much more besides. It might be described as a monument to Greek scholarship. The author was a nineteenth-century professor at King's College, London, as well an honorary fellow at Cambridge. The commentary itself, following the full text of James in one Greek and three Latin versions, is an incisive analysis of the Greek text. In the opening chapters, the author defends in detail the traditional view of the book's date and authorship, furnishes an exhaustive list of parallels between James and earlier writings, examines the book's grammar, and conducts scholars through yet other rooms of informational treasure. Of particular interest is his observation, "On the whole I should be inclined to rate the Greek of this Epistle as approaching more nearly to the standard of classical purity than that of any other book of the N.T. with the exception perhaps of the Epistle to the Hebrews" (p. ccxliv).

Mitton, C. Leslie. *The Epistle of James.* London: Marshall, Morgan & Scott, 1966.

Mitton, who lived in the mid-twentieth century, was principal of Handsworth College in Birmingham, England—a school mainly providing vocational training for adults with lower-class backgrounds. It is evident that his career choice harmonized with, and was perhaps influenced by, the book he so carefully expounded. Next to Hiebert's, Mitton's commentary on James is the best emerging in recent times. It is less useful as a resource for interpreting particular passages because its style is more discursive and subheadings are less frequent, but for sequential devotional reading, it is most rewarding.

Phillips, John. *Exploring the Epistle of James: An Expository Commentary.* Grand Rapids, Mich.: Kregel Publications, 2004.

The utmost in practical applications, Phillips' commentary is a fast-paced, highly readable work full of vivid illustrations drawn from every conceivable source: Scripture itself, historical events, famous works of literature, and the author's own experience. He is uncompromising in upholding both the authority of Scripture and the imperative of holiness. Any preacher or teacher will be grateful for his provision of many alliterative outlines.

Plummer, Alfred. *The General Epistles of St. James and St. Jude.* In *The Expositors' Bible*, edited by W. Robertson Nicoll. New York: Hodder & Stoughton, Publishers, n.d.

> Plummer was an Oxford don in the late nineteenth century. His commentary on James represents a high mark in English evangelical scholarship. The reader can take pleasure in rich Victorian prose setting forth deep spiritual wisdom. For example, when explaining James's admonition not to judge our brother (Jas. 4:11–12), he says, "It is often our own personal acquaintance with iniquity that makes us suppose that others must be like ourselves. It is our own meanness, dishonesty, pride, or impurity that we see reflected on what is perhaps only the surface of a life whose secret springs and motives lie in a sphere quite beyond our groveling comprehension" (p. 258).

Stier, Rudolf. *The Epistle of St. James.* Translated by Rev. William B. Pope. New edition. Edinburgh: T. & T. Clark, 1871; repr., Minneapolis, Minn.: Klock & Klock Christian Publishers, 1982.

> An outstanding work in the German pietistic tradition, this commentary remains a clear guidebook to the right moral applications of James's epistle.

Study Guide

Brooks, Keith L. Brooks. *James: Belief in Action.* Chicago: Correspondence School of Moody Bible Institute, 1962.

> Although my name does not appear in this study guide, much of the writing is mine. When I was in college, I met regularly with some friends for Bible study. My brother-in-law Herbert Klingbeil, who was director of the Correspondence School at Moody, invited us to undertake as a group project the revision of Brooks's original work on the Epistle of James. Most of the other young men contributed very little because of competing demands on their time, but I brought the project to completion, working under the supervision of John Phillips, later a well-known commentator in his own right. The study guide remained in print for at least twenty years. In this present commentary, I have stayed away from reusing any of the writing in this earlier work, since I no longer remember exactly which prose is mine. I believe I retained the substance of Brooks's comments, while editing and expanding them and thoroughly rebuilding all the questions.

Made in the USA
Middletown, DE
12 May 2020

94249965R00119